MURDERERS' LONDON

Ivan Butler was born in Heswall, Cheshire, and is at present living in Northwood, Middlesex. He spent many years in the theatre as writer, director and actor, making his first appearance on tour with the original 'Dracula' Company of Hamilton Deane. He now devotes most of his time to writing, and has published a number of books on the cinema, in addition to plays, radio and television scripts, articles and criticism. He has long been interested in the subject of the supreme crime – particularly its revelations of the motives and eccentricities of human behaviour – and in the surroundings among which such events occur.

Murderers' London
Ivan Butler

ROBERT HALE · LONDON

ISBN 0 7090 4804 1

Robert Hale Limited
Clerkenwell House
Clerkenwell Green
London EC1R 0HT

This book recalls a number of murder cases in
which a charge of murder was brought against
someone. In some of these the accused was
acquitted or convicted of a lesser crime or
had the sentence reduced on the grounds of
diminished responsibility.

Printed in Great Britain by
St Edmundsbury Press Limited,
Bury St Edmunds, Suffolk
Bound by WBC Bookbinders Limited

CONTENTS

ACKNOWLEDGEMENTS

I should like to express my grateful thanks to the reference and local history departments of the following libraries for their unfailingly courteous help in searching through records and providing information, in particular concerning the less recent cases: Brent Public Library (Mr Martin); Bromley Central Library; Chiswick District Library; Croydon Reference Library; Ealing Public Library; Greenwich Public Library; Hornsey Public Library (Mr Campbell); Richmond-upon-Thames Central Library; Southwark Reference Library; Tower Hamlets Central Library; Wandsworth Central Library; City of Westminster Archives Department, Marylebone Branch; Wimbledon Public Library.

I am also indebted to Mr Leslie Boyd, Courts Administrator, Central Criminal Courts, for going to considerable trouble to make various files available to me, and to Mr Philip Weathers, Supervisor of Syon House, for details in particular of the murder of Sylvia Styles.

Last but far from least, my thanks to my wife and my son for helping me in tracing and visiting numerous sites.

I.B.

To my wife Hilda, and
my son Francis

INTRODUCTION

The abiding interest shown in the study of murder and its practitioners is sometimes dismissed as morbid, gruesome, a decadent desire to dabble in gore. It is not such details as these, however, so much as the characters, the motives, the surroundings and circumstances that engage the interest of the student— not the forty whacks which Lizzie Borden (allegedly) gave her mother, but the personality of Lizzie herself, and, even more, the extraordinary life lived in that tall, cramped, oven-hot Fall River house. The motives underlying Field's double confession-retraction long after the death of his victim; the black farce of the appalling Kate Webster hurrying across London bridges to pay lightning visits to 'friends' and dropping portions of her employer's body into the Thames *en route*; the double life of the innocent but suspected 'shabby-genteel' Robert Wood; the mystery of Thomas Anderson's shoes on the mantelpiece of the empty flat near Battersea Park; the grim comedy of Wainwright's trip across the river in a four-wheeler with a dancing-girl, a strong cigar, two parcels containing the remains of his year-dead mistress, and a panting, police-summoning young man running in hot pursuit; the incredible intricacies of jealousy-crazed ex-Minister for Justice Thomas Ley's plotting to take the life of the entirely innocent young barman John Mudie; the grisly programme of death drawn up by the young footman of Lowndes Square; George Joseph Smith playing "Nearer, my God, to Thee" on the harmonium and then slipping out to buy some tomatoes for supper after drowning his 'wife' in her bath in the neat little Highgate lodging house; 22-year-old Sarah Malcolm, after the discovery of £53 stolen money hidden in her hair, sitting dressed in scarlet for her portrait by Hogarth just before her execution—it is in the strange vagaries of human behaviour that the persisting interest lies.

In all such cases—the bizarre, the mysterious, the tragic, the gruesome, the just plain vicious—the setting plays a determining part that is not so often emphasized in books dealing with the subject. Sometimes the scene so aptly fits the crime that its part as a decisive factor is obvious; on other occasions the deed is in lurid and dramatic contrast to its prosaic or inappropriate surroundings. The 'where' has as significant a role as the 'who', the 'what' and the 'why'.

The cases described in this book, amounting to nearly two hundred and ranging in time from the eleventh century to 1971, fall in general within the present Metropolitan Police area, and for convenience are divided by chapters into the London postal districts. Each case is discussed in the district where its main event occurred, but its ramifications may of course extend much farther afield. The mania for changing street names is a disease of long standing and can cause confusion and dismay, but wherever possible both old and new names are given.

Every day another portion of London vanishes for ever. The hand of the planner is heavy on the land, and the drills of the demolishers ceaselessly set up their dismal drumming. Many of the sites of an old drama have gone beyond recall: others that I was still able to see during the course of preparing this book may well have been destroyed by the time it appears in print. Even in these cases, however, the streets themselves remain; and while it may require a greater effort of the imagination, it is still possible to stand near the spot of some bygone tragedy or deed of wickedness and—among the tower blocks and the traffic fumes—recreate in the mind's eye the circumstances of its enactment.

MAP KEY

Note: The numbering, indicating the approximate sites, follows as closely as is practicable the order in which the cases appear in the text, and covers the central district of London. Where street names have been altered the present name is given in brackets.

1 Sidney Street Siege, Sidney Street, E1 (1910)
2 Houndsditch (Sidney Street Siege), EC3 (1910)
3 Jack the Ripper, Bucks Row (Durward Street), E1 (1888)
4 Jack the Ripper, Berner Street (Henriques Street), E1 (1888)
5 Jack the Ripper, Goodman's Yard (Gunthorpe St) E1 (1888)
6 Jack the Ripper, Hanbury Street, E1 (1888)
7 Jack the Ripper, Miller's Court (demolished) (1888)
8 Jack the Ripper, Mitre Square, EC3 (1888)
9 Wainwright, Whitechapel Road, E1 (1864)
10 Cooney (victim), Duval Street (demolished) (1960)
11 Reubens, Rupert Street (Goodman Street), E1 (1909)
12 Goodmacher, Grove Street (Golding Street), E1 (1920)
13 Mullins, James Street (Burslem Street), E1 (1860)
14 Williams, Ratcliffe Highway (The Highway), E1 (1811)
15 Bishop and Williams, Nova Scotia Gdns (demolished) (1831)
16 Overbury, Tower of London, EC3 (1613)
17 Hopwood, Fenchurch Street Station, EC3 (1912)
18 Byron, Post Office Court, EC3 (1902)
19 Millson (victim), Cannon Street, EC4 (1866)
20 Price, Moorfields, EC2 (1718)
21 Ellsome, Wilmington Square, WC1 (1911)
22 Pelizzioni, Saffron Hill, EC1 (1865)
23 Brownrigg, Fleur-de-Lis Court, Fetter Lane, EC4 (1767)
24 Malcolm, Tanfield Court (demolished), Temple, EC4 (1732)

25 Fenning, Chancery Lane, WC2 (1815)
26 Prince (murder of William Terriss), Adelphi Theatre, WC2 (1897)
27 Mountfort (victim), Howard Street, WC2 (1692)
28 Hackman, Covent Garden Opera House, WC2 (1779)
29 Fahmy (tried and acquitted), Savoy Hotel, WC2 (1923)
30 Savage, Charing Cross, WC2 (1727)
31 Gardelle, Leicester Fields (Leicester Square) (1761)
32 Field, Shaftesbury Avenue, WC2 (1931)
33 LaCroix, Little Newport Street, WC2 (1936)
34 Smith (alias Sapwell), Mecklenburgh Square, WC1 (1911)
35 Jones, Montague Place, WC1 (1828)
36 Piernicke (victim), Whitfield Street, W1 (1903)
37 Voisin, Charlotte Street, W1 (1917)
38 De Antiquis (victim), Charlotte Street, W1 (1947)
39 Hermann, Grafton Street (Grafton Way), W1 (1894)
40 Tratsart, Oxford Street, W1 (1945)
41 Cummins, Wardour Street, W1 (1942)
42 Cummins, Montagu Place, W1 (1942)
43 Cummins, Gosfield Street, W1 (1942)
44 Cummins, Sussex Gardens, W2 (1942)
45 Cummins, Southwick Street, W2 (1942)
46 Cummins, Norris Street, SW1 (1942)
47 Fenwick (Ginger Rae) (victim), Broadwick Street, W1 (1948)
48 Freedman (Russian Dora) (victim), Long Acre, WC2 (1948)
49 Barratt (Black Rita) (victim), Rupert Street, W1 (1947)
50 Baxter (convicted of manslaughter), Denman Street, W1 (1913)
51 Martin (victim), Café Royal, Regent Street, W1 (1894)
52 Loynon, Great Pulteney Street, W1 (1871)
53 Cook (victim), Carnaby Street, W1 (1946)
54 Jacoby, Portman Street, W1 (1922)
55 Lees-Smith, George Street, W1 (1942)
55a Lewis, George Street, W1 (1948)
56 Metyard, Bruton Street, W1 (1766)
57 Courvoisier, Norfolk Street (Dunraven Street), W1 (1840)

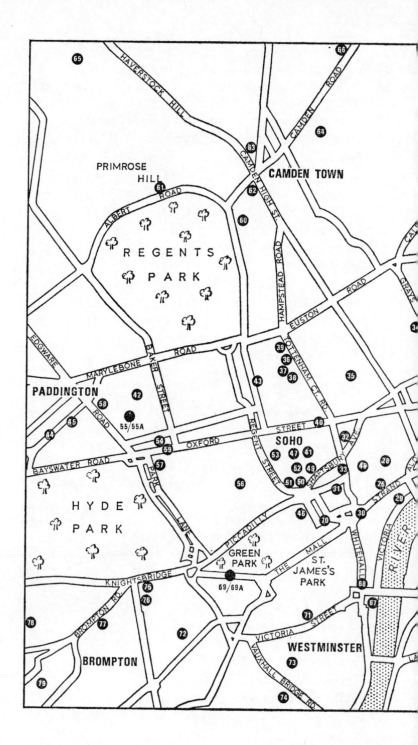

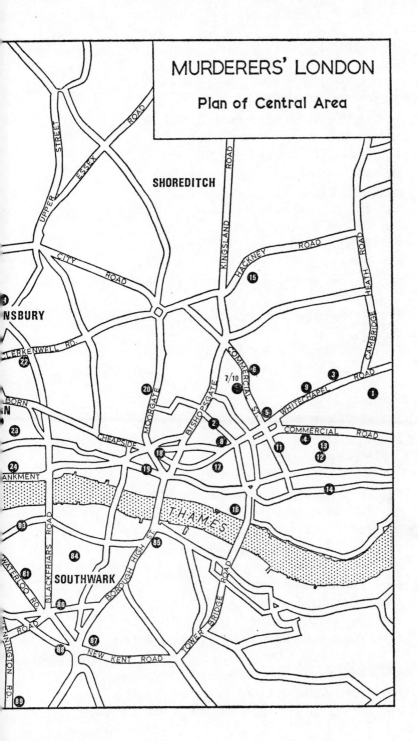

58   Thistlewood, Cato Street, Edgware Road, W1 (1820)

59   Hayes, Tyburn Road (Oxford Street), W1 (1725)

60   Ogilvy, Park Village East, NW1 (1956)

61   Godfrey (victim), Primrose Hill, NW (1678)

62   De Vere, Arlington Road, NW1 (1926)

63   Furnace, Hawley Crescent, NW1 (1933)

64   Wood (tried and acquitted), St Paul's Road (Agar Grove), NW1 (1907)

65   Hocker, Belsize House (demolished), NW3 (1845)

66   Crippen, Hilldrop Crescent, N7 (1910)

67   Bellingham, House of Commons, SW1 (1812)

68   M'Naghten, Parliament Street, SW1 (1843)

69   Oxford (attempted assassination) Constitution Hill, SW1 (1840)

69a McMahon (attempted assassination) Constitution Hill, SW1 (1936)

70   Königsmark, Pall Mall East, SW1 (1681)

71   Udham Singh, Caxton Hall, Westminster, SW1 (1940)

72   Dunn and O'Sullivan, Eaton Place, SW1 (1922)

73   Robinson, Rochester Row, SW1 (1927)

74   Holmyard, Tachbrook Street, SW1 (1929)

75   Barney (tried and acquitted), Williams Mews (William Mews), SW1 (1932)

76   Walker, Lowndes Square, SW1 (1922)

77   Ley and Smith, Beaufort Gardens, SW3 (1947)

78   Lal Dhingra, Imperial Institute, SW7 (1909)

79   Podola, Onslow Square, SW7 (1959)

80   Richards (victim), Waterloo Bridge (1942)

81   Cream, Waterloo Road, SE1 (1891)

82   Cream, Lambeth Road, SE1 (1891)

83   Cream, Stamford Street, SE1 (1892)

84   Chapman, Union Street, SE1 (1901)

85   Chapman, Borough High Street, SE1 (1902)

86   The Mannings, Miniver (Minver) Place (demolished) (1849)

87   Dean, Jacques Court, Thomas Street (demolished) (1818)

88   Bailes (victim), St George's Road, SE1 (1908)

89   Roberts, Chester Street (Chester Way), SE1 (1867)

1

THE RIPPER'S STREETS
East London: Hackney and Bow, Whitechapel, Stepney

We start our journey, appropriately enough, on the railway—the first British train murder, in fact—9th July 1864. Mr Thomas Briggs, a senior bank clerk, spent the evening dining with his niece at 23 Nelson Square (now the northern part of Furley Road), Peckham, and then caught the train at Fenchurch Street station on his way home to 5 Clapton Square, Hackney. When it arrived at Hackney Wick his carriage was found to be empty and spattered with blood: Mr Briggs was seen lying between the rails about a mile and a quarter north of Bow, and died without recovering consciousness.

His gold watch and chain, and also his silk hat, were missing. In place of the latter, the police found a hat with an unusually low crown for the style of the period, and it was chiefly through this unfashionable headgear that the murder was traced to a German tailor, one Franz Müller, lodging at 16 Park Terrace, then part of the Old Ford Road, Victoria Park, Hackney. By this time, however, Müller had left the country and was on a sailing vessel bound for New York. Anticipating the procedure adopted for the capture of Crippen, detectives and witnesses travelled across the Atlantic on a fast steamship, and were awaiting his arrival. Suspicion had been first directed to Müller by a cabman friend who recognized a small box the tailor had given to his little daughter. On it was the name of a jeweller with whom Müller had exchanged the dead man's gold watch chain for other articles. The tracing of this insignificant item, and of the hat which Müller had so unwisely exchanged for his victim's smart silk one, brought about his downfall. The case caused considerable anxiety among travellers and demonstrated the dangers of the compartments in use at the time on the railways—badly lit (or totally unlit) and with no means of inter-communication. The jeweller's shop at which Müller made his exchange was at 55 Cheapside, EC, and the name of the proprietor—Death.

A mile or two farther west another railway station, Dalston Junction, was the setting for a particularly cruel and callous child murder. Louisa Masset, daughter of a Frenchman and an English woman, had a son by a lover in France whose name she refused to divulge even to her own family. To conceal the disgrace—in 1899—of having given birth to an illegitimate child, she came to England, left him in the care of a foster mother in Clyde Road, Tottenham, and found work for herself as a governess. The arrangement, however, did not last, neither did her money. Early in October the foster mother received a letter from Louisa (who was staying with her sister at 29 Bethune Road, Stoke Newington) to say that she had made arrangements to send the boy, Manfred Louis, to his father in France. On the morning of 27th October Louisa collected him, together with a small parcel containing his clothes. According to the foster mother, the boy cried bitterly at having to go, but at 1.45 p.m. mother and son were seen together at London Bridge Station, Manfred Louis laughing and chattering and obviously delighted to be with her again.

At 6 p.m. that evening a woman entered the ladies' cloakroom on Number 3 platform, Dalston Junction, and on opening the lavatory door was horrified to see a dead child lying on the floor. There were wounds on the face and neck, and the body was naked except for the black shawl in which it was wrapped. A bloodstained stone lay nearby. A day or two later the foster mother read a description in the newspaper and identified the body as Manfred Louis. On being questioned, Louisa Masset said she had handed the child over to two women at London Bridge Station who promised to care for him, and had then caught the train to Brighton, where she spent the week-end with her lover—a Frenchman who lived next door to Louisa's sister in Bethune Road. There was absolutely no corroboration of the unlikely first part of this story, but the second part was undoubtedly true, and did much to hang her. A paper parcel containing the boy's clothes was found in Brighton Station, the black shawl was identified as one Louisa had recently bought in Stoke Newington, the stone fitted a hole in the garden rockery of Bethune Road. It appears that, after taking the boy from the foster mother at London Bridge, she returned to Dalston Junction, a station with which she was familiar, to kill him. Louisa Masset might well have escaped with a lesser sentence—an unmarried mother desperate to know how to support herself and her child —had it not been for the general horror felt at her action in travelling to Brighton immediately after the murder, to spend the night with her lover.

In Bow Road, between the wars, stood the Eastern Palace cinema. On 7th August 1934, John Stockwell, a 19-year-old member of the staff, attacked the manager with an axe and stole a little under £100 from the office safe. The manager, found by a cleaner lying unconscious in the circle of the cinema, died without speaking. Stockwell deposited the money in a case at Aldgate East Station and put into operation an elaborate fake suicide-by-drowning plan. This, however, miscarried—partly through a slip he made in signing a hotel register, partly through his clothes being discovered on the seashore *before* the time at which a letter to the police was postmarked. Stockwell was discovered, under an alias, at the Metropole Hotel, Great Yarmouth, charged and found guilty of murder.

Moving westward, we come to Sidney Street, running from Whitechapel Road to Commercial Road, and famous for the siege attended, in his capacity as Home Secretary, by Winston Churchill. The events directly culminating in the siege had their beginnings in Houndsditch, where, in December 1910, a group of members of the anarchist movement who had fled from Tsarist Russia, planned to rob a jeweller's shop to obtain funds. Their headquarters was the Anarchist Club in Jubilee Street, running parallel and adjacent to Sidney Street. To execute the robbery, they rented two small houses, numbers 9 and 11 Exchange Buildings, a little cul-de-sac backing on to the jeweller's at 119 Houndsditch. The site is at present occupied by the City of London Polytechnic, which extends through to cover both the shop and the houses behind, but until a few years ago it was still possible to see the actual numbers on the doors in Exchange Buildings, and the deep little cul-de-sac itself probably looks not too different today. The noise made by the inefficient gang as they tried to tunnel their way through the wall caused a man living next door to the shop to raise the alarm, and the result was a gun battle and the death and wounding of several police. The anarchists' leader, George Gardstein, was fatally wounded by one of his own party.

Gardstein had been living at 44 Gold Street (which until recently led from Stepney Green to Redman's Road), and the escaping gang tried to carry him back there, groping their dim, gaslit way along Cutler Street, Harrow Alley (now Harrow Place), Middlesex Street (altered from Petticoat Lane in 1846 but still popularly known by its old name) and Aldgate High Street. Here they changed their plan, and headed instead for the nearer Grove Street, off Commercial Road, where one of the party, known as Peter the Painter, lived at No 59. (Grove Street later became Golding Street and still exists, though truncated by new buildings in Burslem Street.) There they left the dying Gardstein, and scattered. Several were caught very shortly afterwards, and on 3rd January word was received that at least two were hiding in the second floor of 100 Sidney Street, in a room occupied by a Mrs Gersham, whose skirt and boots they had removed in the hope, presumably, that in those less permissive days such a deprivation would shame her into remaining as hostage. Together with the other occupants, however, she managed to escape, and at 7.30 in the morning, the house having been quietly surrounded, the famous siege began. A detachment of Scots Guards arrived later from the Tower, and after a morning of constant firing from both sides the house burst into flames, and the two men known to have been in it perished. Peter the Painter, the most mysterious character of all, was never found, and many rumours have surrounded him ever since, partly no doubt because of his enigmatic name, the prosaic explanation of which was probably that he painted the scenery for the anarchist playlets put on by the group.

The southern end of Sidney Street commemorates its moment of fame by a large block of flats proudly entitled Siege House. No 100 was some way further along: it was gutted during the battle and all its neighbours have been replaced by modern estates. A solitary building remains, used as a garage and small car park and retaining its number—82. From this anchorage, a distance can be approximately measured by the enthusiast anxious to place his feet on the spot—and use his imagination.

Houses nearby, and those in Sidney Square, can help to create the scene in the mind's eye.

Links have been suggested between Jack the Ripper, Steinie Morrison, George Chapman (Severin Klosowski) and the Sidney Street anarchists: how strong such links actually are—if they exist at all—is never likely to be established, but the theories and counter-theories make perennially enjoyable reading.

A quarter of a century before Sidney Street, one of the most macabre and strange of all journeys through the district (and, indeed, through any district) took place when Henry Wainwright, in 1875, transported the dismembered body of his ex-mistress from his warehouse in Whitechapel Road to the Borough High Street in a four-wheeler, accompanied by a ballet dancer, and chased on foot by a perspiring and horrified young maker of brushes. This unusual concatenation of circumstances arose as follows. Wainwright, a popular, prosperous, floridly handsome family man, lived with his wife and children in 40 Tredegar Square, Bow. In partnership with his brother, he ran a successful business as a mat and brush maker, owning a shop at No 84 Whitechapel Road, and a warehouse almost opposite at No 215. He was a keen amateur actor and reciter, and a constant and welcome visitor to the Pavilion Theatre next door to his shop. In 1871 he met at Broxbourne Gardens, a London pleasure resort, Miss Harriet Lane, a petite and lively girl with pretty golden hair, who had been employed as a milliner's apprentice at Waltham Abbey. It was a fateful encounter. Harriet became his mistress and later, as Mr Cecil King, he 'married' her. With, we must assume, considerable ingenuity, he managed to live with her as his wife, entirely unknown to Mrs Wainwright and her friends, first at 14 St Peter Street (now Cephas Street), Mile End, where a daughter was born, then at Alfred Street, Bedford Square, at Cecil Street, Strand, and back at St Peter Street, No 70, for the arrival of a second daughter. In 1874 she went to lodge with a Mrs Foster in Sidney Square, off Sidney Street.

By this time, however, things in general were not so satisfactory. Wainwright's financial affairs had wilted under the strain of two families (and possibly further entanglements), and his brother had dissolved their partnership. Concurrently, his relationship with Harriet deteriorated. She began to drink heavily, refused to be shaken off, and became a menace to both his reputation and security. She made scenes at No 84. On 11th September 1874, Wainwright induced her to come to the shop, and she was never seen again. To explain her disappearance, he said that she had gone off with a 'friend' (impersonated shortly beforehand in an effort to palm her off, by the obliging brother Thomas), called Teddy Frieake. With almost incredible stupidity, Wainwright chose this highly unusual name of an actual friend of his, a respectable man who was understandably astonished to find another such outlandishly spelt surname (with the same Christian name) as his own, in the one small circle. When the truth came to light he was, besides astonished, also highly indignant.

In actual fact, Harriet was lying, shot dead, buried deep in chloride of lime under the floor of a paintroom in Wainwright's warehouse. In November 1874 the shop at No 84 was burnt down, but Harriet remained undisturbed across the road for a whole year until, Wainwright having been made bankrupt and the warehouse taken over, it became imperative to move her. Meanwhile, Thomas had opened an ironmongery business in a building oddly called 'The Hen and Chickens' (it does not appear to have been a pub) across the river at the corner of Southwark Street and Borough High Street. This singularly accommodating relative agreed to let Henry store poor little Harriet's bones in the deep cellars of these premises. However, when Henry (probably helped by Thomas) set about the grisly task of digging her up, he found he had more than bones to contend with—the lime had preserved rather than destroyed the body. He therefore cut it up and made it into two parcels, which he wrapped in American cloth. At four o'clock on Saturday, 11th September, a year to the day after the murder, Henry Wainwright set out on his fearful odyssey.

When his shop had been burnt to the ground (a little suspiciously, it appears), Henry had given up his own business and taken a position as manager of a similar concern at 78 New Road, off Whitechapel Road nearby. Also in the firm was a young man named Stokes, who lived at 34 Bakers' Row (now Vallance Road) exactly opposite New Road. Wainwright met Stokes and asked him if he would help carry a couple of parcels. Anxious to oblige his manager, the young man agreed. Together they went through Vine Court, adjoining the warehouse, to the back entrance, picked up the packages, and set off towards St Mary's Church (bombed in 1941 and now a green space). As they reached it, about a quarter of a mile westwards, Stokes, who had already noticed a most unpleasant smell, panted that his parcel was too heavy and he must rest. "For God's sake don't drop it," said Wainwright, "you might break it." He then, again with unbelievable stupidity, himself went off to fetch a cab. Stokes at once pulled open a corner of his parcel (he afterwards declared a Voice from on High had commanded him to do so)—and discovered a woman's hand sticking out. Henry Wainwright returned with a cab, put the parcels inside and drove off. Recovering from his shock, Stokes ran after the cab, calling on passers-by for help. The cab went down Church Lane (afterwards White Church Lane) to Commercial Road. At the corner, Henry stopped the cab, dismounted, and walked to the corner of Greenfield Street, where he had spotted Miss Alice Day, a ballet dancer from the Pavilion Theatre. He was now, somewhat belatedly, smoking a large cigar in an effort to counteract the stench of his parcels. He offered Miss Day the pleasure of a drive across the river— asking her, however, not to talk as he had some thinking to do. Followed by a breathless, constable-calling (and derided) Stokes, the cab drove through the City to the river, rattled over London Bridge, and drew up near the Hen and Chickens. The place was empty as Thomas had now sold up his business and cleared out the stock. Henry took one parcel inside and returned for the second: but by now Stokes had at last attracted attention, and two policemen were waiting. "May we see inside your parcel, sir?" one asked politely. "We have reason to believe it is wrong." It was, indeed, 'wrong'. Desperately, Wainwright tried to bribe the constables, only to be curtly informed that they put duty above riches. Together with the horrified Miss Day, Wainwright was taken to Stone's End Police Station. Tried and convicted, Henry Wainwright was sentenced to death, Thomas to seven years penal servitude as accomplice after the fact—the precise share of his responsibility has never been established. Stokes was commended for his public-spirited sprint and awarded the slightly significant figure of thirty pounds.

Though the buildings have long since gone, and the present street numbering is different, the sites of the Wainwright story are easy to trace. The Pavilion Theatre was by the west corner of Vallance Road: it was burnt down, rebuilt, bombed, became a Yiddish Theatre and a cinema, and in 1961 was demolished. No 84 adjoined it, and is now replaced by a synagogue. The T-shaped Vine Court retains much of its old appearance. No 215 was the next shop but one to the Royal Oak Tavern, which still stands on the corner of the Court.

Henry Wainwright was hanged at Newgate on 21st December 1875—behaving, it is recorded, with some courage and dignity. Some sixty eminent persons had been invited to the yard of Newgate Prison for the pleasure of watching his execution. Looking scornfully round the privileged group he said, with icy contempt, "Come to see a man die, have you, you curs?"

Wainwright's favourite recital piece during happier days had been Thomas Hood's "The Dream of Eugene Aram", with its closing verse:

> Two stern-faced men set out from Lynn
> Through the cold and heavy mist,
> And Eugene Aram walked between
> With gyves upon his wrist.

We are now well into Jack the Ripper country. So much has been written about this most notorious of London murderers that we shall not deal with him here in close detail, but concern ourselves mainly with the sites—or what is left of them, for of all the scenes we shall be visiting, those of the Ripper's dark Victorian deeds have undergone the most thorough destruction. No-one can say for certain now whether he committed all of, or more than, the murders attributed to him, but the generally accepted number of his victims is six. All were killed within the comparatively small area of about a mile square, and within the comparatively short period of three months. The site of the first is probably the least changed today. On 7th August 1888 the body of Martha Turner, or Tabram, a 35-year-old prostitute living at 4 Star Place, Commercial Road (long vanished), was found on the first floor of George Yard Buildings, off White-chapel Road. She had been stabbed repeatedly, with two different weapons. The body was found by a lodger in the Buildings as he left for work at 5 a.m. George Yard, now Gunthorpe Street, runs parallel to and just east of Commercial Street—a narrow passage between gaunt buildings, arched at its southern end, and with the yard still to be seen.

Just over three weeks later, on 31st August, the Ripper's

second victim, Mary Ann Nicholls, was found lying partly in the road and partly across the pavement of Bucks Row (now Durward Street), towards the Brady Street end and just beyond the spot where it splits in two, retaining its own name on the northern side and becoming Winthrop Street on the southern. A carter passing along Bucks Row with another man in the darkness found the body, and hurried to Brady Street where they met a police constable. Meanwhile another policeman advancing on his beat from the opposite direction, Old Montague Street, had also discovered the dead woman, and she was taken to Old Montague Street workhouse mortuary. Altogether four people, two of them constables, had arrived on the scene from different directions within half an hour or less of the murder, and no-one had heard or seen anything unusual. Forty-two years old, separated from her husband, with no fixed abode, Mary Ann Nicholls had been scraping a bare existence on the streets. She was in the habit of sleeping in a room at 18 Thrawl Street, a short, narrow road joining Brick Lane to Commercial Street, but had recently been turned out because of inability to pay for a night's lodging. She then spent a few days in the adjoining Flower and Dean Street before being turned away here also, on the night she met her death. Thrawl Street and the incongruously named Flower and Dean Street (where neither deans nor flowers could have often been seen) are grim and gloomy enough today. In the 1880s they were among the most squalid spots in the district, the filthy haunts of prostitutes and thieves, the wretched and the wicked. Mary Ann Nicholls was last seen by a friend staggering drunkenly along a wall in nearby Osborn Street. The pathetic remark to the lodging-house keeper, "Don't let my 'doss', I'll soon be back with the money—see what a fine new bonnet I've got", has been variously attributed to her and to the next victim, Annie Chapman.

The western end of Durward Street (Bucks Row) is rapidly being opened up, and Vallance Road, at the far end from the murder spot, is a teeming mass of traffic. The spot itself, however, just beyond the split with Winthrop Street, is still a narrow, gloomy passage, though one side has been demolished save for a brick wall. The rows of small, shabby two-storey houses on the inner sides of the two streets are just as they were on that night. Though probably for but a brief while longer, they still conjure up the dismal surroundings in which poor,

wretched Mary Ann Nicholls became assured of a fame out-
lasting her death by over eighty years. In earlier years, Winthrop Street had been known as Ducking Pond Row, leading
to a place of punishment for scolding wives.

The mutilated body of Annie Chapman, the third victim, was
found in the backyard of 29 Hanbury Street in the early morning of 8th September. Though of slightly better class originally
than her associates, she was in many ways the most hopeless and
helpless of them all. She had been married to a veterinary
surgeon and was the mother of three children, but her addiction
to strong drink had broken the family up and for some years
(she was 47 when she met her death) she had eked out a miserable existence as a prostitute, creeping into a dosshouse bed
whenever she had been able to trade herself for a few pence.
Her most usual haunt was at 35 Dorset Street, off Commercial
Street. No 29 Hanbury Street was on the northern side between
Wilkes and Commercial Streets. No sign of it remains, the whole
section being long taken over by commercial buildings: the
houses opposite, however, are not greatly changed in appearance.

It was with the murder of Annie Chapman that the great
Ripper scare really began, and three weeks later he achieved his
most startling effect with the famous two-in-one night, 30th
September. The first of these was in Berner Street, now Henriques Street, a turning south of Commercial Road. In the backyard of No 40, then partly occupied by a working men's club,
the body of Elizabeth Stride (a Swede whose maiden name was
Gustafsdotter) was found by a hawker when he drove his cart
into the yard. Her throat had been cut, but it looked as if the
Ripper had been interrupted before he had time to complete
his usual work of mutilation. Elizabeth Stride was at one time
married to a carpenter and had several children. They managed
a coffee house in Poplar until—according to her own, uncor-
roborated story—tragedy struck her when both husband and
children were drowned in the pleasure steamer *Princess Alice*,
which sank in the Thames. This catastrophe, she was in the
habit of declaring, drove her to drink and later to prostitution.
In her final months her most frequent lodging place was in
Flower and Dean Street. Berner (Henriques) Street is much
changed now: a school stands partly on the site of No 40, and
the whole street is dominated by the high Post Office Data
Processing Building.

At the moment that the hawker was crying out in horror on finding Elizabeth Stride's body in Berner Street, another prostitute, Catherine Eddowes, aged 43, was released from Bishopsgate Police Station where she had been taken earlier in the evening, hopelessly drunk. Her home was in Fashion Street, just north of Flower and Dean Street, where she lived with a man named Kelly—the surname, by chance, of the Ripper's final victim. As the murderer turned out of Berner Street and, frustrated in his first attempt, made his way along Commercial Road towards the City, Catherine Eddowes was turning left out of Bishopsgate into Houndsditch. In all probability they encountered each other at the corner of Aldgate High Street, he having watched her half-drunken approach. She then suggested the nearby Mitre Square as suitable for their purpose, whereupon they went together up Duke's Place towards the dim, narrow Church Passage (now St James's Passage), through which the local constable on his beat came at 1.30 a.m., as he himself stated later. He had passed through the square from its main entrance on the far side, having seen and heard nothing. As he turned away from Church Passage, Catherine Eddowes and her escort entered Mitre Square through it—and on the constable's return at 1.45 she was lying, dead and mutilated, in the south-west corner. The Ripper's probable escape route was through Creechurch Lane, across Houndsditch and Middlesex Street, for a bloodstained fragment of Catherine Eddowes' apron was found in Goulston Street a few hours later.

Mitre Square, a cobblestoned courtyard about twenty by thirty yards in size, was much the most 'respectable' of the Ripper sites, but even so its situation, in the midst of a confusion of little passages and alleyways, provided useful spots to hide and then slip away. Today all this is exposed to the vulgar gaze— but the square itself is largely unchanged, save that the three-storey dwelling house at the corner where Catherine Eddowes was found has now gone.

The murder in Mitre Square was probably the nearest that Jack the Ripper ever came to being discovered, had he but known it. In the warehouse of Messrs Kearley and Tonge, forming one side of the square, was a nightwatchman whose habit it was to stand in the doorway just around the crucial time, for a breath of air and a smoke; but for some unexpected interruption of his routine on that particular night he might well have seen, from his shadowy viewpoint, the Ripper at his work.

After this night of double-feature horror there was quiet for five whole weeks, and Whitechapel was starting to think all might be over, when, on 9th November, the most appalling and revolting murder of all—the only occasion on which the Ripper was able to proceed with his ghastly work indoors and un-disturbed—took place in Miller's Court. The victim, Marie Kelly, was younger and more presentable than the pathetic, prematurely aged drabs he had attacked hitherto. Twenty-four years of age at the time of her death, she had married at 16, lost her husband in an accident four years later, and since then had been living—at first with a lover, then alone—in the single ground-floor room where her mangled body was found. The discovery was made at about 11 o'clock on the morning of the 9th, by a man who went to collect the rent. On receiving no reply, he put his hand through a broken window-pane, pulled aside a rag of curtain, and looked inside. The room was a shambles. Marie Kelly's naked body, or what was left of it, lay on the bed—practically every organ had been removed and was draped or scattered around the room. Her heart was placed on the pillow by her head, which had been cut almost clean from the trunk. The fireplace was piled with charred clothing. This may have been burnt to provide light for his work (the heat had been so intense that a metal kettle had partly melted), but it has also given rise to some of the numerous theories as to the Ripper's identity—including one that he may have worn a woman's clothes as a disguise.

Miller's Court opened off Dorset Street (where Annie Chap-man slept when she could afford a bed), a turning off Com-mercial Street just south of Spitalfields Market. After the crime, Dorset Street was changed to Duval Street. In 1928 Miller's Court was demolished to make way for an extension of the market. Now everything is gone, including Duval Street itself, and the space is filled by an enormous multi-storey car park, bounded on the south by White's Row, which ran parallel with Dorset Street, and may still afford some reminder of its neigh-bour's appearance. Miller's Court was never a true courtyard, but rather a shallow passage between the house backs. Leonard Matters, probably the last visitor to the place before its disap-pearance, describes it in his book, *The Mystery of Jack the*

Ripper, as a "dirty, damp and dismal hovel, with boarded-up windows and a padlocked door, as though the place had not been occupied since the crime was committed".

After this fearful climax Jack the Ripper disappeared into obscurity—and into history. More than any other murderer, he belongs to his period and his setting; as the sites of his crimes are increasingly and more thoroughly obliterated, so the dark, shadowy figure fades into a vanished, but not forgotten, past. In Mitre Square are two commemorative plaques—one to the site of St James's Church, the other to that of the Priory of the Holy Trinity. To the most famous, if least illustrious figure of its past there is no such tribute.

Before finally leaving Jack the Ripper we may note one or two murders sometimes, though probably mistakenly, laid to his charge. On 3rd April 1888, before the first 'official' Ripper killing, Emma Smith, 45-year-old prostitute, was attacked in Osborn Street, Whitechapel, and died as a result of her injuries. This was probably the work of a robber gang. Emma Smith lived in George Street, which ran parallel to Brick Lane near Shoreditch Station. On 21st November, in a house in George Street itself, a man tried to cut the throat of a woman named Annie Farmer, but made off when she screamed. On 17th July in the following year Alice Mackenzie, known as 'Clay Pipe Annie', who lived in Gun Street, Spitalfields, was found with her throat cut and wounds on her body, in Castle Alley, a cramped and secluded passageway off Whitechapel Road. Two years later, in February 1891, Frances Coles, of Thrawl Street, was killed in the same way under a dark railway arch leading from Chamber Street to Royal Mint Street (once Rosemary Lane). All these, and doubtless others, were added to the score, but six is the generally accepted toll. Some investigators even favour five only, having doubts as to whether Martha Turner in George Yard Buildings was a genuine Ripper murder.

Duval Street, before it was demolished, was the scene of another killing seventy years later. On 8th February 1960 Selwyn Keith Cooney was shot dead at the incongruously named Pen Club. Cooney was manager of another club, the 'New Cabinet', Gerrard Street, Soho, and the shooting was a climax in an underworld gang war. Three men were arrested and charged, but despite the presence of over thirty witnesses in the club, none was found guilty of murder. The verdicts were one of causing grievous bodily harm and two of being accessories after the fact. The case was marked by the unwillingness, or fear, of bystanders to give evidence. A second start to the trial had to be made after one of the jury, in all innocence, visited a prison where an acquaintance was being held on remand in a cell next to one of the accused.

Running from Whitechapel High Street towards the river, and essentially a continuation of Commercial Street, is Leman Street, with its well-known and—at least during the period we have been considering—extremely busy police station. Parallel with part of it is Goodman Street, a reminder that this district was once part of a farm belonging to the Abbey of the Nuns of St Clair and known as Goodman's Fields. In earlier years Goodman Street was known as Rupert Street, and an even earlier Goodman Street ran where Goodman's Yard runs now—if there is one occupation that street-planners enjoy more than any other it is surely that of creating a condition of utter confusion.

Rupert Street (Goodman Street) in 1909 consisted partly of lodging houses where sailors would spend their leave, and their pay, with the prostitutes who lived there. On 15th March of that year two members of the crew of S.S. *Dorset*, newly docked from Australia, picked up Ellen Stevens and Emily Allen and were taken by them, after a few hours of pub-crawling, to No 3. A constable from Leman Street noticed two men peering through the shuttered windows from the pavement, and then enter the house. Later in the night he was summoned back to Rupert Street, to find one sailor lying on the opposite side of the road, stabbed through the heart. His companion was afterwards found wandering along Whitechapel Road in a dazed condition, muttering something about a fight. A trail of silver threepenny pieces, often collected by sailors to distribute among small boys when on leave, led to the door of No 3. Inside the house were the two girls (one in a drunken sleep) and two brothers, Morris and Marks Reubens (or Rubens) known to the police as pimps and thieves. All four were arrested, and Morris Reubens immediately began to accuse his brother. Charges against the girls were dropped, and one of them gave what was accepted as a substantially true story of robbery and murder. Sir Travers Humphreys, who appeared for the Crown, has described the outburst from Morris Reubens when the verdict of guilty was delivered—screaming, "Vot, gentlemen? No recommendation? Oh my poor mother! Vot, no recommendation?" Both were hanged.

Goodman Street is now a dark, cobbled, silent channel between vast murky warehouses, crossed at one stage by a covered bridgeway—changed no doubt from its Rupert Street days, but not difficult to picture as the setting for this cowardly and sordid crime.

Writing in 1927, S. T. Felstead notes (in his life of Sir Richard Muir) that apart from the Reubens brothers only one orthodox Jew had been executed in London for murder. This was Mark Goodmacher, a tailor living in Grove Street (now Golding Street), St George-in-the-East, who killed his married daughter, Fanny Zeitoun, on 20th September 1920. Relations had apparently been strained for some time between father, daughter and son-in-law, who all lived together in the same house. When the latter came home from work on that day he found his wife lying dead with her throat cut, and Goodmacher stretched out by her side. Her personal belongings, linen, jewellery, even money, had been destroyed. Goodmacher was sentenced to death. It seems that he had been upset because his daughter and her husband refused to speak to him on the Day of Atonement—a time for reconciliation. It seems an inadequate motive, however, for murder.

Ajoining Golding Street is Burslem Street. In 1860, when its appearance was very different and it went by the name of James Street, an elderly widow was found dead at No 9, killed by a blow from a hammer. Left comfortably off by her husband, a dust-contractor and brickmaker, Mrs Elmsley lived on rents she collected herself from various house properties. The obvious motive was robbery, though in fact only a few valuables were missing. A man named Mullins volunteered information against a Mr Emms, one of the woman's agents, but was himself eventually convicted and hanged, protesting his innocence to the last, before a vast crowd at Newgate. An odd feature of the case was the presence of several rolls of wallpaper on the table in the front room. Presumably the widow had either been selecting patterns for herself or showing them to somebody else, but in spite of appeals no explanation of either their presence or their source was ever forthcoming. Neither was it discovered how Mullins could have got into the house. The empty air where once stood 9 James Street, may one feels, preserve a mystery still unsolved, and Mullins' violent protests against his conviction could well have been a genuine cry against injustice done.

Turning south from Burslem Street down Cannon Street Road, we cross Cable Street and so arrive at what was known in 1811 as the Ratcliffe Highway—later renamed George Street and now joined with its continuation to the Regents Canal Dock as The Highway. During the year in question, when the Ratcliffe Highway was notorious for its dens of thieves and general skulduggery, there occurred a number of murders that caused at least as great a sensation as those of the Ripper nearly eighty years later. Macaulay wrote of London being in a state of terror, of doors barred and stocks of blunderbusses and other weapons bought up. One shopkeeper sold three hundred rattles in ten hours for use as alarms.

The first victim was Mr Marr, a young man who kept a lace and hosiery shop at No 29. On the night of 7th September he sent his servant girl out to buy some oysters for supper. On her return, she found herself locked out and the house in darkness. Her calls for help resulted in the discovery of Marr, his wife, their baby and an apprentice boy of 13, all violently slaughtered, their heads smashed in and their throats cut. Little or nothing of any value had been taken. Twelve days later a much older man named Williamson, landlord of the 'King's Arms', 81 New Gravel Lane (now Garnet Street), his wife and an elderly maidservant were found similarly treated. Their lodger, a man of 26, heard noises, investigated, saw a figure looming over a body and, placing discretion before valour, escaped through his bedroom window, using his sheets as a rope, and gave the alarm. It was certainly this interruption alone that saved the life of the landlord's 14-year-old daughter. The discovery of a sailor's maul, or hammer, led to the apprehension of a labourer named John Williams who was lodging at the Pear Tree Inn down by the river, near Cinnamon Street. Among the inmates were several sailors, including the owner of the weapon. The motives for the killings were not clearly established : that for the first seems to have been some sort of grudge against Marr, the second was most probably robbery.

Williams hanged himself in his cell in Cold Bath Fields prison shortly after his arrest. In accordance with gruesome contemporary custom, his body was placed on a cart and driven past the homes of the victims through gloating crowds before being buried beneath the pavement at the crossroads of Cannon Street Road and New Road (now part of Cable Street). Time, bombs and demolishers have long since eradicated all trace of both the appearance and the atmosphere of the evil old Ratcliffe Highway, but—as so often happens in even the most devastated districts—the street shapes remain and the former names can be traced. The block that contained Marr's shop was almost opposite Betts Street, bound on three of its sides by The Highway, Pennington Street and Artichoke Hill, where Cuttle Court flats now stand.*

It was of Williams and the Ratcliffe Highway murders that Thomas de Quincey wrote in his essay "On Murder, Considered as One of the Fine Arts."

Another Ratcliffe Highway murder (among many, for a certainty, that are unrecorded) was that of John Pegsworth, who kept a tobacconist's shop at No 69. A few doors along lived John Holiday Ready, a tailor at No 137. The two men often did business together. At the beginning of January 1837 Pegsworth gave up his tobacco selling and closed the shop. For some time he had owed Ready £1 for a jacket supplied to his son, and now the tailor, thinking perhaps that the closing of the shop indicated Pegsworth was not doing too well, began to press for his money. When nothing was forthcoming, he threatened to sue. On 10th January Pegsworth bought a large knife, called on the tailor in his shop, and stabbed him to death. Though he attempted to withdraw the knife from the wound, Pegsworth did not try to escape and never denied his guilt. He was duly executed. According to contemporary reports "the wretched convict went to his death with becoming resignation"—which did not, however, give the unfortunate Mr Ready back his life.

Returning now to the northern part of our district we arrive at Columbia Road, Bethnal Green, leading from Hackney Road near Shoreditch Church. Here until quite recently stood Columbia Market, erected through the good offices of Baroness

---

* In an excellent recent book on the Ratcliffe Highway Murders, T. A. Critchley and P. D. James argue interestingly that Williams may well have been much maligned, and that his supposed suicide in prison was, in fact, one more murder. This exciting and probably definitive study includes a detailed map of the district pointing the various sites. (*The Maul and the Pear Tree*, Constable, 1971)

Burdett-Coutts (Baroness Road runs to north of the site) on what was once a crowded, pestilential jumble of hovels and tenements euphemistically called Nova Scotia Gardens. Here in 1831 a pair of wretches named Bishop and Williams, plying a trade similar to that of Edinburgh's Burke and Hare, decoyed a poor Italian boy into their hut, drugged him with laudanum, drowned him in a well, and asked twelve guineas for his body at King's College. Their execution at Newgate was watched, it is said, by thirty thousand people.

Finally, though the crime of which he was convicted took place on Clapham Common, Steinie Morrison was so much a man of Whitechapel that it seems appropriate to record the case here. The victim whose body was found on the morning of 1st January 1911, lying by some bushes beside a pathway leading from the bandstand to Battersea Rise, was a 48-year-old Russian Jew named Leon Beron. He had been in England for some time, living with his brother at 133 Jubilee Street, Stepney. Although his sole income was some £25 a year levied from property he had the reputation among his associates of being a gentleman of means, and was known to carry around with him a considerable number of sovereigns, in addition to a heavy gold watch. Both money and jewellery were missing when the body was found. He had been killed by violent blows on the head, and had then been stabbed several times. In addition, cuts vaguely resembling the letter S had been made on his face after death.

Beron was one of a group of foreign *emigrés*, mainly Russian Jews, who used to gather at a small establishment run by a man named Snelwar, known as the Warsaw Restaurant, 32 Osborn Street. There they spent the entire day talking, reminiscing, discussing and, as a secondary consideration, eating and drinking. For some time before his death Beron's constant companion had been a compatriot known as Steinie Morrison; he had several aliases and his real name was thought to be Alexander Petropavloff. Morrison was a strikingly handsome and popular young man—he was also a professional burglar and petty crook. He was staying with a Mr and Mrs Zimmerman, 91 Newark Street, which runs parallel to Whitechapel Road, joining New Road to Sidney Street of the siege. Before this he had lodged briefly at 4 Whitfield Street (now Kiffen Street) near Old Street, and at 5 Grove Street off the Commercial Road. After the murder Morrison appeared to be suddenly flush of money. He had been seen with Beron late on the night of 31st December, and during the preceding months was working at a bakery at 213 Lavender Hill, close to a turning which led to the spot on Clapham Common where the body was found. This would indicate a familiarity with the district and provide at least some ground for speculation as to why Beron should have been found dead so far from his usual haunts. Morrison now left his lodgings and stopped visiting the Warsaw Restaurant, spending the night of 2nd January at 72 Fieldgate Mansions, near Newark Street, and then crossing the river to stay with a prostitute at 116 York Road, Lambeth. It was in Whitechapel that he was arrested, however, as he sat down to breakfast at Cohen's Restaurant in Fieldgate Street, on 8th January. He was taken to Leman Street Police Station.

The main evidence against him was provided by three cabmen who identified him as a man they had driven, in company with another, between the East End and Clapham Common during the hours of the night in question. Morrison's chief defence was an alibi provided by the Zimmermans. The trial was notable for the hysterical atmosphere generated by the excitable and often defiant witnesses, one of whom went completely off his head. Typical of the exchanges was this one, between counsel for the defence (Edward Abinger) and a Mrs Deitch:

Q. What is your husband?
A. He is a gasfitter.
Q. And what are you?
A. What am I? I'm a woman, of course.
Q. I can see that, but what is your occupation?
A. Well, that's a fine question to ask me! I'm at home in my house, looking after my children.

In actual fact, by suggesting that Mrs Deitch used her house for less admirable purposes, and thus attacking a prosecution witness, Abinger, despite the judge's warning, opened the way for the revelation of his client's activities as a criminal. Morrison spent ten years in prison, violent, protesting his innocence, longing to die. Eventually he accomplished his purpose by persistent fasting, at the age of 39.

Few of the buildings connected with this famous case remain today. Osborn Street was practically laid bare in the 1940–41 blitz, and numbers 32–38 now comprise a smart modern block of offices and flats. Nearby, however, is a small café perhaps not so very different, in externals at any rate, from the 'Warsaw'. Only a few small houses remain at the northern end of Jubilee Street to suggest its former apperarance. Cohen's Restaurant has long gone, but Fieldgate Mansions, somewhat grim but strongly and imposingly built, still stand. 213 Lavender Hill may be traced, and so, surprisingly, may 91 Newark Street, Whitechapel, though shuttered, derelict and obviously doomed soon to disappear. The real mystery—Beron's agreeing to make the journey to lonely Clapham Common—has caused lasting interest in the Morrison case. Coincidences of time and place (and even the mystic cuts on the dead man's face) have led some people to form theories linking the murder with the Sidney Street siege. Others scorn the idea. As with such mysteries as Lizzie Borden, William Wallace and Charles Bravo, it is rather a case of "you reads your books and you takes your choice".

2

A NOSEGAY BEFORE HANGING
The City: The Tower, Newgate, Old Bailey

The Tower of London, with feet in both camps, is situated in the Borough of Stepney but in the postal district of the City of London. Despite its formidable history it has but slight concern with our present purpose, for only two notable murders are linked with its name (unless, of course, one considers the Tower Hill bloodbaths of the Tudors as such), and of these two, one is wholly unproven.

This is not the place to enquire into the tragic story of Richard III and the blackening of his character and reign by the unscrupulous and sycophantic scribes who survived him. The legend, planted and nurtured by the usurpers, has persisted to this day, though eaten away by time and research until little remains. His 'murder' of his nephews was alleged, on the flimsiest and most suspect of evidence, to have taken place in the Bloody Tower. Cases have been made for both Henry VII and the Duke of Buckingham having equal, or greater, interest in the deaths of the unfortunate princes—if, indeed, they were done to death in the Tower at all. The discovery of a small heap of bones during the reign of Charles II means little in such grim surroundings despite the solemn pomp with which they were conveyed to Westminster Abbey for burial, though dental evidence derived from an examination in 1933 lends a certain weight to the argument that they might be those of the boys. The murder could, just conceivably, if we put our faith in contemporary and biased writers, have happened, and could, just conceivably (though not very probably) have been committed with the connivance of Richard. That is the limit to which the most devoted follower of the devious, rapacious, fish-cold Henry VII can conscientiously go.

The one undoubted murder in the Tower was that of Sir Thomas Overbury in 1613. Overbury, a poet and statesman, was a youthful friend of Robert Carr, a page to the Earl of Dunbar, whom he met in Edinburgh while on a holiday. They came to London together, and Carr attracted the homosexual eye of James I, who made him first his favourite and later Lord Rochester. Overbury retained his influence over his friend, and it could be said Rochester ruled James, and Overbury ruled Rochester. In 1611, however, the latter fell in love with the young Countess of Essex, Frances Howard. Overbury was violently opposed to this alliance, particularly when it became evident that Rochester intended to marry her if she could obtain her divorce (Essex was abroad and the marriage apparently un-consummated). Never one to curb his tongue with the reins of niceties, Overbury roused both Rochester's and the Countess's fury with his attacks, and eventually, on a trumped-up charge, he was imprisoned in the Bloody Tower. Even this, however, did not satisfy the rage of Frances Howard. Through the agency of the Lieutenant of the Tower, Sir Gervaise Helwyss, with the assistance of a physician's widow named Mrs Turner, Overbury was poisoned in a slow and ghastly manner, with copper vitriol.

Months passed in silence, but Overbury's friends were un-easy, and their suspicions gradually grew stronger that all had not been natural about his death. Then a young man who had been employed in the Tower when a boy, fell ill in Flanders and, when he learnt that he was dying, confessed to a share in the plot. Despite the efforts of James to keep things nice and quiet the truth came out. Helwyss, Mrs Turner and others concerned were hanged in chains on Tower Hill. Mrs Turner also incurred harsh criticism for popularising the use of yellow starch in ruffs, cuffs and bands. Her executioner used the same colour, and as a result it became 'generally detested and disused' thence-forth.

The last prisoner of note to be incarcerated in the Bloody Tower was Arthur Thistlewood, the Cato Street conspirator (see page 79), and the last of the long line of executions in the melancholy history of the Tower itself was that of Simon Lord Lovat on 9th April 1747. He seems to have been involved equally in Jacobite and anti-Jacobite intrigues, but it was on account of the former that, after the Battle of Culloden, he went to his death. A scaffolding built to accommodate some thousand spectators collapsed during the proceedings, killing twelve. Lord Lovat, it was said, seemed to enjoy seeing the downfall of so many Whigs.

Leaving, perhaps with a lightening of the spirit, the Tower and its dismal record, we move further into the City proper. On 28th September 1912, a married man in his forties named Edward Hopwood shot an actress, Florence Dudley, in a taxi outside Fenchurch Street Station and then attempted to commit suicide. He had made her acquaintance at a Manchester theatre, and fallen violently in love with her. Jealous and possessive, he even went so far as to have her watched when unable to be with her himself. Apparently she had met him earlier that day in the Holborn Viaduct Hotel and told him she wanted to break off their relationship immediately. There was no doubt of his guilt, and Hopwood was hanged. His affection for the actress, however, seems to have been genuine and deep, and it may well be that a less abrupt, a more gently suggested severance, might have avoided a double tragedy.

A short distance farther west, on 8th December 1944, there occurred a robbery which ended in a particularly cruel and vicious murder. Ronald Hedley, Thomas Jenkins and two other men planned a smash-and-grab raid on a jeweller's shop in Birchin Lane, between Cornhill and Lombard Street. The crime took place in the afternoon, when the street was crowded with City workers. Having smashed the steel grille with an axe, three of the gang snatched as much jewellery as they could hold—several thousand pounds' worth—and bundled into the car where Hedley sat ready to drive off. A retired naval officer in his late fifties, Captain Binney, tried to block their way. Hedley accelerated and drove right over him, then reversed into Lombard Street and made for London Bridge, dragging him beneath the car for over a mile. After passing over the bridge and along the Borough High Street, Hedley turned abruptly into St Thomas Street to the left, flinging Binney clear. He died in hospital of his injuries shortly afterwards. The car was found abandoned near the Elephant and Castle, but Hedley and Jenkins, both known criminals, were quickly traced. The Binney Medal Award for bravery in attempting to stop an escaping criminal was instituted by his family in memory of his courage. Hedley was sentenced to death, then reprieved. He served nine years in prison. For Captain Binney there was no reprieve.

Forty years previously, in 1902, a much more understandable reprieve had been granted following a tragedy that occurred a stone's throw away, in Post Office Court, off Lombard Street. A young woman named Emma (or Kitty) Byron sent a note by post office messenger to a stockbroker, Arthur Reginald Baker, at his office near the Exchange. In response to her request, Baker returned with the messenger to meet her at the post office. Customers at the counter noticed the pair in violent discussion, and as they emerged into Post Office Court she drew a knife from her muff and stabbed him several times. He died almost at once, whereupon she threw herself on the body, sobbing bitterly. It transpired at the trial that she had been living with Baker for some time in Duke Street, Oxford Street, and that he had treated her with the greatest harshness, amounting to actual physical cruelty when he was drunk, which was frequently. He spent her meagre wages (she worked as a milliner's assistant) and their life together was so violent that their landlady, Madame Liard, though sympathizing with the girl, threatened to throw them out. Despite all this, Kitty Byron remained infatuated with her lover. There was no real answer to the charge of murder except that she may have bought the knife originally with the intention of committing suicide in Baker's presence, until he goaded her into using it on himself. Following an intensely moving speech in her defence by Sir Henry Dickens, son of Charles Dickens, the jury added to their verdict a strong recommendation to mercy. Kitty Byron was reprieved and released from prison after six years. It is pleasant to note that, when the true story became known to them, the money for her defence was provided by Baker's fellow members on the Stock Exchange.

Moving still further back in time, and towards the river, we come to Cannon Street in a period when it was inhabited at night to a greater and more domestic extent than is the case today. At nine o'clock on an evening in April 1866 Sarah Millson, a widow employed as housekeeper on the premises of Messrs Bevington, leather-sellers, was sitting by the fire on the first floor, chatting with another servant, when a bell rang in the hall below. Saying she knew who it was, Sarah went downstairs. For one whole hour she did not return, while her companion continued, with a singular lack of curiosity, to enjoy the warmth of the blazing coals. Sarah, she said later, always had a habit of gossiping on the doorstep. One senses a certain righteous disapproval in the remark. Eventually, however, presumably deciding that even for talkative Sarah this was a bit much, she went downstairs to investigate, and found the unfortunate woman lying dead in the hall, with severe wounds in the head. Her shoes, strangely, were on a table beside her, free from bloodstains. A small crowbar used to open packing-cases was lying near the body, also unstained. Another was missing. As the horrified servant opened the door to give the alarm, she found a woman sheltering, she thought, from the rain. On being asked to help, the woman exclaimed, "Oh dear no, I can't come in," and hurried away. The Cannon Street mystery was never solved.

Moorfields, in 1718, was mainly an open space, and there one John Price, known as Jack Ketch, ravished and murdered Elizabeth White, who sold gingerbread in the streets of London. He was, in fact, the hangman. All members of the profession were popularly called after the true and original Ketch, who, in the line of duty, executed Lord Russell in 1683 "in a butcherly manner"—he seems in fact to have been generally inefficient at his job. For depriving the gingerbread girl of her young life John Price, the Ketch of 1718, suffered the fate he had often meted out to others, being hanged at Bunhill Fields, a short distance away from his crime.

Though we are concerned in this book with the act of murder rather than its punishment, a few paragraphs must be included on Newgate and the Old Bailey, close to which we pass on our way from Moorfields. Newgate was originally the Prison Over the Gate (in the City wall), as was Ludgate, and as such is known to have been in existence in 1189, used as a county gaol for London and Middlesex. It was rebuilt, enlarged and strengthened in the fifteenth century, when it crossed the western end of Newgate Street. The prison was broken into by Wat Tyler and his peasants in 1381, and again by the Lord George Gordon rioters in 1780, who also set it on fire. In 1770 the gate was demolished during further rebuilding, and the edifice itself was demolished in 1902. Between that year and 1907 the present building, housing the Central Criminal Court (constituted in 1834), was erected to the plans of the architect Edward W. Mountford. This building was badly damaged in the big 'May air-raid' of 1941, when part of the Newgate Street side was destroyed.

The old prison had been surrounded by a wall broken by barred windows and niches containing statues. It was from here that Jack Sheppard, highwayman, made his most famous escapes, the first with the help of Edgeworth Bess, a footsoldier's doxy and a gold-digger who became his mistress and led to his downfall. The first break-out from Newgate was on 31st August 1724; on 8th September he committed a robbery in Fleet Street; on 10th September he was caught on Finchley Common; his greatest escape followed on 15th October; on the 29th he was caught in Drury Lane, returned once more to Newgate, and left it on 16th November for Tyburn and death, aged 22.

It was outside the debtors' door (where the entrance to the Central Criminal Court now stands) that the public executions took place, the first on 9th December 1783. The hangman in this instance was Edward Dennis—immortalized in Dickens' *Barnaby Rudge*—who executed twenty felons. An inn, the 'Magpie and Stump', stood across the way; a 'Magpie and Stump' stands there today. At St Sepulchre's Church it was the custom to present a nosegay to every criminal who set out on the journey to Tyburn—a gentle thought, perhaps, for those unhappy wretches about to leave for ever the flowers and fruits of this world.

The last public execution took place in 1868, that of Michael Barrett, a member of the Fenian Brotherhood whose object was to establish a republic in Ireland, for attempting to blow up the Middlesex House of Detention.

The last criminal to be hanged inside Newgate gaol was 24-year-old George Woolf (than whom few deserved it more) for the murder in 1902 of Charlotte Cheeseman on Tottenham Marshes. Charlotte, who worked in a cigar factory at Hoxton, was expecting to marry him when, with the utmost callousness, he wrote saying he had met someone he liked better and had therefore finished with her forthwith. "I hope I shall never hear of you or see you again, as I am indeed thankful I have got rid of you so easily," he said, adding in a postscript that it would be no good trying to put the blame on him if she found herself "in a certain condition". He even wrote to her employer warning him, without apparent reason and totally without truth, that she was not to be trusted—a letter the man very sensibly reported to the police. Charlotte's reply to the young man's dismissal of her is as pathetic a reproach as one may read anywhere: "Dear George, Don't be offended because I am writing this letter to you. Will you go out with me again as you know what you have done to me. I think it is a shame how you have treated me, but I will forget that and think of you all the more. You don't know how much I love you."

On the evening of 25th January they were seen having a drink together in the 'Rosemary Branch', a pub in Southgate Road. On the following morning some boys were playing on the Tottenham Marshes, at that time a desolate, waterlogged waste of ill repute, traversed by the Great Eastern Railway, when their ball ran into a ditch. There they found the body of Charlotte Cheeseman, her face and hands covered with blood, her nose broken, her hair matted with frozen blood. Woolf was swiftly apprehended and brought to trial. It was proved that he had beaten the girl about the head and face with a chisel. S. T. Felstead records that Sir Richard Muir, who prosecuted, rarely felt any satisfaction at having sent a criminal to his death, but the case of this disgustingly cruel and vicious young man was an exception.

The name Old Bailey probably derives from the ballium of the city wall between New and Lud gates—bailly in middle English signifying enclosure. The first Old Bailey Court was built in 1539 (for £6,000), trials before then having taken place in ordinary halls or in the prison itself. A new Hall of Justice was opened in 1774, followed by the present Central Criminal Court, as stated in 1907. In 1965 work started on a massive modern extension, due for completion in the early 1970s. Number One Court, Old Bailey, is probably the most famous criminal court in the world.

The story of London prisons is outside the scope of this book, but mention may be made of the vanished Tothill Fields Penitentiary, erected in 1618, demolished in 1885 and now replaced by Westminster Cathedral; the Millbank, built in 1799 to a design by Jeremy Bentham on the site now occupied by the Tate Gallery, and demolished in 1903; and the Fleet, which stood in the square formed by Ludgate Hill, Farringdon Street,

Fleet Lane and Old Bailey. It was destroyed in the Great Fire of 1666, rebuilt, burnt again during the riots of 1780, rebuilt, demolished finally in 1846. For some 800 years in all a prison of some sort had occupied the site, over part of which the railway now runs.

Returning from the punishment to the crime, and moving north-westward, we come to Turnmill Street, off Clerkenwell Road along and above the railway to Farringdon Station. Today merely a dull thoroughfare with commercial buildings on one side and a low wall masking the tracks on the other, it was looked on two hundred years ago as one of the most disreputable streets in all London—no mere achievement at the time. In Shakespeare's *King Henry IV*, Part II, Falstaff refers to Shallow's prating to him about "the wildness of his youth and the feats he hath done about Turnbull Street"—Turnbull being the early version of Turnmill. By the southern end was Chick Lane, later West Street, long since swept away by Farringdon Street and the railway. It was here that the infamous Metyards in 1758 tried to get rid of the remains of Anne Naylor (see page 74) by throwing them in parcels down the common sewer. Finding they were not being carried away, the two women hid them in the mud gathered before the grating—a story which throws a ghastly light on the hygienic conditions of the period.

Though it is in fact just outside the area covered by this chapter it may be convenient to record here a crime that occurred at the northern end of Farringdon Street, within a parcel's throw of Mount Pleasant Post Office. (The latter, incidentally, is built on the site of the Cold Bath Fields House of Correction.) Two narrow streets away is Wilmington Square, now a quiet and surprisingly restful little oasis surrounded by the traffic's roar. In 1911 the district was less respectable, so that when a man on his way to work early on an August morning heard a girl screaming, "Don't, Charles—don't!" he passed prudently by on the other side. A few hours later her body was found lying on the pavement, stabbed to death. She was identified as Rose Pender, 19, who had been living with, and supporting, a man of 22 named Charles Ellsome. She had broken with him shortly before she was murdered. The following day Ellsome reported to the police, giving the name of Brown, and saying he knew he would be wanted for questioning and was anxious to clear himself. His defence was a far from watertight alibi, but the chief prosecution witness (who claimed that Ellsome had confessed to him) was a professed and proud thief, and subject to epileptic fits. The case is interesting in that, though it appears virtually certain Ellsome was guilty (he was proved, for instance, to have bought a large knife shortly beforehand), the verdict was set aside by the Court of Criminal Appeal on account of a misdirection in the summing up, after an unusually exhausting day, by the eminent Horace Avory.

Nearby is Saffron Hill, named from the saffron that once grew in the garden of the old Palace of the Bishops of Ely. At the corner with Castle Street, near where Saffron Street is today, there stood in 1865 the Golden Anchor Inn, run by a Mr Shaw. The district at that time was crowded with Italians, and racial disturbances were frequent. Trouble blew up on Boxing Day of that year when Shaw allegedly insulted an Italian customer and threw him out of the bar into Castle Street. Britons and Italians gathered their rival forces, tempers flared and a short sharp fight took place. When things quietened down, two Englishmen were found lying in the 'Golden Anchor' severely wounded, the potboy and a man named Michael Harrington. The former recovered eventually, but Harrington died. An Italian picture-frame maker, Serafino Pelizzioni, was accused of the killing, though he protested that in fact he had been summoned from another pub in Cross Street (now St Cross Street) to act as peacemaker. He was convicted and sentenced to death. Considerable doubt was felt as to his guilt, however, and the case aroused the interest of Mr Negretti, a glass-blower from Como who had become one of the partners of Negretti and Zamba, the famous makers of optical and other scientific instruments. After enquiries, Mr Negretti traced a cousin of Pelizzioni's to Birmingham, and accused him of responsibility for the killing. Eventually this man was sentenced to imprisonment for manslaughter and Pelizzioni released. The famous building of Negretti and Zamba, with its meteorological station on the roof, was completely destroyed in the blitz of 1940–41.

Moving south to Fleet Street and turning up Fetter Lane on our left, we come to Fleur de Lis Court, a narrow L-shaped little passage ending now in a tiny open space. This quiet, poky spot was the setting in 1767 for a nightmare of horror, and an idea of the general character of the district may be gathered from the fact that the name Fetter Lane is said to have been derived not from any prison manacles but from the fewters—or beggars, vagrants, impostors and cheats—who crowded along it.

In the court dwelt the notorious Elizabeth Brownrigg and her wretched apprentices. After working as a domestic servant, Elizabeth had married James Brownrigg, who made a good living as a plumber. Apart from the house in Fleur-de-Lis Court they owned a place in Islington for use as a week-end retreat. They had a large family, though only one son appears to have been living with them at the time of the scandal. Mrs Brownrigg worked as a midwife, and had a responsible position caring for the poor women of St Dunstan's during their confinements. She also made use of her own home for private cases. The general housework was done by girl apprentices from poor homes, who were hired out by the parish. Elizabeth Brownrigg seems to have developed her violent sadistic impulses quite suddenly, perhaps on reaching the menopause. Three girls in particular, all named Mary (Jones, Mitchell and Clifford) received the most appalling treatment at her hands. On the slightest provocation —or indeed on none—they were stripped and beaten, their clothes were taken away, they were starved, and one of them, Mary Clifford, who may have suffered from some physical deformity, was forced to sleep on a mat in the coal cellar. James Brownrigg and the son, John, also took part in these orgies of cruelty. The girls' hands were tied together by a cord which was then passed over a waterpipe in the kitchen ceiling and drawn up until they were hanging by their wrists; the beatings then began and might continue for hours. When the piping at length collapsed, Brownrigg screwed a large hook into one of the ceiling beams to replace it.

The parish took little interest in the fate of the girls, and visitors and patients in the house seemed strangely ignorant— or careless—of what was going on. It was not until some years later that anything much was done. Then one of the neighbours, disturbed by the screams and yells of pain, managed to peep through a skylight over a covered yard and saw a girl lying on the ground too ill to speak or respond to her in any way. As a result of steps this woman took the authorities were compelled to look into the matter, and officials of St Dunstan's visited the house and demanded to see the girls. Mary Mitchell was taken away with wounds on her back of such severity that it was impossible to remove her clothing because of the dried blood which had sealed the material onto her skin, but the Brownriggs denied that Mary Clifford was in the house. She was found, however, pushed into a cupboard in a dying condition, and removed to St Bartholomew's Hospital, where she lingered on for a few more agonizing days. James Brownrigg was arrested immediately. Elizabeth and her son escaped for a brief period, hiding from place to place, until they were recognized lodging in a chandler's shop in Wandsworth. All three were tried at the Old Bailey and convicted of murder. Elizabeth was sentenced to death, James and John received the scandalously light sentence of six months' imprisonment each. The frightful, motiveless cruelty of these sadistic crimes roused the fury of the watching crowd, who gave vent to their own sadistic impulses by pelting and screaming at the miserable woman on her journey to Tyburn, 14th September 1767.

Emerging from the still dark but now scream-free little court, and crossing Fleet Street, we face Old Mitre Court, leading to the Temple. Opposite this spot in 1732 Sarah Malcolm, aged 22, was hanged for triple murder. She was a girl from a good family which had become impoverished by the spendthrift habits of her father, so that she was forced to work as a laundress. In the course of her labours she had access to the rooms of a wealthy old lady, Mrs Duncomb, and one day she strangled her, an elderly maidservant and a young girl, and robbed the house. Bloodstained clothing belonging to Sarah, and a silver tankard of Mrs Duncomb's, were found in the rooms of an employer of Sarah at Tanfield Court, Temple. Tanfield Court, described one hundred years ago as "a dull nook on the east side of the Temple", was destroyed during the bombing raid and is now no more than an archway opposite the Temple Church. On being accused of the murders Sarah tried to implicate two brothers and another woman but they were able to prove themselves innocent—or at any rate were never brought to trial. Sarah herself was taken to Newgate and searched—£53 was found hidden in her hair. She was apparently a girl of striking appearance. Two days before her execution she dressed in scarlet and sat for a sketch by William Hogarth; it was bought later by

Horace Walpole for the sum of £5.* After death, her body was taken to an undertakers in Snow Hill and exhibited for money. Later it was dissected and the skeleton sent to the Cambridge Botanical Gardens.

As the unceasing traffic pollutes the air of Fleet Street, the pedestrian, coughing out his fume-filled lungs by Old Mitre Court, probably has little time or inclination to ponder on the fate of 22-year-old Sarah Malcolm, rightly done to death on that very spot—but she appears to have been a more interesting character than this necessarily brief account of her sordidly materialistic crime might indicate.

---

* Hogarth also drew a pre-execution portrait of Elizabeth Adams, who in 1738, aided by Thomas Carr (a "low attorney" of Elm Court) robbed and murdered a gentleman named Quarrington at the 'Angel and Crown' tavern in Shire Lane, off Fleet Street. Shire Lane was swept away when the Law Courts were built: at the 'Bible' public house, No 13, there was a room with a secret trap to a subterranean passage emerging in nearby Bell Yard, of which Jack Sheppard made use when it was necessary to escape from the clutches of the law.

3

"IN COVENT GARDEN SHOT HER"
West Central: Chancery Lane, Strand, Theatreland, Charing Cross, Leicester Square

Just within the West-Central district is Chancery Lane, once in truth a lane winding through the open countryside, then built up as New Street and changing to Chancellor's Lane before receiving its present name. In 1815, at No 68, a merchant by the unusual name of Orlebar Turner, whose home was in Lambeth, carried on a business as a law stationers. His son Robert lived in the large building with his wife, two male apprentices, a maid, and a cook—Elizabeth Fenning, 21 years of age, small, pretty and of a gentle disposition. The house was overrun with rats and mice—a natural condition of domestic dwellings in those days, but a serious matter in a place where valuable papers and parchments were stored. In an attempt to keep the menace down a stock of arsenic was kept handy, the packet being clearly labelled in an unlocked drawer. Robert Turner seems to have been a neurotic man, and his wife an imperious nagger. She ruled her staff with a heavy hand and allowed them few personal rights. When Elizabeth's father, who lived and worked in a potato warehouse at Red Lion Passage, Holborn, called to see her a few days before the events to be described, he was refused admission. In March 1815 Elizabeth had been with the family for only six weeks. There had already been a spot of bother when one of the apprentices had tried to flirt with the pretty cook and she had resented it. Mrs Turner, unjustly it would appear, had sacked Elizabeth rather than the amorous apprentice, but a reconciliation had taken place, and Elizabeth herself said later that she was very happy indeed with this seemingly less than idyllic household. One evening in March, Orlebar took a meal with his son and daughter-in-law at which they all—servants included—tucked into a considerable number of dumplings prepared by Elizabeth. Shortly afterwards the entire household, including the cook, became violently ill. The arsenic packet had disappeared, and a white powder was said to have been discovered in the dumplings. On what seems the flimsiest of evidence Elizabeth was accused of trying to poison the family, who with one accord turned on her. No real motive was forthcoming, and rumours put about later that she had made previous attempts at murder remained completely unsubstantiated. Nevertheless, after the judge had summed up right against her, she was convicted and sentenced to death. Despite the fact that none of the family actually died, and all might well have been suffering from one of the many forms of food poisoning prevalent in those unrefrigerated days with rats abounding, she was executed at Newgate. The people of London, it is said—in those none too sensitive days—wept for the death of young Elizabeth Fenning.

Moving down the Strand towards the West End we come to the site of the most notorious of theatrical murders—that of William Charles James Lewin, better known as William Terriss, father of Ellaline who married Seymour Hicks, at his private entrance to the Adelphi Theatre on the evening of 16th December 1897. The murderer was a demented young actor named Richard A. Prince and the motive was jealousy. Terriss had earlier made a name for himself in Henry Irving's company at the 'Lyceum', but it was not until he started playing heroes in somewhat fustian melodramas at the 'Adelphi' that he became the popular idol of the day. Prince had been a small-part member of his company—a strange, twisted, tormented young man with a heavy waxed moustache, a squint, a strong Scots accent, and a decidedly inflated opinion of himself both as actor and dramatist. The fact that he was successful in neither field preyed on his mind to such an extent that he became a victim to persecution mania, and was known to his colleagues as Mad Archie. He was also an inveterate letter-writer, either of abuse to theatrical managers who had offended him, or to royalty and other celebrities in condolence or congratulation on events in their personal lives. The latter effusions were often in doggerel verse. In 1895 he tried to kill himself by jumping into the Regents Canal.

Terriss seems to have put up with both importunities and actual insults with admirable patience, but at last he refused to see him any more (he had already been dismissed from the Adelphi company), and Prince's seething envy finally boiled over into madness. On 13th December he tried in vain to get a complimentary ticket for the Vaudeville Theatre, which adjoined the 'Adelphi' and was under the same management. On being refused, he created a disturbance at the box-office, then returned to his lodgings near Victoria Station and brooded over his wrongs. He was out of work, unrecognized, insulted, penniless. He made up his mind to take vengeance.

Terriss was appearing at this time in William Gillette's drama *Secret Service*. In the early evening of 16th December he left the Green Room Club, where he had been playing poker, and drove with a friend in a cab to Maiden Lane, behind the theatre, walking on from there the few yards to his private entrance. In the dim gaslight he probably never even noticed the dark figure hovering on the opposite side of the lane, near Rule's well-known restaurant. As he started to unlock his door, Prince ran to him, drew a knife and stabbed him several times. He died less than half an hour afterwards. Prince was taken at once to Bow Street and charged. He had several pawn-tickets on him but no money, and his first words were to ask for something to eat. He made no attempt to escape and no defence. He was convicted of murder, but found insane and committed to Broadmoor, where he was seen by a visitor in after years conducting a concert given by the prisoners, with full dramatic flourishes, and evidently enjoying himself to the full.

It might be convenient here to mention two other murders connected with London's West End theatres. In 1692 Will Mountfort, an actor, was killed in Howard Street, which then, as now, runs across Norfolk Street from Arundel to Surrey Streets between the Strand and Temple Place. A certain Captain Hill, who swaggered around as a gallant, had developed a desire to 'possess' Mrs Bracegirdle, the famous actress then appearing at the Drury Lane Theatre. He worked out a wildly impossible plan to abduct her, inducing his equally irresponsible friend, Lord Mohun, to help him. The first attempt went wrong, so the pair decided to try again one night as she was returning home from the theatre. An additional annoyance to Captain Hill for some time had been the suspicion that Mrs Bracegirdle rejected him because she was carrying on with Will Mountfort—a highly improbable supposition as Mountfort was very happily married and both he and his wife were close friends of the actress. On the evening in question Hill and Mohun obtained a bottle of canary from the Horseshoe Tavern and proceeded to drink it while roistering about in the middle of the street. Later, while waiting for Mrs Bracegirdle to finish her performance, they started to hunt around for Will Mountfort. It seems that Mrs Bracegirdle had some idea of what was going on because she sent her servant to Howard Street to warn the Mountforts. Will, however, was out. On his way home he was stoppped by Hill and Mohun. The former hit him on the ear and told him to draw. Whether Mountfort actually did so or not is uncertain, but without any doubt Hill ran him through the stomach, and he died the next day in his Howard Street home.

It was inside the Drury Lane Theatre that James Hadfield fired from the pit at King George III and his family as they bowed to the audience from the royal box on an evening in 1800. Hadfield, who had been a soldier, was considered insane to have made such an attempt and was kept in custody until his death some forty years later. The King faced the situation with courageous imperturbability, and the orchestra and audience, after cheering wildly, performed "God Save the King" three times running, including a final verse written on the spot—with surely unsurpassed celerity of invention—by Richard Brinsley Sheridan, who happened to be present and composed a few lines of what might be called instant anthem.

The piazza of Covent Garden was the scene of the death of Martha Reay, or Ray, mistress of the Earl of Sandwich, who was shot by the Reverend James Hackman as she left the theatre on 7th April 1779. Hackman had at one time been an officer in the army, and had become acquainted with Martha Reay at the Earl's house near Hinchbrooke. They fell in love, but she would not leave Lord Sandwich, who had treated her with great kindness for years and by whom she had had several children. Still hoping she might one day change her mind and marry him, Hackman resigned his commission and joined the Church—presumably he thought that thereby his prospects would be improved. In time, however, he seems to have become convinced that there was no hope for him. One day he saw her by chance walking along Whitehall, followed her to Covent Garden, went back to his rooms for two pistols, then returned there and waited for the end of the performance. As she emerged from the crowd, he shot her. At his trial Hackman said that he intended originally to commit suicide before her eyes and the second pistol was in case the first misfired. Lord Sandwich, with notable generosity, offered Hackman any help he wished in his defence, but the distraught man wanted only to die. Martha Reay was the daughter of a labourer who lived at Elstree, Hertfordshire, and it is there that she is buried. Hackman was executed at Tyburn. An anonymous versifier, with high moral purpose if less than immortal poetry, commented on the tragedy :

> O Clergyman ! O wicked one !
> In Covent Garden shot her.
> No time to cry upon her God—
> It's hoped He's not forgot her.

Sometimes a natural phenomenon is so dramatically apt a background to a human drama that it is difficult to regard their coinciding as a matter of mere chance. On 10th July 1923, at the Savoy Hotel, Strand, a tragedy was reaching its climax to the accompaniment of the most violent storm to hit London for many years. For hours the flashes of lightning and rumble of thunder continued almost without break. At about two o'clock on the morning of the 11th a porter in one of the hotel corridors heard, faintly above the storm, several shots. They came from a suite occupied by an Egyptian, Prince Fahmy Bey, his wife and his confidential secretary Said Enani. When the alarmed porter managed to get into the room Fahmy Bey was lying dead on the ground in his pyjamas and his wife was standing by him with an automatic pistol. Three empty cartridges were on the floor nearby.

Madame Fahmy was a cultured and elegant Frenchwoman who had been previously married to a Monsieur Laurent. There was never any doubt that it was she who had fired the shots, but in one of the most dramatic defence speeches he ever delivered Marshall Hall secured for her a verdict of not guilty of either murder or manslaughter. In his cross-examination of prosecution witnesses he elicited from Fahmy Bey's devoted secretary (whom it was necessary to handle with extreme care to avoid any attack on his character) that Madame Fahmy was a sadly changed person from the "gay, cheerful, entertaining

and fascinating woman" she had been before her second marriage, that her husband had been "a bit unkind" to her, and
that she had said both secretary and husband were always
against her. From the doctor who arrived on the scene just
after the tragedy Hall obtained information that Madame Fahmy
had told him the Prince had treated her with cruelty and
brutality; and from the gunsmith confirmation that the pistol
was very easily triggered and someone unused to weapons might
reload it by firing a shot while thinking she had emptied it. By
the time Madame Fahmy entered the witness box to give evidence in her own defence the groundwork had been well laid.
It was soon apparent that her married life with a man of perverted and sadistic habits had become an unbearable misery.
Hall also established that she was totally ignorant of firearms
and, as she said, had merely meant to frighten him with the
pistol when he attacked her. During his final speech Marshall
Hall performed a dramatic—not to say melodramatic—piece of
business with the pistol and, in what was even for those days
a highly emotional peroration, concluded—after a reference to
Robert Hitchens' novel *The Garden of Allah*: "You will remember the final scene, where this woman goes out of the gates of the
garden into the dark night of the desert. Members of the jury,
I want you to open the gates where this Western woman can
go out, not into the dark night of the desert, but back to her
friends, who love her in spite of her weaknesses—back to her
friends who will be glad to receive her—back to her child who
will be waiting for her with open arms. You will open the gate,
and let this woman go back into the light of God's great Western
sun." Then, quoting another great advocate's words, "I don't
ask you for a verdict, I demand it at your hands." It is pleasant
to record that the jury complied.

Near Charing Cross in 1727 stood 'Robinson's', a noted Coffee
House. On an evening of that year Richard Savage, poet and
close associate of Samuel Johnson, was enjoying himself drink-
ing and rioting. A quarrel flared up, steel flashed, and a Mr
James Sinclair dropped dead, run through by Savage's sword.
He was tried, convicted of murder, and imprisoned in Newgate.
Fortunate in possessing friends in high places, however, he
was granted a King's Pardon through the mediation of the
Countess of Hertford, Lord Tyrconnell and Mrs Oldfield the
actress.

On the western side of Leicester Square—known in earlier days as Leicester Fields—stood the house of Sir Joshua Reynolds, destroyed despite indignant opposition in 1936 to make room for an enlargement of the A.A. building. Nearby in 1761 lived a fellow painter, less illustrious in his art but for a time even more widely known for less estimable reasons. Theodore Gardelle was a Swiss miniaturist who lodged with a Mrs King. On a day early in February of that year he sent the servant out on an errand, and when she returned told her he had been instructed by her mistress to pay her what was due and sack her forthwith. With surprisingly meek acceptance of so abrupt and unexplained a dismissal, the girl departed. For the next ten days or so Gardelle told enquirers that Mrs King had gone to the West Country. He even let a room to a lady seeking lodgings, and engaged a charwoman. Very shortly the latter found the cistern choked with bedding—and with pieces of flesh. The authorities were called in and found Mrs King's private room spotted with bloodstains. Charred bones and further pieces of flesh were hidden about the house. Gardelle declared that during a row he lost his head and stabbed her with a pointed comb—then lost it again and attempted to dispose of the body (in a notably ineffectual manner) instead of summoning a doctor. His whole behaviour after the crime, in fact, seems rash to the point of imbecility. The apparent motive was robbery. Watched by the usual crowds, Gardelle was hanged in the Haymarket, at the point where it is joined by Panton Street.

From Cambridge Circus north to Princes Circus, Shaftesbury Avenue is designated West-Central and thus comes within our present district. During 1931 the shop numbered 173–9 on the northern side (which has a back entry onto New Compton Street) had been empty for some time. In September of that year Frederick Field, a 32-year-old sign-fitter who lived at 148 Clensham Road, Sutton, was given the key by his employers and told to take down a 'to let' notice. When asked a day or two later what he had done with the keys he said that he had given them to a man with gold fillings in his teeth who had authority to inspect the premises. Since nothing was known of any such man, gold fillings or not, the firm's manager accompanied Field to the empty shop and broke in. There they found the dead body of a woman who had been strangled with her own belt. Her skirt had been removed, and her jumper used as a gag. She was identified as Norah Upchurch, a 20-year-old prostitute who had been staying at 82 Warwick Street, Pimlico, and was also in the habit of visiting a house at No 7 Bear Street, Leicester Square. Field's behaviour hereafter is a choice example of the inexplicable vagaries of the human character. At the inquest he identified a man as the one to whom he had referred, but when the coroner, Mr Ingleby Oddie, asked the latter to open his mouth it was clear he had not a single gold tooth in his head. This palpable and seemingly pointless lie increased suspicions already held by the police, but there was nothing really solid to work on, and no charge was made. In all likelihood that would have been the end of it, but nearly two years later, in July 1933, Field contacted a couple of journalists and told them that he killed Norah Upchurch, requesting the cost of his defence in exchange for the full story. After investigating the claim, the newspapermen called in the police. Field told the latter that after the murder he had stolen the girl's handbag and then thrown it away. As might be expected after so long an interval, this was never found, and the only evidence against Field was his own confession. This he suddenly retracted at the trial, declaring that his intention was to have his innocence proclaimed. The judge, Mr Justice Swift, directed the jury to acquit him.

Field's behaviour up to now could be considered strange, but the sequel was stranger still. At the time of his confession Field was in the R.A.F. Two and a half years later, in 1936, another prostitute, Beatrice Vilna Sutton, was found strangled on the bed in her flat at Elmhurst Mansions, Clapham. She had been dead for about twelve hours. Eleven hours previously the police had picked up a deserter from the R.A.F. who had been staying in Manor Street, Clapham. The man, Field, confessed to the murder (though at the time he could not have known she was dead), first to the R.A.F. guards, then to the police. He then followed the same procedure as before, declaring that he had killed the girl, a complete stranger to him, merely because he was fed up; then withdrawing the confession and substituting a vague story of having seen a man rush out of the flat after a quarrel and afterwards finding her dead. His reason for confessing, he stated, was that he wanted to commit suicide and had not the courage. This time, however, Field overreached himself—too many details of the crime could have been known only to the killer. His answer to the prosecution's question as to how he knew so much—"It was pure supposition"—understandably failed to carry any weight with the jury. They took only a few minutes to reach their verdict, and this extreme example of a murderer's subconscious urge towards self-destruction was ended. No suspicion in regard to Beatrice Sutton's death was directed towards Field until his confession. Had he kept silent on each or either case he might well have been living today.

Little Newport Street is a narrow thoroughfare linking the east end of Lisle Street (once part of the gardens of Leicester House, built 1632–36, destroyed 1806, and the temporary residence of King George III when Prince of Wales) and Charing Cross Road. On one side is a tall old block housing some rather tired shops; across the road is the back of the Hippodrome Theatre. Several miles away is Cecil Barnes Lane, on the outskirts of St Albans and in 1936 still an unfrequented and countrified spot. The link between these two dissimilar settings was forged in that year by the body of a murdered man. Emile Allard, better known as Max Kassel, or Red (or Ginger) Max, was either a Russian or a French Canadian—the matter was never fully cleared up. He was a dealer in cheap jewellery. He was also a pimp. Pierre Alexandre was the proprietor of a garage in Soho Square and the lessor of a maisonette comprising the second and third floors of a house in Little Newport Street. Georges LaCroix was a Frenchman living with a woman called Suzanne Naylor (or Bertron) in the maisonette leased by Pierre Alexandre. He was also an escapee from Devil's Island. Another inhabitant of the maisonette was a maid, Marcelle Aubin. On a certain night in 1936 this interesting quintet became involved in a drama which, for four of them, led to disaster. Kassell, it appeared later, owed Suzanne Bertron £25, probably in connection with various petty crimes in which he and LaCroix were associated. In some way he was lured to the maisonette and there shot by LaCroix while the two women sat listening in a bedroom. LaCroix then summoned Alexandre, over whom he appears to have had some hold, and made him help to load Kassel's body into the back of his Chrysler and dump it out in the countryside near St Albans. While they were doing so, Suzanne and Marcelle endeavoured to remove all traces of the shooting, washing bloodstains, burning the dead man's hat and the lace window-curtains, even trimming off the bottoms of the main curtains, which had become spotted with blood. Nemesis was not long delayed. Identification of the body led the police to Alexandre and LaCroix, neighbours told of hearing the noise of a quarrel followed by shots and breaking glass—and Marcelle Aubin filled in the rest. LaCroix fled to France, where he was joined later by Suzanne. He was caught and returned to Devil's Island. Alexandre received five years penal servitude. Life in Little Newport Street went on. Suzanne Bertron was found not guilty.

Moving across to the north-east boundary of our present area, we come to Gray's Inn Road, the southern portion of which in 1830 was still known as Gray's Inn Lane. While on duty in this section at 12.30 a.m. on 16th August, P.C. Long, of the recently established Metropolitan Police Force, saw three men behaving in what struck him as a suspicious manner. He followed them up the lane, past Theobalds Road and the then tantalizingly named Liquorpond Road, along Guilford Street and Doughty Street to Mecklenburgh Square. There the group stopped and talked. Suspecting a burglary was being plotted, P.C. Long went up to them and advised them to be on their way. One of them immediately drew a knife and stabbed him. He died within a minute, but another constable had heard the noise. He gave chase and caught one of the men, John Smith, alias William Sapwell. Housebreaking implements were found lying on the road where the murder occurred. It is thought that this may well be the first instance of a constable being killed in the execution of his duty. He left a wife and several children, for whom, one is glad to note, "a liberal public subscription was raised".

In nearby Russell Square is the solidly respectable and long-standing Russell Hotel. It was here that the decidedly unrespectable, in fact infamous, conceited and excitable Jean Pierre Vaquier stayed with Mrs Alfred Jones before poisoning her landlord husband with strychnine at the Blue Anchor Hotel, Byfleet, Surrey in 1924. They had met first at Biarritz, where Mrs Jones was taking a solitary holiday. A friendship sprang up, and they conversed—and later conducted a love affair—by means of two-way dictionaries. Vaquier later stayed some weeks at her husband's hotel, trying to sell the patent right of his brain-child, a new type of sausage machine. The strychnine with which he poisoned the unfortunate man, causing him to die in fearful agony, was bought from a chemist's shop at No 134 Southampton Row. After shouting, screaming, and gesticulating violently throughout his trial this vain, mean and abominably callous murderer was hanged at Wandsworth Prison in August 1924.

It was at the Russell Hotel also that Harry Roberts stayed a night with Mrs Perry after the killing of three policemen at Shepherd's Bush in 1966 (see page 94).

Off the opposite side of the square, behind the august walls of the British Museum, an elderly housekeeper living alone at 11 Montague Place in the early part of the nineteenth century, was found dead one morning, her throat savagely cut. The house, which was ransacked, belonged to a gentleman named Lett, living in Dulwich. Mrs Jeffe, the housekeeper, had been seen the previous evening talking to a young man dressed in a blue coat and wearing a white apron—soon to be identified as William Jones. Stephen Jones, the young man's father, was well known as an author and as the compiler of a dictionary resoundingly if somewhat puzzlingly called *Jones's Sheridan Improved*. His son had once gone to sea and latterly become something of a wastrel. At the time of the murder he was living with his mistress in Mitre Street (now Mitre Road), Lambeth. He had been in the habit of calling on Mr Lett with his father and in this way became acquainted with kindly old Mrs Jeffe, who would quietly help him with money. He repaid her by taking her life. Jones was not hanged, but transported to Van Diemen's Land for seven years. It has been suggested that certain 'persons of respectability'—perhaps in gratitude for the existence of *Jones's Sheridan Improved*—used their influence to save him from the penalty he so richly deserved.

4

TWO PARCELS AND A CASK
West One: Tottenham Court Road, Marylebone, Edgware Road and Hyde Park, Piccadilly and Soho

The area within the above bounds has the dubious distinction of providing the longest single list in our collection.

At the eastern border, parallel with and adjacent to Tottenham Court Road, Whitfield Street was the scene of an unsolved crime on the last day of 1903. Dora Piernicke, a Polish streetwalker, was found lying on her bed with her throat cut when the police, summoned by the landlady, broke open the door of her room. A lodger said that he heard strange noises during the night but, the neighbourhood being what it was, concluded they were merely indications that business was proceeding normally and enquired no further. The murderer, probably a client, was never found. Four years later a prostitute discovered in very similar circumstances formed the starting point of the famous Camden Town murder case (see page 110), but the death of Dora Piernicke from Poland caused little stir.

Whitfield Street and its surroundings were badly damaged by the blitz and the flying bombs: the Whitefield Tabernacle, between Whitfield Street and Tottenham Court Road, originally opened by George Whitefield the religious leader and rebuilt in 1903, was destroyed on 25th March 1945 in almost the last major rocket incident of the war, when seven people were killed.

The air-raids of the previous war were far less destructive, but because of their novelty and the general feeling of unprotectedness, almost as terrifying. A plane attack on the last night of October 1917 was the precipitating factor in a particularly bloody and gruesome murder. Charlotte Street (named after the wife of George III) runs parallel to Whitfield Street from Fitzroy Street to Rathbone Place. In the basement flat of No 101—not far from the house where the painter John Constable lived and died—lodged a 42-year-old French butcher named Louis Voisin, a hulking brute of great strength and little intelligence. He had sufficient cunning, however, to keep two affairs running simultaneously without either partner being aware of the existence of the other. The first, to become the indirect victim of a German air-raid, was a Belgian, Emilienne Gerard, 32, wife of a French army chef. The second was a Frenchwoman named Berthe Roche.

When the raid started, Mme Gerard left her rooms at 50 Munster Square and, following the custom in both wars, descended into the safety of the London Tube. When the 'all clear' sounded she surfaced, and was seen no more. On 2nd November a roadsweeper at work in Regent Square, about a mile to the east of Charlotte Street, found a parcel wrapped in a sheet and some sacking, lying just inside the railings. To his horror, he found it contained the headless torso of a woman, still partially clothed, together with a scrap of paper on which were scrawled the words "Blodie Belgiam". Nearby was a second parcel, of brown paper, in which were the legs. The remains were identified, through a laundrymark on the sheet, as those of Emilienne Gerard, and following the discovery of a photograph and an IOU signed Louis Voisin in her room, the police went to call on the basement flat in Charlotte Street. There they found the butcher sitting cosily with Berthe Roche. The squalid kitchen was fearsome enough in the ordinary way, with its dirt and mess, its big knife-sharpening wheel, its butcher's saws and other implements hanging on the walls; but in addition it was now splashed with blood which proved to be human. In the filthy outhouse were further horrors—the head and hands of Emilienne Gerard concealed in a cask and covered with sawdust. Even Voisin's pony and trap standing outside the house were stained with blood. At the police station he was asked to write the words "Bloody Belgiam" several times. Slowly and painstakingly he traced the letters: "Blodie Belgiam". His story, that he called at Munster Square, found the dismembered body, thought a trap had been laid for him, went out and had some lunch, then later cleaned up the place and removed the pieces, proved singularly unconvincing. He was found guilty, sentenced (in French) to death, and hanged at Pentonville prison. Berthe Roche was tried as an accessory and sentenced to seven years penal servitude. After a year or so she was found to be insane, and died in a mental institution the following May. What really happened that night in the loathsome Charlotte Street kitchen can only be conjectured now. Probably the two women met for the first time when Mme Gerard arrived unexpectedly for company after the raid; a quarrel flared up and Voisin, with or without Berthe's help, attacked and killed her. What is certain is that those two scribbled words "Blodie Belgiam", evidently intended as a brilliant device to divert suspicion from Voisin, were largely instrumental in sealing his fate.

101 Charlotte Street has gone, swallowed up by the huge building of Astor College, the Middlesex Hospital Medical School. Up to 97, however, the houses still stand and 101, with its basement below, must have been very similar.

Thirty years later, farther down the same street, the courageous Alec de Antiquis, owner of a little motor-cycle shop in South London and the father of six children, was shot and killed while attempting to foil a raid on a jeweller's shop at the corner with Tottenham Street. As three men came running from the shop, one of them brandishing a revolver, Antiquis, who was riding a motor-bicycle, drove it in front of them. One of the gang shot him through the head. A surveyor, George Grimshaw, who also tried to hold the thieves, was knocked to the ground and kicked. In the ensuing confusion all three got away, running down Tottenham Street towards Euston. Their abandoned escape car, stolen from Whitfield Street just before the raid, was taken to Scotland Yard. After a day or two of fruitless enquiries a taxi-driver reported that he had seen two men going inside the doorway of Brook House, 191 Tottenham Court Road, on the day of the crime with handkerchiefs round their chins. A search resulted in the discovery of articles of clothing in one of the empty rooms, and from there led eventually to the apprehension of Charles Henry Jenkins, 23, younger brother of the killer of Captain Binney (see page 41), Christopher Geraghty, 21, and Terence Rolt, 17. The murder weapon and, later, another gun were found on the bank of the Thames at Wapping. By about three weeks after the crime all three men had been arrested and charged with murder. It was revealed that Geraghty had been working in a paint shop almost directly across Tottenham Court Road from the police station at the time, and had watched the detectives moving in and out as they worked on the case. Jenkins and Geraghty were executed, Rolt, being under age, was sentenced to be detained during the King's pleasure.

Jay's the jewellers is no longer in Charlotte Street: the Scala Theatre, with all its theatrical history, having survived the bombs of a foreign enemy, has been demolished by destroyers nearer home; the opposite corner is now taken up by the James Pringle House of Middlesex Hospital. Alec de Antiquis, however, needs no material memorial to perpetuate his memory as a brave and selfless man who lost his life in an attempt to foil three ruthless young thugs. And a comment from Ex-Detective-Superintendent Robert Higgins, who worked on the Antiquis murder, sounds significant today: "Many criminals went as far as throwing away their guns", he writes, "when they heard that two young men were destined for the gallows."*

Leading off the south side of Fitzroy Square towards Tottenham Court Road is Grafton Way, once Grafton Street and probably retitled to avoid confusion with the Grafton Street off Bond Street. In 1894 it was the scene of the crime that gave Marshall Hall, in the words of his biographer Edward Marjoribanks, "his great opportunity". On the first floor of No 51 there lived a middle-aged Austrian woman who described herself as a music teacher visited from time to time by her husband. In reality, she had at one time been a governess, but now, with three children to support—one of them blind—she had for some years earned a precarious living by prostitution. In the old days, grand and generous, she had been known as the 'Duchess'; by 1894, ageing and with her looks gone, she was facing penury.

During the evening of 15th March Louise Hutchins, a young girl who lived on the floor above, was busy preparing to go off to a dance. Suddenly she heard odd noises, a crash and a man's voice moaning "murder" from the rooms below. Not to be put off from her evening's entertainment by such trifles she said good-bye to her mother and left the house. Later on Mrs Hutchins herself heard more voices, then saw Marie Hermann, the Austrian woman, go out and return later with a bottle of

* *In the Name of the Law*, John Long, 1958.

brandy. At 3.30 a.m. she was awakened by a loud thud and the sound of breaking wood. In the morning (after, presumably, a fairly sleepless night) she discovered blood in a common sink used by all the occupants. A short while later Marie Hermann met her on the stairs and said she was leaving and going to live elsewhere. She then went out and bought some furniture, surprisingly in view of her supposed poverty, and engaged two men to help carry downstairs a very heavy trunk. They were, she said, to handle it with great care as it contained her most treasured possessions. It was loaded into a van, and Mrs Hermann set off for her new address, 56 Upper Marylebone Street, which is now roughly that portion of New Cavendish Street between Cleveland and Great Portland Streets, about a quarter of a mile away. Mrs Hutchins, her detective instincts now at full stretch, followed the van, then reported the matter to the police, who as it happened already knew of Mrs Hermann. They called on her in Upper Marylebone Street, opened the trunk, and found the body of a heavily-built elderly man with several wounds about the head. He was identified as a retired cab-driver who lived in Albany Street. Against very considerable odds— the woman's reputation, her sudden possession of unaccountable money, the brutally injured body of a 70-year-old man—Marshall Hall managed to persuade the jury that Mrs Hermann had struck the blows in self-defence, and secured a verdict of manslaughter with a strong recommendation to mercy. Mrs Hermann was sentenced to six years penal servitude. Edward Marjoribanks notes that she was all gratitude to her counsel and solicitor, calling them "her saviours"; immediately after her release, however, she employed an attorney to write to the latter, Arthur Newton, demanding an account of all the money spent on her defence, to which, incidentally, she had made no contribution herself. "Dear Sir," Newton replied with cutting brevity, "We saved your client from the gallows. Yours sincerely. . . ."

As seems to happen so often, the actual house, No 51 Grafton Street, has now disappeared, replaced by a large modern block at the corner of Whitfield Street, but up to No 45 the old ones remain, if somewhat modernized; and those opposite gaze across at the site of the crime much as they did on the night it was committed.

Now to a tragedy in Oxford Street: Jack Adrian Tratsart, 27 years of age, was a toolmaker living in Norbury. During the

Second World War his father, stepmother, two sisters and younger brother had been living in Northampton while he stayed in Norbury to carry on his trade. In 1945 the family were happily preparing to return home, and on 20th April he arranged a little celebration at the Oxford Street Lyons Corner House. All except the stepmother assembled in the crowded ground-floor restaurant, together with an aunt who was already living in London. In the middle of the tea-party, without warning, Tratsart pulled out a gun, pointed it at Claire, the elder sister, and pulled the trigger. Everyone thought he was joking, and laughed—perhaps a little uneasily—as he tried a second shot, also without result. On the third attempt he fired two bullets at Claire, then two each at his father and brother. Not realizing the chamber was now empty, he put the barrel to his own forehead and again pulled the trigger. When nothing happened, he threw the weapon up into one of the hanging bowl lights. By this time, of course, the whole place was in an uproar. Claire and Mr Tratsart senior were dead, the boy badly wounded in the face. Jack Tratsart alone sat unmoved, waiting until the police arrived. In his statement he said he had been thinking of killing his brother and sister for years—she was an epileptic, the boy suffered from an inability to use his hands properly, neither stood any chance of living a decent life—and his father was "miserly, terribly bigoted and the worst person to have as a father". He was charged with murder, but found unfit to plead and committed to Broadmoor. He had apparently suffered from depression for a long time, not only over his private concerns but over the whole condition of the war-torn world. He died a few years later, closing one of the most tragic and strange cases of that shattered period.

Crossing Oxford Street to the south, and entering the heart of Soho, we come to Wardour Street, formerly known as Princes Street. On 10th February 1942, an ex-actress in her thirties known as Nita Ward (her real name was Evelyn Oatley) was found dead in her flat at No 153. Her throat had been slashed and her body mutilated with a tin-opener. The following June a 28-year-old R.A.F. cadet, Gordon Frederick Cummins, was sentenced to death at the Old Bailey for her murder. This was the final act in a series of murder cases that took place in a darkened London during the darkest period of a dark and dreary war, more closely resembling the crimes of Jack the Ripper than any others to date. In normal times, with fewer reports of mass slaughter elsewhere to fill the headlines, they would certainly have shocked the whole country. The murder for which Cummins was tried was actually the second of four for which he was indicted—he was also charged with two attempted killings. The case opened the previous day, 9th February, with the discovery of the body of Evelyn Hamilton, a 40-year-old schoolmistress, in the centre one of three surface air-raid shelters in Montagu Place, between Baker Street and Edgware Road. She had been strangled, but not sexually assaulted, and her handbag was missing. Evelyn Oatley's handbag also had been ransacked. On 11th February Mrs Florence (or Margaret) Lowe, 43, was found by her teenage evacuee daughter in the flat where she was living alone, No 4, 9–10 Gosfield Street, Marylebone. She had been strangled with a stocking, then cut about the body with a razor. A fourth murder was discovered very shortly afterwards, that of 32-year-old Mrs Doris Jouannet, at 187 Sussex Gardens, off Edgware Road, who had been attacked in much the same manner.

Two of the victims were known to the police as prostitutes. Mrs Jouannet had been soliciting men from the armed forces while her elderly husband was on night duty at a Paddington hotel. Understandable alarm now reigned in the blacked-out West End streets, particularly among members of 'the profession'. The police came up against the customary unwillingness to talk, but further stories began to come to light. Chief Inspector Greeno, in charge of the investigations, heard from a Mrs Mulcahy of an attack on her by a young airman whom she took to her flat at 29 Southwick Street, near Paddington. She had resisted so violently that he had fled, leaving behind him a belt. As Chief Inspector Greeno was dealing with this, news came in that George Frederick Cummins had been arrested and charged with an assault made immediately before that on Mrs Mulcahy. A Mrs Margaret Hayward had been taken by him to the 'Trocadero' for a drink, and they then went on to the 'Captain's Cabin', by Norris Street and St Alban's Street. Apparently she told him she didn't want to spend any more time with him, whereupon he pressed her against the wall just outside the 'Captain's Cabin' and grabbed her by the throat. She lost consciousness, but before she did so her cries attracted the attention of an off-licence delivery man and her attacker ran away—leaving behind him the most convenient clue he could have chosen, his gas-mask with his service number printed on the case. Cummins was swiftly traced to his billet in Prince Albert Road, NW8 (his home was at 21 Westmoreland Road, Barnes), and brought in for questioning. He pleaded drunkenness and declared he remembered nothing, but in his possession were found numerous small handbag items belonging to the murdered women. Cummins was executed on 25th June 1942, after a second trial, the first having to be cut short owing to the introduction of evidence connecting him with murders other than the one of which he stood accused. Had he not carelessly dropped pieces of his equipment behind him the killer might well have remained unknown to this day, except by the inevitable title of the Ripper of World War Two.

Leading off Wardour Street to the west is Broadwick Street, which was once known as Broad Street and consisted of a collection of hovels and huts shared alike by criminals and animals. On 26th September 1948 Rachel Fenwick, 41-year-old prostitute, was found dead in her flat overlooking the street. She was lying on the floor with her head under a settee and had been stabbed several times with, it is thought, a stiletto. Because of her bright auburn hair she had been known as Ginger, or Red, Rae. The flat, described by Detective-Superintendent Higgins as well furnished and clean, but very untidy, was almost opposite Trenchard House, named after Lord Trenchard, Commissioner of Metropolitan Police, in which were living-quarters for unmarried members of the Force. The circumstances resembled those of the killing of another prostitute, Helen Freedman, a Lithuanian known as Russian Dora, a few months previously in Long Acre. She was nearly 60 years of age. Neither crime was ever solved, so that speculations on whether they were connected (suggestions were advanced that the killers may have been members of a vice gang) must remain unsatisfied.

Yet another unsolved murder of a prostitute had occurred the previous year in nearby Rupert Street, when Rita Barratt (known as Black Rita) was found dead at about 7 p.m. on 8th September 1947. During the afternoon she had been seen walking around Lisle and Wardour Streets, though most of her clientèle seem to have been engaged by appointment. At 5 p.m. she had a meal with another woman in a café and was later noticed walking in the direction of Rupert Street accompanied by a young man. People in the house heard footsteps going upstairs and, almost as soon as these stopped outside her flat, the sound of shots. Black Rita had been killed by three bullets in her back. A man was seen hurrying from the house around the critical time, carrying a gladstone bag, but he was never traced.

During the pioneering days of aviation just before the First World War a young airman, Julian Hall, lived in a flat in Denman Street, a short cross-street just before Shaftesbury Avenue joins Piccadilly. There he was shot and killed by his mistress, Jeannie Baxter, an unusually beautiful girl with striking red hair. They had met in a nightclub and quickly became lovers, each giving up a former relationship to be together. Jeannie herself, in fact, had thrown over a far richer man in favour of her airman. Hall seems to have been a typical early example of the handsome, physically courageous, but hard-drinking, reckless and womanizing flyer—more frequently found in fiction than in fact. Soon after meeting Jeannie he challenged her former lover to a duel, saying she must choose between them. She chose Hall, who set her up in a flat in Carlton Mansions, Maida Vale. It was an unhappy decision for Jeannie, and there were soon terrible rows between her violent lover and herself. At one time he promised to marry her but later, on the strong encouragement of a male friend, backed out of the arrangement. What with drinking, arguments and fights, Jeannie began to yearn for the peace and luxury of her former less disruptive alliance. One day six shots rang out from Hall's flat. The next moment Jeannie Baxter ran into the hall sobbing that she had shot him, that he dared her to do it, saying he couldn't keep his promise, it was better to finish it, the drink was killing him.

Jeannie was fortunate in her defender, Marshall Hall. Her story was that Julian had been teasing her about suicide, had turned the gun on himself and dared her to pull the trigger. She had tried to snatch it away, and in the struggle it had gone off. Hall pointed to the double significance of the words "finish it"—did they refer to the affair—or to his own life? He implanted sufficient doubt in the jury's mind for them to find Jeannie Baxter guilty of manslaughter only, and she was sentenced to three years penal servitude.

In 1894 the Café Royal, Piccadilly (originally opened in 1865 with its main entrance in Glasshouse Street) was at the height of its fame, frequented by Oscar Wilde and his circle, sparkling with wit and bright lights. Below stairs, however, life was not so pleasant, largely owing to an over-zealous and arrogant night-watchman named Marius Martin, who seems to have incurred the hostility of practically the entire staff. When, therefore, early on 6th December his lifeless body was found in a passage off Glasshouse Street, shot in the face, there was probably only a modicum of grief among his colleagues, and not much more surprise. No-one, however, seemed anxious to claim credit for the deed, in spite of searching investigations by the authorities. The absence of any signs of a break-in indicated that the killer had probably hidden himself (or herself) in the building during the day, but the closest the police ever got to anything positive was a mention by one of the staff of a man who had been hanging about one of the lavatories. The light was found still burning the following morning, which may have had some significance, but the trail petered out. Nothing had been stolen, either from Martin or the café safe, and the case of the nasty night-watchman will doubtless remain a mystery for all time.

Returning to Oxford Street via Golden Square (and passing near Great Pulteney Street where in March 1871 a Frenchman named Victor Loynon, depressed by the loss of his two children and the destruction of his property in the Siege of Paris, shot his wife and then committed suicide), we arrive at Carnaby Street, one-time symbol of the now somewhat tarnished 'swinging London' of the sixties. Here, in November 1946, occurred the still unsolved 'Blue Lagoon' Murder. On his way to open the club of that name at around 9 p.m., Jack Lazarus was told by passers-by of a shot they had just heard. He found the body of a young woman lying on some rubbish in an adjoining passage-way. A man had been seen running towards Oxford Circus, where he disappeared among the crowds. The victim was a 26-year-old ex-Borstal girl named Margaret Cook who lived in Devonshire Terrace, Paddington, and had no connection with the 'Blue Lagoon'. It transpired that she had been warned that a man with whom she was associating had a gun and was better avoided, though the woman who warned her did not know his name. Miss Cook retorted, inaccurately as it turned out, that she could look after herself. A large National Fire Service tank which was still situated beside the club was drained and searched for the weapon, without result. No motive came to light, no murderer was found. It was at the 'Blue Lagoon' that Marina Jones, of the Hammersmith Cleft Chin case (see page 96) claimed to have performed her striptease dances.

Crossing Oxford Street and turning west, we find on our right Portman Street, a short road leading to Portman Square and thereafter turning into Gloucester Place. At Spencer's Hotel, Portman Street, in 1922 resided the elderly widow of Sir Edward White, a former chairman of the London County Council. Among the lower ranks of the hotel staff was an 18-year-old pantry-boy, Henry Jacoby. On the night of 14th March, when he had been at work there for less than a month, he told the porter he had heard some men whispering outside his basement room. Nothing untoward was found, however, and the porter returned to his duties, the pantry-boy to his bed. The following morning Lady White was found in her room beaten to death with some heavy instrument. No suspicion fell on Jacoby, and the case might have remained unsolved had he not given himself up to the police a few days later. The motive was robbery, and Lady White was the victim simply because he was able to get into her room—he had tried another door first and found it locked. Jacoby had bludgeoned the old lady to death with a hammer that he had extracted from a bag of tools left by a workman in the basement. After the crime he washed it and returned it where he found it. Jacoby was hanged. A good deal of agitation arose over his execution, comparisons being made with the case of Ronald True that occurred around the same time (see page 154). But, unlike True, Jacoby was not found to be insane. The talk of whispering men beforehand suggests some sort of plan and points to obvious premeditation. The facts were clear—an elderly widow was viciously battered to death by a panic-stricken thief anxious to avoid discovery. That he gave himself up is all that could be said in his favour, and was of little help to Lady White. Spencer's Hotel is now known as the Mostyn Hotel, still retaining an air of discreet, slightly old-fashioned dignity and quiet comfort—separated by narrow Bryanston Street from a huge Littlewood's store on one side, and close to the ultra-modern Churchill Hotel on the other.

A little north of Portman Street is George Street, running from Edgware Road across Gloucester Place and Baker Street to Thayer Street. Towards the Edgware Road end it passes the southern side of Bryanston Square, once known as Millionaire's Square and built on Ward's Fields, replacing a group of slum dwellings euphemistically called Apple Village. Facing each other almost exactly, just beyond the square, are two imposing blocks of flats, Bryanston Court and Fursecroft, each of which was the scene of a murder in the 1940s. Bryanston Court is in two separate houses, one of which turns the corner of a quiet road called Stourcliffe Street. In Flat 112 on 31st December 1942, a young man of 20, Derek Thayer Lees-Smith, stabbed and killed his mother, a widow. His history was a tragic one. He had suffered from deafness from infancy and there was evidence of hereditary insanity. A medical examination, however, revealed no actual mental illness or epilepsy in the young man himself. Instead the doctors diagnosed a condition known as hypoglycaemia, a deficiency of sugar in the blood that could lead at times to breathlessness, excitement and partial unconsciousness, resulting in an impairment of judgment. It was suggested that the deed was done during such a period, though admittedly this was the first time, so far as could be ascertained, that any such loss of control had occurred. As E. Spencer Shew points out in his account of the case,* it was only by giving a very wide interpretation to the M'Naghten Rules that the jury were able to find Lees-Smith guilty but insane. Nevertheless, this was clearly a verdict based on both mercy and common sense, and Derek Lees-Smith was ordered to be detained during His Majesty's pleasure.

The second George Street crime was more commonplace—yet another instance of a vicious attack by a surprised thief. Early on Boxing Day morning 1948, a porter on duty at Fursecroft heard cries for help coming from a basement flat, No 75, which faced towards the corner of Brown Street and Nutford Place. He found the tenant, a commercial artist named Harry Michaelson, supporting himself against the outside of his front door with blood streaming from wounds in the head. He was fully conscious, was in fact trying to staunch the flow of blood with a towel, but had no memory whatever of what had happened. His wife, a professional pianist, was away on an engagement. Michaelson was taken to hospital and died shortly afterwards, following an operation on his brain which, though critical, was considered to be the only chance of saving his life. Fingerprints

* A *Second Companion to Murder*, Cassell, 1961.

and palm prints on a metal chair in the bedroom led the police to Harry Lewis, 22, a known thief. He was arrested and charged about three weeks after the murder. Lewis said that he had no plan in mind that evening. He was penniless, saw a window of the basement flat open, jumped over the railing, and climbed into the room—which happened to be the bedroom where Harry Michaelson was sleeping. He stole a wallet and had gone out to the hall when he heard a voice behind him demanding to know who was there. He went back and saw a man getting out of bed. He picked up the chair and "gave him two bashes". The defence suggested that Michaelson might have lived had he not undergone the operation, but this was countered by Dr Donald Teare, the pathologist. In his summing-up the judge, Lord Goddard, emphasized that a burglar who killed a householder to escape apprehension was guilty of murder. The jury so found in the case of Lewis, most generously adding a recommendation to mercy for a known criminal who had shown no mercy to his victim. Lewis was hanged.

We now retrace our steps a little to take in three crimes that occurred in the select district south of Oxford Street between Bond Street and Park Lane. The first was in Bruton Street (or Brudon Street, as it was spelt in the 1760s, the period with which we are concerned). Mrs Sarah Metyard, a milliner, and her daughter, a girl under 20 years of age and also called Sarah, employed five apprentice girls whom they obtained from the local parish—and ill-treated in as brutal a way as did the infamous Elizabeth Brownrigg of Fleur-de-Lis Court. In particular their viciousness was directed against two sisters, one of whom, Anne Naylor, was of a sickly constitution and unable to do her full share of the work. When the unhappy girl tried to run away the Metyards tied her hands behind her back and fastened the rope to a doorknob in such a way that she could neither sit nor lie down. For three whole days they left her like this, at the same time refusing her anything to eat. When at the end of that time she died, they hid the body in a box in the garret for two whole months, explaining her absence to the other girls by saying she had thrown a fit and been taken to hospital. Whatever the poor wretches may have surmised, they knew better than to enquire too deeply into this story. When the deteriorating condition of the corpse made it imperative that they should remove it, they cut it up and disposed of it in Chick Lane as described in a previous chapter. At the inquest on the remains it was concluded they were those of a body taken from a grave and dissected by a doctor.

For four years this verdict was undisturbed. During this time, however, the mother Metyard had begun to treat her own daughter almost as badly as the apprentices. A Mr Rooker, who for a brief time lodged with the Metyards, was appalled at the older woman's cruelty, and when he moved to his own house offered young Sarah a position as servant to his family. There, eventually, she confessed to him about Anne Naylor and the others. It did not save her. Both mother and daughter were executed at Tyburn.

Norfolk Street, a short, quiet narrow road between North Row and Wood Mews behind the northern end of Park Lane, consisted in 1840 of small but elegant three-storied houses of which No 14 was a typical example. Here lived Lord William Russell, a 73-year-old widower, and his modest staff of three servants—a maid, a female cook and his valet, François Benjamin Courvoisier, 23 years old and Swiss. On the morning of 6th May the housemaid, on going downstairs to start her work, discovered the main rooms in a state of confusion, drawers opened and overturned, articles scattered around, cupboards forced. Calling Courvoisier in alarm, she went to her master's room and found him lying dead on his bloodstained bed. She rushed out into the street and rang the bell of a house opposite. When no-one answered, she crossed back and did the same at No 22. Meantime a footman at the first house emerged, so she sent him to Hanover Square for the police and despatched someone else to 22 Cleveland Row, by St James's Palace, for the physician. Neither the cook nor the valet appear to have helped this efficient girl in the slightest. The authorities were soon on the spot and the news spread rapidly, causing widespread horror and excitement. The first supposition was that Lord Russell had committed suicide, but this quickly proved false. The old gentleman's throat had been cut from ear to ear, a towel lying over his face was soaked with blood, as were pillows and bedding. Apart from this, the room was clear of stains. Certain articles of value, including silver, were missing. At first Courvoisier did little except sit about with his head in his hands and moan over the impossibility of his ever obtaining another situation, but later he suddenly appeared all eagerness to help. Despite this, however, he very soon became the prime object of suspicion, and before long was arrested and held in Tothill Fields prison. There he was visited, among others, by the diarist Charles Greville, who described him as "rather ill-looking, a baddish countenance; but his manner was calm though dejected and he was civil and respectful, not sulky". Meanwhile the authorities were busy unearthing a number of the vanished objects, which had been clumsily hidden around the house. Other evidence against the valet mounted up, and he was charged with the murder.

The first day of the trial, which opened on 18th June, was spent mainly on the evidence of the cook, housemaid and police —and all of it weighed heavily against the accused, despite the fact that no trace of blood was found anywhere upon him or his clothing. That night, however, something far more damning occurred. In Leicester Place, leading off Leicester Square to Lisle Street, was a small hotel, the 'Dieppe', run by a Frenchman named Louis Piolaine and his wife's cousin, Joseph Vincent. A few years before the crime Courvoisier had worked there for about a month. Some six weeks before the murder he had called on Madame Piolaine, who did not at first recognize him. A little later he called again and asked her to look after a brown paper parcel for him. He said he would collect it in a short while, but never did so. When Monsieur Vincent read the details of the case in the paper the parcel was opened and found to contain silverware missing from Lord Russell's house. Madame Piolaine was taken to Tothill Fields and at once recognized Courvoisier. When her evidence remained unshaken in the witness-box the following day the valet seemed to realize there was no hope for him. He confessed in a whisper to his counsel, Mr Charles Phillips, demanding at the same time that he be defended to the utmost. Phillips then took the extraordinary step of telling one of the judges, Baron Parke, of the confession and asking what he should do. The judge told him he must accede to his client's wishes and use "all fair argument arising on the evidence". Phillips's subsequent conduct of the defence aroused considerable criticism on account of its generous interpretation of the phrase "all fair arguments". At the end of it all, however, his client was found guilty. At the last moment before his death he made a further and very full confession, including the now well-known fact that he committed the murder while stripped naked.

An interesting sideline to the case which, though cloaked in anonymity, seems to have been well authenticated, is that a gentleman looking through a landing window of a house opposite on the fatal night had actually seen the crime committed (or more probably, as Yseult Bridges suggests in her book *Two Studies in Crime*, had glimpsed the figure of a naked man carrying a lighted candle past the corresponding landing window in No 14), but had kept his peace in order to save the honour of the lady in whose company he was. The situation was used in a successful play by a dramatist named Percival Landon entitled *The House Opposite*; it was produced at the Queens Theatre, Shaftesbury Avenue in November 1909 by the keen criminologist and actor-manager son of Sir Henry—H. B. Irving.

Courvoisier was executed outside the Old Bailey on 6th July 1840, before a crowd estimated to number 20,000. Thackeray, spurred by curiosity, was present, and was moved by pity and disgust at the event being made a public spectacle, as Dickens was to be by the death of the Mannings a few years later.

Norfolk Street was renamed Dunraven Street not so very long ago: though considerably rebuilt and housing many offices it still remains a surprisingly quiet and dignified backwater beside the busy Park Lane. No trace of No 14 is apparent; nor will the seeker find, in cinema-dominated Leicester Place, the little hotel wherein Courvoisier's merited fate was finally sealed.

Now to Park Lane itself, and the year 1872. At No 13 there lived a lady by the name of Marie Caroline Riel. For much of the time she was alone, but her daughter Julie, an actress, stayed with her in the intervals of touring, and she had many personal friends, the majority of them of French nationality. In 1871 she engaged a somewhat slow-witted personal maid, Eliza Watts, and at the end of the year added to her small staff a muscular Belgian cook, 29-year-old Marguerite Diblanc. The latter appointment, however, was not a success, and quarrels between mistress and servant were frequent. Eventually Julie on her mother's behalf dismissed the cook, giving her a week's wages and refusing an indignant demand for more. Then, having arranged her mother's domestic affairs, she went off to France for a brief holiday. On the Sunday morning after Julie's departure Eliza saw her mistress going downstairs on her way to exercise her dog in the park; later she noticed the dog alone on the stairs. At eight o'clock the same evening Marguerite Diblanc went out, saying she would be back by ten. At midnight there was no sign of either woman. Eliza, who apparently couldn't care less, went to bed. On her return from holiday the next evening Julie found her mother's body in the pantry—she had been strangled. A rope was tied loosely round her neck, but there was no question of suicide. A sum of money was missing. Marguerite Diblanc, who was naturally suspected at once, was found in France. She confessed her guilt to the authorities there, giving as her motive resentment at the high-handed way in which she had been treated. According to her story she strangled Mme Riel manually in the cellar and then dragged the body to the pantry by the rope which was afterwards found round the dead woman's neck. After a certain amount of delay and complication she was extradited, brought to the police station at King Street, Westminster and there charged. She was found guilty of murder, but reprieved.

An intriguing feature of the trial was the presence as a witness of General Lord Lucan. When Julie, alarmed at finding neither the cook nor her mother around on her return from France, sent Eliza to fetch 'somebody' for help, Eliza went, without further instruction, to the general's house, 36 South Street. It appeared later that shortly before the crime Lucan had given Julie £30 (in notes that were to incriminate Marguerite Diblanc) to be passed on to her mother as the proceeds of a dividend warrant cashed on her behalf. It seemed that Mme Riel did not possess a banking account. As Jack Smith-Hughes notes in his entertaining essay on the case: "This makes her possession of a residence in so select a district as Park Lane all the more remarkable: one would like to know who paid the rent, though it is not difficult to make a shrewd guess."*

Hyde Park, once the Manor of Hyde, of the old Abbey of Westminster, has a long and interesting history of its own. For our purpose it is significant as the starting point of the modern Metropolitan Police. Some two centuries ago the open space was so dangerous to cross after dark, so infested with highwaymen and villains generally that travellers were summoned by a bell at fixed hours to a point from which they could move off in company. One night the King himself was robbed on his way back from a hunting trip. This was considered to be carrying things a bit too far, and the very next day a company of armed men on horseback was formed to patrol the streets and public places

* *Unfair Comment on Some Victorian Murder Trials*, Cassell, 1951.

of the city. From this body developed the police force of today.

A recent and as yet unsolved murder in the park was that of Andres Mizelas, head of a fashionable hair stylists, Andre Bernard of Mayfair, who was found slumped over the wheel of his red sports car in Rotten Row on 9th November 1970. He had been shot dead. Almost exactly one year later another man was found shot dead only about three hundred yards away: this, however, proved to be a case of suicide, and no connection existed between the two incidents.

A little over a quarter of a mile along the Edgware Road from Marble Arch is Harrowby Street, a turning off to our right. Second left along it is a tiny road, not much more than a passage-way, barely the width of a car. This is Cato Street, noted in every history book for its conspiracy of 1820. The plot was, in truth, a bungled and harebrained undertaking, scarcely deserving its grandiose name, though it caused something of a sensation at the time. A group of extreme radicals, militant protesters of their day, formed a plan to express their displeasure with certain government legislature; notably the Six Acts, the general effect of which was to curb the power of the press and to make popular assemblies legal in an attempt to curb a serious increase in rick-burning, machine-breaking and general vandalism and violence. The idea behind the conspiracy was to murder all the Cabinet Ministers at one swoop while they were dining with Lord Harrowby, President of the Council, at his house, No 29 Grosvenor Square.

The conspirators met, and the plot was hatched, in the upper room of a three-stall stable in Cato Street. The originator and leader was one Arthur Thistlewood, a known agitator, man of violence, and petty criminal, who had gathered round him a gang of roughs, hotheads and illiterates. Among their number he had been foolish enough to recruit a police informer, and each step of the plan was passed on to the authorities as the group took it. At the appropriate moment the stable room was raided, and during the ensuing fraças Thistlewood stabbed a Constable Smithers to death. He escaped with some others, but was arrested later at 8 White Street, Little Moorfields, now engulfed but existing until quite recently a little north of Moorgate station. He was convicted of high treason and murder, and together with four of his fellow plotters—Ings, Brunt, Tidd and Davidson— was hanged and then beheaded at Newgate. The initial horror of the spectators, it was reported, turned to uncontrollable laughter as the fifth head fell.

The street names surrounding the tiny district have undergone some interesting, not to say confusing, changes since. Presumably to blot out its shame Cato Street was quickly changed to Horace Street (as Rillington Place, after Christie, became Ruston Close). On an 1832 map the thoroughfare linking it to Edgware Road is Newnham Street and the roads into which it runs are John Street to the north and Queen Street to the south. Thereafter Queen Street becomes the present Harrowby Street, doubtless to commemorate his happy escape. One hundred years later, in 1930, John Street has become Crawford Place, and Newnham Street is Brendon Street. So they remain, except that today Horace Street is once more Cato Street, thus continuing to perpetuate the memory of a would-be violent protest that came to grief.

One of the most gruesome of murder dramas, with a woman as its protagonist, took place in the Tyburn Road (Oxford Street) in 1725. Dark deeds began to come to light when a night-watchman found a human head on the bank of the Thames opposite the penitentiary—near the present Tate Gallery. The grisly object, after the custom of the day, was exhibited to the public for identification purposes, and eventually recognized as that of John Hayes—a successful (until now) pawnbroker and moneylender who had once owned a shop in Tyburn Road and had done well enough later to buy a house in the same district. There he had dwelt with his wife Catherine, two lodgers named Wood and Billings, and, apparently, a rather mysterious couple, Mr and Mrs Springate—though these may not have turned up until later. Catherine Hayes had been a servant of her husband's father, a Warwickshire farmer, until John married her secretly. She seems to have been an extremely neurotic and excitable young woman and in the course of time their relationship had deteriorated badly. When her husband suddenly disappeared she told enquirers the not too likely story that he had killed somebody and fled to Portugal. When nothing more definite was heard of him, suspicions that all was not as it should be grew into certainties, and Catherine was arrested, together with Billings, and later Wood, who was away at the time. Confronted with the severed head she cried yes it was her beloved husband; with commendable courage she then kissed it and put on a dramatic show of grief. As the strain of continuing enquiries increased, however, young Wood's nerve gave way and he suddenly broke down and confessed. Seeing all was up, the others followed suit and the whole grim story came out.

Catherine admitted that she had been determined to get rid of her unwanted spouse and had induced the two lodgers to help her. Each had already shared her bed at various times during his temporary absences; she was then 34, Wood and Billings considerably younger. From her fertile imagination she produced numerous reasons why he should be despatched—he was mean; he had killed their two children and buried them under two fruit trees; above all, he was an atheist. One night the four of them had a drinking bout at the Brawn's Head Inn, New Bond Street, then returned home and deliberately continued the session until John Hayes lost consciousness. They then killed him with a coal hatchet—one of his former occupations had been that of coal merchant and there were several such tools lying around. Under Catherine's cool and competent supervision the two young men cut off the head and put it in a bucket. She wished, reasonably enough, to boil the flesh off and make it unrecognizable, but this was too much for mere males and she allowed the idea to drop. Wood and Billings then emptied the blood from the bucket down the sink and carried it, with the head inside, along the street, down Whitehall and Westminster to Horseferry Wharf, at the end of the present Horseferry Road under Lambeth Bridge, where they threw it into the Thames. Catherine meanwhile, with the headless body lying near her on the bed, was busy washing up. On their return, the indefatigable and obliging (though by now surely a little breathless) pair cut the body to pieces and put some in a blanket, others in a box. They then set off again and threw the packages into a pond in Marylebone Fields, where they were later found by the authorities.

All this tiring work, however, went for nothing. Tried and condemned, Wood fell sick and died in prison, and Billings was hanged at a spot near Upper Wimpole Street. Catherine herself, who expressed a somewhat tardy regret at having involved the two young men, was executed at Tyburn. She suffered a terrible retribution. It has been recorded that she was burnt alive by the mob, who were so outraged that they would not wait for the hangman. The truth probably is that death by burning was her ordained punishment, the murder of a husband being treated in those days as petty treason and not to be expiated by mere hanging. What is certain is that she should have been mercifully strangled first, but the executioner was too slow and could not get to her through the flames.

The mysterious and shadowy character of Mrs Springate and her even more shadowy husband has never been clearly explained. She moved with Catherine to another address just after the murder, but little is known of the extent of her knowledge of, or complicity in, what was going on—and even less regarding her husband. Colin Wilson, in *A Casebook of Murder*, suggests he may have been an invalid, or was simply lazy and left his wife after the murder. Both husband and wife remained in the dark wings of the stage on which the drama was enacted, and they are not likely to emerge from them now.

5

'COLONEL' HEATH, MR CHRISTIE
Bayswater, North and West Kensington, Hammersmith, Ealing, Turnham Green

The main thoroughfare leading off the Bayswater Road opposite Hyde Park is Queensway, and the main store in Queensway is that of William Whiteley, "Universal Providers". Until 1831 Queensway was known as Westbourne Green Lane and Black Lion Lane, and consisted of a few small scattered houses. In honour of Queen Victoria it was then christened Queen's Road and grew rapidly. The retitling to Queensway is fairly recent. Whiteley's occupied its present main site (on that of the old Paddington Swimming Baths) in 1911. Until that date it was located in Westbourne Grove adjoining, and it was here that its famous founder met his death on 24th January 1907. A handsome, well-dressed young man entered the shop and said he had an introduction to Whiteley from the latter's solicitor Sir George Lewis. He was admitted to the presence. A short while later Whiteley opened his office door and sent one of the staff to fetch a policeman. Another employee saw the young man follow Whiteley out of the room and push him. After a brief, angry exchange he pulled out a gun and shot Whiteley, killing him instantly. He then fired a bullet into his own head. As may be imagined, the place was instantly in an uproar. The young man was taken to hospital and for some time his condition was critical, though he retained sufficient consciousness to declare that he was Whiteley's illegitimate son. By 19th February he had recovered enough to be charged with murder.

His name was given as Horace George Rayner, living in Grove Park Road, Tottenham. The pattern of human relationships which was revealed at the trial was a complicated one, and was never fully cleared up. Rayner's mother was a woman named Emily Turner who had been living for some years with a Mr George Rayner at 13 Greville Road, Kilburn—a house taken by Whiteley in Rayner's name for her use and that of her sister Louisa. The latter had been employed in the store and thereafter became Whiteley's mistress. Louisa gave birth to a son she called Cecil Whiteley, but she was not asked at the trial who the father was. Whiteley later became interested in Emily also, and in due course Horace Rayner was born. Horace at first regarded George Rayner as his father, though the latter had more than once repudiated him and told him that it was to William Whiteley he should look. In due course his mother died, and he lived with George Rayner in Craven Street, off the Strand, ultimately marrying and moving to the Grove Park Road address. At the time of the murder Horace Rayner was in grave financial difficulties and, as he said at the trial, went to Whiteley to claim help on the grounds of their relationship. This was refused, and in desperation he drew the gun and fired.

His story in the witness-box was not cross-examined by prosecuting counsel Sir Richard Muir, a fact that caused considerable surprise. A self-confessed murderer with no evidence of insanity, Rayner was sentenced to death, but later reprieved and given twenty years penal servitude. Whatever the true facts of the case, considerable sympathy was felt for him. The face that looks out from his photograph is a sensitive and tragic one. He had suffered terrible injuries from his self-inflicted wound— one eye was blinded, and he was in constant pain. He died two years after his release from prison, having served twelve.

Turning left along Westbourne Grove to Pembridge Villas we come, again on our left, to Chepstow Place where, early on the morning of 1st November 1945, a man was found sprawled on the back seat of a car, shot through the head. He was identified as an Armenian named Martirosoff, or Russian Robert, well-known to the police as a thief, receiver and black marketeer. News was soon received of the car having been seen standing in Kensington Park Road some hours before it was found in Chepstow Place—three men were noticed walking away from it, one a Polish naval officer. Police enquiries revealed that among the dead man's associates were two men, a Pole and a Spaniard, who carried on a rather odd business making handbags in a

Notting Hill flat. The address was traced, but the place had been empty for some weeks. Then word arrived of more handbag-making going on in Maida Vale—but here also enquiries were too late. The man, described as 'a Spaniard', had left the day before Martirosoff was killed. Eventually the police were led to Marian Grondkowski, a Pole, who was arrested in the East India Dock Road, and thereafter to another Pole, a naval officer called Henryk Malinowski, with whom Grondkowski had roomed in Castellain Road, off Elgin Avenue. Articles belonging to Martirosoff were found in the possession of both men, as well as two pistols. In statements both admitted the crime but, following the usual procedure, each accused the other of having fired the actual shot. J. D. Casswell, Q.C., who defended Malinowski, puts up a strong case for the probability that he may have had the lesser share of guilt, but both men were convicted, and hanged on 2nd April 1946. Despite the complicated enquiries, they had both been apprehended barely two days after the murder was discovered. Sir Richard Jackson, who was concerned in the case, states in his book* that the police believed another murder committed two weeks previously was by the same hands. The body of a taxi-driver, Frank Everett (who was also a black marketeer) was found in a National Fire Service shelter on Lambeth Bridge. He had been shot through the head from behind and robbed. His taxi was found in Notting Hill with a bullet in the framework and the electric-light leads ripped away. There were a number of other similarities between the two cases, though both men denied all knowledge of it.

Two minutes away from Chepstow Place across Pembridge Square is Pembridge Gardens. Two months after the closing of the case of Russian Robert this quiet little street was flung into a glare of publicity with the discovery, on 21st June 1946, in Room No 4, Pembridge Court Hotel, of the dead and horribly mutilated body of Mrs Margery Gardner. It was found by Mrs Alice Wyatt, manageress of the hotel, at two o'clock in the afternoon, after a chambermaid had expressed the fear that something might be wrong as nothing had been heard all day from the man who had booked the room, and no meals had been ordered. Mrs Gardner was lying with the bedclothes covering her, but only a glance was necessary for Mrs Wyatt to see that this was a matter for the police. The actual cause of death was

* *Occupied with Crime*, Harrap, 1967.

suffocation, probably by a pillow, but the body had also been lacerated, bitten and lashed with a woven thong. Mrs Gardner was 33 years of age, separated from her husband, a commercial artist and at one time a film extra. The room had been booked by a civil air pilot describing himself as 'Colonel' Heath, who lived in Wimbledon. Heath, Christie and Haigh are probably the best-known murderers names of their period, and all have been written about more fully elsewhere than is possible in the space available here.*

There was at first nothing to connect Heath with Mrs Gardner, whose presence in the hotel was not even known until Mrs Wyatt entered the bedroom. Eventually a cab driver identified both Heath and Mrs Gardner from photographs, having driven them from the Panama Club, South Kensington, to the hotel just after midnight on the previous evening. Heath was finally traced to a hotel in Bournemouth, the 'Tollard Royal', where he was staying as Group Captain Rupert Brooke. He was detained, after himself getting in touch with the police as Brooke, on 6th July—but not before he had killed. with even more bestial savagery, a second woman, 21-year-old Doreen Marshall, with whom he had dined at the hotel on 3rd July, and whose body was found in Branksome Dene Chine. It was pointed out severely that had a photograph of Heath been given to the press for publication, Miss Marshall might well have recognized her companion, and thus saved her life.

Heath was charged with the murder of Margery Gardner. There was never any doubt that he had killed her—the question was as to his mental condition at the time. It came out in evidence that he had already spent the night of 16th June in the same hotel room with a young girl under promise of marriage. He treated her with all gentleness and courtesy, and on meeting her on the 22nd had discussed the coincidence of the murder happening there so soon afterwards. The plea of insanity was commented on by the judge, Mr Justice Morris, in his summing-up: ". . . in order to establish a defence on the grounds of insanity, it must be clearly proved that, at the time of committing the act, accused was labouring under such defect of reason from

---

* See *Ten Rillington Place* by Ludovic Kennedy (Gollancz, 1961) for Christie; *Murder with a Difference* by Molly Lefebure (Heinemann, 1958) for Christie and Haigh; *Murder for Sex* by Robert Traini (Kimber, 1960) for Christie and Heath.

disease of the mind as not to know the nature and quality of the act he was doing, or if he did know that, he did not know he was doing what was wrong. . . . A strong sexual instinct is not of itself insanity. Mere love of lust, mere recklessness, are not in themselves insanity. Inability to resist temptation is not in itself insanity. A perverted impulse could not be excused on the ground of insanity. Legal insanity could not be permitted to become an easy or vague explanation of some conduct which was shocking because it was also startling." Heath was found guilty and executed at Pentonville.

Leading off Holland Park Avenue close to the underground station is Clarendon Road, a variegated mixture of old and new, smart and shabby houses. It covers part of the site of an old racecourse known as the Hippodrome which existed from 1837 to 1841 and was then demolished, despite bitter opposition from the sporting fraternity, because of the unsuitability of the soil. This origin probably accounts for the course-like shapes of several crescents in the locality. In 1919 the neighbourhood, at any rate towards the southern end of Clarendon Road, was eminently respectable upper middle-class. Numbers 13 and 15 are large, three-storey semi-detached dwellings on the corner of Ladbroke Road, set somewhat apart from their neighbours by reason of their having been built several yards farther back from the road.

At No 15 lived two elderly ladies, the Misses Halse. As they sat quietly in their drawing-room late on the evening of 13th January they were startled to hear, through the party wall, what sounded like several shots in rapid succession. Their neighbours, with whom they were on very friendly terms, were Sir Malcolm and Lady Seton, and one of the ladies, Miss Emmeline Halse, bravely went to see if all was well. A stranger, whom she described as a swarthy man, opened the door, calmly said he would enquire if Lady Seton was all right, and returned with a message of "thank you, but at the moment she did not wish to see anyone". "At the moment", in fact, Lady Seton was in the dining-room supporting the body of Sir Malcolm's cousin, Miles Seton. Sir Malcolm had rushed out for the doctor. The swarthy man was the killer. Had she succeeded in entering the house, Miss Emmeline Halse would certainly have needed all her courage.

The story was a tragic one of jealousy and insanity exacerbated by shellshock incurred in the recent war. Years beforehand,

Miles Seton had been coached for examinations in medicine by a young doctor named Norman Cecil Rutherford, and the two men had remained friends. Rutherford, who lived at Mill Hill and also had a place at Carshalton, was married with a family of several children. There was a history of insanity in the family and he was subject to fits of furious jealousy and rage against his wife. During the war he was commissioned in the R.A.M.C., and won the D.S.O. Seton had been in Australia, but returned with the A.N.Z.A.C. Corps and resumed his friendship with both Rutherford and his wife. The latter, unable to bear any longer with her husband's outbursts, had decided to divorce him, and turned for advice and help to Seton. Meanwhile Rutherford, now promoted to the rank of colonel, was shellshocked in France, which considerably aggravated his condition of instability. Unwisely, if understandably, Mrs Rutherford told him of her decision to leave him while he was away at the front. In January, two months after the Armistice, he came home to Carshalton on leave. On the night of the 13th he locked his wife in her bedroom, picked up a revolver and made the journey to Clarendon Road, fuming with rage over the imagined relationship between her and Miles Seton. It was never made quite clear how he knew that the latter would be at Sir Malcolm's house that evening. On arrival he was shown into the dining-room, which adjoined the drawing-room of the Misses Halse next door. Miles came down to him alone, and a few moments later Sir Malcolm and Lady Seton heard shots. On rushing down, they found Miles dead and Rutherford dazedly waving the gun about. With admirable coolness Lady Seton took the gun from him, while Sir Malcolm went for help. This was the scene on which Miss Halse intruded. The shock seems to have temporarily quietened Rutherford; the police even permitted him to write a note for his wife before they took him away. He declared to his counsel, Travers Humphreys, that he intended to claim the "unwritten law" in his defence, but the latter managed to dissuade him from so disastrous a course, and put forward a plea of insanity. Rutherford was sent to Broadmoor, bringing to a close a tragic story of mental illness and war injuries.

Continuing up Clarendon Road, right along Blenheim Crescent and left along St Mark's Road, we arrive at the most famous— or infamous—criminal address of the post-war years: 10 Rillington Place. In this dismal, decaying little cul-de-sac, brickwalled at one end and dominated by an old foundry chimney, John Reginald Halliday Christie took up residence in 1938, and five years later—and for ten years more—lived with his hideous secrets. Here in 1948 came Timothy Evans with his pregnant young wife and baby Geraldine (or Jeraldine, as they preferred to spell it) to rent the top-floor flat and encounter, in Ludovic Kennedy's words, "the unique and terrible thing" that was to happen to him. Christie, who was born in Halifax in 1908, first arrived in London in 1924, parting from his wife in Sheffield when their relationship deteriorated. Not much is known of his life during the following years, but in 1929 he was living in Almeric Road, Battersea, whence he was sent to prison for hitting a woman on the head with a cricket bat. In 1933 he was again in trouble, for stealing a car, and wrote to his wife asking her to rejoin him. She did so on his release, and they settled in Rillington Place. In 1946 Evans and his family moved from Cornwall Road, now Westbourne Park Road, to 11 St Mark's Road, a short walk away. In 1948, when Beryl found she was pregnant and there would be no room for the four of them, they moved into the empty flat in Rillington Place. By this time, during periods while his wife was away, Christie had already committed two murders. His first victim, in 1943, was Margaret Fuerst, who lived in a room at 41 Oxford Gardens; his second, the following year, was Muriel Eady. Both bodies he buried in the tiny patch of garden behind the house.

In the middle of November 1949, having sold the furniture in his flat to a dealer, Mr Hookway, of 319 Portobello Road, Evans arrived unexpectedly at his aunt's home in Wales, alone. At the end of the month he went to the police and made two statements, in the second of which he said that Christie had given his wife some "stuff" to procure an abortion, that he later found her dead, and that Christie later told him he had put her body down a drain by the house. Nothing was found in the spot he had indicated, but later the bodies of both Beryl and the baby were discovered hidden in a small outdoor washhouse. It transpired much later that while the police were searching for Beryl Evans, Christie himself saw that the skull of one of his earlier victims had become exposed in the garden. He quickly concealed it, and that night took it to a bombed and derelict house, 133 St Mark's Road, and dropped it into one of the shattered rooms. Evans meanwhile was brought back to London, and confessed to the killing of his wife and child. Later he re-tracted this, and accused Christie of killing Beryl. He was, nevertheless, executed, and hanged on 9th March 1950. Time passed. In December 1952 Christie, probably worried that she might give him away, strangled his wife and buried her under the floorboards. The actual extent of Mrs Christie's knowledge of events was never known.

During the first three months of 1953 Christie killed and *then* sexually assaulted three women, afterwards placing their bodies in a tiny recess in the kitchen which he covered with ordinary wallpaper. After this he seems, not surprisingly, to have lost both his nerve and what little sense he had left. He saw a Mrs Reilly in Ladbroke Grove reading an "Accommodation to Let" notice, and offered her the shabby little flat and its ghastly secrets. She moved in with her husband, and Christie left it for ever. The Reillys were turned out the next day by the landlord, who pointed out that Christie had no right to sublet. The land-lord's own tenant, a Jamaican, arrived and, while cleaning up the place as he settled in, pulled away a small piece of the paper covering the recess—and looked inside.

Christie was found by a policeman wandering near Putney Bridge—he had been sleeping at Rowton House in King's Cross Road. The constable asked him to remove his hat, which he did, revealing that unmistakable bald domed head which was soon to become familiar through the country. Christie confessed eventually to all the murders—except that of the baby. This is a necessarily brief outline of a complex story which, as already stated, has been fully told elsewhere. Many students of the case—but not all—are convinced of Evans's innocence of the actual murders, whatever steps he may have taken afterwards. On the other hand at least one writer, Molly Lefebure, has stated her view that Evans *may* have killed his wife and very probably *did* kill his daughter.

The Western Avenue extension now joins the railway in cutting across the settings of this dismal tale. 133 St Mark's Road, where Christie hid the skull, was the end house next to a tennis court adjoining Kensington Memorial Park. It has now gone completely and only a grass space remains. Rillington Place quickly changed it name to Ruston Close. In 1970–71 a film of the crime directed by Richard Fleischer, and notable for Richard Attenborough's remarkable performance, was shot on the actual locations. The house used was not No 10, but another in the same row. Though some of the chronology and details were twisted around the film preserves an almost completely photographic record of the places concerned. Ruston Close itself has now disappeared. All the houses are down and the open space is at present used for council vans and other vehicles. For the moment, at the far end, three dingy fireplaces can be seen one above the other—the last remaining walls of that house of horror torn open to the sky. Soon, doubtless, these last relics will disappear—no cause here, surely, for nostalgia.

A short distance farther north, in Appleford Road, Kensal Green (now a redevelopment area) a young housewife, Moira Burdett, was discovered dead in her home after returning from doing the household shopping. The date was 27th November 1956. The cause of death was cyanide, which she had drunk in a cup of tea. Her husband, who seems to have delayed calling for help an unusually long time, was charged with murder. He admitted stealing the cyanide from his place of work, but said it was for the purpose of committing suicide on account of his unhappy relationship with his wife. Later he found the empty bottle and concluded she had had the same idea and forestalled him. He thereupon hid the bottle to save her name from the stigma of having taken her own life. The question before the jury was whether it was a case of suicide, or of murder, that he was trying to conceal. They decided on the latter, but Burdett, though sentenced to death, was later reprieved.

Until about one hundred years ago each end of Addison Road, W14, was closed by a toll-gate, a restriction which—had it still remained in force—might have prevented the road being the scene of a tragic discovery in 1931. On 16th December of that year the body of a little girl was found lying on her back behind the tradesman's entrance of No 89, near the Holland Park Avenue end. She had been sexually assaulted and then strangled. Her clothing was soiled with soot and coal-dust and there were two or three spots of candle-grease near her right shoulder. A fingerstall with a piece of lint was caught in a fold of her coat. It smelt of ammonia. From the condition of the body it was concluded that the crime had taken place indoors some time previously, and that the murderer had placed her in the Addison Road garden only shortly before she was found.

The child was identified as Vera Page, 11 years old, living at

22 Blenheim Crescent on the other side of the wide Holland Park Avenue. Her movements on the afternoon when she was last seen alive were traced in some detail. She called briefly on her aunt in 70 Blenheim Crescent, arriving at 4.30, leaving at 4.45. At five o'clock she was seen looking in a shop window at a corner of Blenheim Crescent, and the last glimpse of her was on the right-hand side of Montpelier Road (now renamed Lansdowne Rise) walking towards Lansdowne Crescent, into which she turned. A few days after the body was discovered a beret, identified as belonging to Vera Page, was found in the area of No 23 Stanley Crescent, which forms roughly the eastern half of a circle with Lansdowne Crescent.

The mystery of her death was never solved. Among those questioned at the inquest was a man of 41 with the striking name of Percy Orlando Rush. He worked as flannel washer at Whiteley's Laundry, near the Olympia, where ammonia was used, and he had been seen wearing a fingerstall of the sort found in the girl's clothing. He lived with his wife at 128 Talbot Road, a continuation of Blenheim Crescent: candles were found in the house, and there were marks of coal-dust and soot on his clothing. He knew Vera Page, as his parents lived on the top floor of the same address in Blenheim Crescent and he had a key to the house. He was unable to produce any confirmation of his stated movements during the period after the little girl was last seen. A woman testified at the inquest that at 7 a.m. on the morning of 16th December she was crossing Holland Park Avenue and saw a man wheeling a barrow, with a bundle wrapped in a red tablecloth, towards Addison Road. A similar tablecloth was found in Rush's home. The woman, however, failed to pick him out in an identity parade and said that his cloth, though of the same colour, had a different fringe from the one she had seen on the barrow. During the inquest another woman called out, "Sir, this man is telling lies." The weight of purely circumstantial evidence, however, was considered insufficient to justify any verdict other than an open one, and this was returned.

In those days crimes of this horrible nature against small children were infrequently reported, and the case caused widespread and long-lasting horror. No 89 Addison Road is gone now, replaced by modern-style school buildings; 87 on the one side, and 90 on the other, remain probably much as they were on the morning of that grim discovery in a placid and self-respecting neighbourhood.

Three minutes walk away, across the once smart and arrow-straight but now beheaded and sadly decaying Holland Road, is another staid street of three-storey Victorian houses, Elsham Road. Most of them have long been divided first into flats and then further into bed-sitters. On 14th October 1941 in her home at No 71a, 65-year-old Mrs Theodora Jessie Greenhill, widow of an army officer, was discovered lying on the floor by her desk, with a handkerchief over her face. She had been stunned by a blow on the head from a milk bottle and then strangled. The flat had been ransacked, and the crime in itself was just one more vicious case of robbery with violence. The interest lies in the character of the killer—one Harold Dorien Trevor. Aged about 60 at the time, he had spent less than one year of the past thirty or so out of prison. He was, in fact, a petty crook with a long record of small thefts and minor offences, and a large genius for being found out. But he had no reputation whatever for violence. He liked to pose as a man of position, affecting an eyeglass (he was known as the Monocle Man), and gave himself a variety of military titles. On occasion he knighted himself. Eleven days before the murder, on 3rd October, he had been discharged from Parkhurst prison and until the 13th stayed at the St Martin's Hotel, Upper St Martin's Lane. During this period he robbed a flat at 8 Sloane Square, obtaining entry by getting the address from an estate agent and posing as a possible tenant. He followed the same procedure with Mrs Greenhill, apparently presenting himself on this occasion with a medical degree, for he killed her as she was writing out a receipt for the first rent instalment, starting: "Received from Dr H. D. Trevor the s . . ."—the last word being smudged as she fell. He then summoned a taxi into which he loaded various articles from the flat, went to King's Cross and thence to Birmingham. By leaving behind not only the receipt but a large number of fingerprints, however, he had ensured that the police would not be put to much trouble in finding who the criminal was, and ensured his speedy apprehension. Trevor was found guilty of this cruel and blundering murder and deservedly hanged—but it is interesting to speculate what momentary madness tipped an incorrigible but non-violent thief into a brutal killer.

Shepherd's Bush Green (as it is generally called, though

Shepherd's Bush Common would be more accurate) is now no more than a dusty patch in the middle of a constant stream of traffic, surrounded by dirt, noise and general pollution. A century ago it was a small village green, and as late as 1890 there still stood in the centre of it a thatched cottage well over three hundred years old. Here lived, in 1657, a gentleman named Miles Syndercombe, who appears to have taken up residence for the sole purpose of being within reasonable distance of Oliver Cromwell, whom he intended to assassinate. His plan was discovered and Cromwell—following his own interpretation of his much proclaimed Christian principles—showed his love for his enemy by having the wretched Miles condemned to death. He was imprisoned in the Tower, but managed to take poison (smuggled in, it was thought, by his sister) the night before his execution. With further Puritan religious zeal, his body was dragged to his intended gallows behind a horse and a stake was driven, Dracula-fashion, through his heart.

At about midday on 12th August 1966 three men were sitting in the 'Clay Pigeon', a public house in Field End Road, Eastcote, Ruislip. They were John E. Witney, John Duddy and Harry Roberts. Their car, an old Vanguard, was parked outside; in it was a canvas bag containing three guns. Witney, 36, was an unemployed lorry-driver living in Paddington, Duddy, 38, a Scotsman, came from the Gorbals district of Glasgow and Roberts, 30, from Wanstead. All three were criminals. Having finished their drinks, they got into the car and drove to Braybrook Street, a small road running along Old Oak Common and Wormwood Scrubs, adjacent to the prison. Their purpose was to sit on the common and complete plans to steal a car, ditch the old one and rob a rent collector. As they still sat in the car in Braybrook Street at a little after 3 p.m., a police patrol vehicle drew up. In it were Detective-Sergeant Christopher Head, Detective-Constable David Wombwell and the driver, P.C. Geoffrey Fox. Stationary cars outside prisons must always arouse police interest: what happened during the next few moments was pieced together during the ensuing weeks of investigation and at the eventual trial. Roberts was in the passenger seat beside Witney, and Duddy sat behind. Detective-Sergeant Head and Detective-Constable Wombwell got out of the police car and approached the Vanguard, and asked Witney for his driving licence. Instantly Roberts drew out a gun and shot Wombell through the left eye. Head started back to the police car, and Roberts got out of the Vanguard and shot him in the back. At the same time Duddy also got out of the car, ran across and fired three shots at P.C. Fox, one of them passing through his eye. As Fox slumped forward, dying, his foot pressed the accelerator and the police car ran forward, passing over the body of Detective-Sergeant Head. Roberts and Duddy rushed back into the Vanguard, which drove off at high speed, leaving behind a horrifying scene of blood, broken bodies, and shocked, appalled people hurrying to the spot.

Witney was traced through the Vanguard to his basement flat at Fernhead Road, Paddington and himself led the police first to Wymering Mansions, Wymering Road, Maida Vale, where Roberts had been staying, and then to another block of flats, Treverton Towers, Ladbroke Grove, for Duddy. Neither was to be found. Roberts, it later transpired, had spent a night at the Russell Hotel, Russell Square, with Mrs Lillian Perry who had been with him in the flat belonging to Mrs Colin Howard at Wymering Mansions. He afterwards parted from her at the 'Wake Arms' public house, Epping Forest, and disappeared. Duddy was arrested after a short interval, in Glasgow (his two young daughters were found alone in Treverton Towers), but the search for Roberts was to be long and exhausting, leading to one disheartening dead-end after another. Reports that he had been seen came in from all over the country, from the Isle of Man, Wales, Ireland, Oxhey in Hertfordshire, Dolphin Square by the river in Pimlico, cafés and clubs in the East and West Ends of London. One of the most exhaustive searches took place in and around the Sadlers Wells Theatre following a call that he had been spotted in the vicinity. Preparations for the trial of Witney and Duddy went ahead meanwhile, and it was due to open on 15th November. On the 11th a farmhand named John Cunningham reported finding a tent concealed in Thorley Wood, near Bishop's Stortford, Hertfordshire. A day or two later, in a deserted building filled with straw in Matham's Wood close by, Roberts was at last run to earth.

All three were found guilty of murder and sentenced to life imprisonment, which, said the judge, Mr Justice Glyn-Jones, "may well be treated in this case as meaning exactly what it says". These appalling and senseless killings roused revulsion and indignation throughout the country. Help poured in during the hunt for Roberts, as did expressions of sympathy and subscriptions to a fund for the bereaved families of the murdered policemen. Nor were they the only ones to suffer. No-one could have listened unmoved to Mrs Roberts' broken voice as she broadcast an appeal to her son to give himself up. It brought no response from Roberts, who may never have heard it: two radios were found among his belongings where he camped, but the batteries of both had run down. That the deaths of three courageous men in the execution of their duty shocked the public to a realization of what they are asking their paid protectors to face on their behalf may, perhaps, be some small consolation to their bereaved families and friends. It is a realization that should not have to be periodically reawakened by tragedies such as this.*

In a single room at 311 King Street, Hammersmith during the autumn of 1944 lived Elizabeth Marina Jones, calling herself Georgina Grayson, self-styled strip-tease dancer working in clubs such as the 'Panama', Knightsbridge and the 'Blue Lagoon' in Carnaby Street. In her home town in Ireland, where she was born in 1926, she had been known as a problem child. Finding her unmanageable when her father was called up, her mother sent her to an approved school. While on leave from this at the age of 16 she married a childhood friend, Corporal Stanley Jones, apparently taking this step as a means of avoiding a return to the school, for she left him almost at once and came to London—to seek, no doubt, her fortune. For a while she stayed in Lexham Mews, off the Earls Court Road, then returned to Ireland.

In 1944 she was back again in England, this time in Hammersmith, and on 23rd October was introduced by a friend to a man wearing an American officer's uniform and calling himself Second Lieutenant Ricky Allen. His real name was Karl Gustav Hulten and he was a private A.W.O.L. The place of this ill-starred meeting was a café near the junction of Hammersmith Broadway and Queen Caroline Street, now much altered and shadowed by a fly-over. Hulten was 22, a Swiss-American who

---

* Tom Tullett's excellent full-length account of the case, *No Answer from Foxtrot Eleven* (Michael Joseph, 1967) contains a sharply pertinent foreword from Sir Richard Jackson, formerly Assistant Commissioner C.I.D. New Scotland Yard.

before being drafted had worked as a shoe salesman. He had no record of criminal activities. Marina Jones herself seemed to have been merely unstable rather than anything more sinister until now: it needed a chance encounter and a chance (and misunderstood) remark to light the fuse leading to robbery and murder—the gunpowder lay ready to hand in the silly and dangerous romanticizing in which the pair indulged. He told her he was a Chicago gangster, and she enjoyed seeing herself as his moll. They arranged to meet again the same evening outside the Broadway Cinema. He was late, and Marina, giving him up, started to walk home. Then she heard him calling out to her from the cabin of an American army truck—and she got in beside him for a ride. "During the night", she said, "he taught me to drive." She told him that she wanted to do something dangerous "meaning, to go over Germany in a bomber. But he got me wrong. He showed me a gun which he pulled out from an inside pocket." The match was struck—the fuse lit. Anxious to impress his foolish companion, he said he was going to hold up a hotel in Maidenhead. On their way through the darkened roads he stopped the truck as they passed a girl on a bicycle, knocked her down and gave Marina her handbag. He told her they would have to abandon the hotel hold-up because they were being watched. Thereafter for a few days they cruised around in the truck—which was, of course, stolen—and indulged in a series of mean and vicious crimes. An attempt to rob a taxi-driver in a stationary car came to an abrupt halt when an unseen passenger (an American army officer, of all people) called out to know what was going on. Another imbecilic plan to steal a prostitute's fur coat in the West End also came to nothing. With pedestrians or cyclists in the dim, V-bomb threatened streets they were more successful. One girl who accepted a lift was taken to a deserted spot, battered on the head with an iron bar, partially strangled, robbed, then thrown out unconscious by the river.

On the night of 6th October they walked along Hammersmith Road and stood in the doorway of Cadby Hall, close to the 'Olympia'. After a few minutes a car came along which they hailed, thinking it to be a taxi. It turned out. in fact, that it was a private-hire vehicle. That, however, suited their nefarious purpose well enough, so they got in and told the driver, a man of 34 named George Heath, to take them to the western end of

King Street. When they got there they asked him to continue on along the Great West Road. This in 1944 started farther west than it does today, being then an extension of Chiswick High Road, itself a continuation of King Street. After Heath had driven about three hundred yards Hulten told him to stop, and the next moment, according to Marina's story, "I saw a flash and heard a bang." Hulten then took Heath's place in the driving seat and went on, while she rifled the dying man's pockets. It must be remembered that all this took place in blacked-out and comparatively deserted streets.

Heath's body was found the next morning dumped in a ditch on Knowle Green, Staines. Articles belonging to him were scattered on the Great West Road. After the crime Hulten drove back, left the car in the old Gaumont Cinema parking lot, and the two of them went to their café for a meal. It was about 3.45 a.m. For the next day or two they drove around in the dead man's car—he had been quickly identified and a description of the vehicle circulated to all police. It was seen in Lurgan Avenue, a turning off Fulham Palace Road close to the hospital. A watch was kept, and after a very short time Hulten emerged from No 159 Fulham Palace Road and got in. He was arrested, and in the first instance handed over to the American army authorities. Eventually both he and Marina Jones were tried at the Old Bailey and found guilty of murder. Hulten was hanged, Marina reprieved and sent to prison, whence she emerged in 1954. J. D. Casswell, Q.C., who defended her with great skill, has described her as a "fragile little person, colourless and pathetic", and was of the opinion that she was very much under Hulten's influence—and indeed very frightened of him, having witnessed the brutality of which he was capable in his treatment of women. He doubts whether, keen though she was on dancing, she had ever actually performed a strip-tease.

Heath's murder was at first suspected as being the work of a black market gang, and had it not been for the almost incredible stupidity with which (fortunately for justice) the pair behaved afterwards, the case might never have been cleared up. Together they drove around in the wanted car; Hulten went to a barber's shop at 18 Queen Caroline Street and offered Heath's watch for sale the day after the murder; Marina Jones, when her pale appearance was remarked on by a *policeman* she knew, replied that if he had seen someone do what she had seen, he wouldn't be able to sleep at night either. This second-rate Bonnie and Clyde story became known as the Cleft Chin Murder because of that noticeable feature—not in either of the killers but in their victim, car-hire driver George Heath.

On 2nd February 1964 the body of Hannah Tailford, a prostitute, was found on the bank of the Thames near Hammersmith Bridge. She was naked except for her stockings and part of her clothing had been stuffed into her mouth. This was the first in a series of murders by an unknown killer who became known —inevitably—as Jack the Stripper. Hannah Tailford, who was also known by three or four other names, lived at Thurlby Road, West Norwood, and had last been seen leaving that address on 24th January. There was some evidence that she may have been in the habit of taking compromising photographs of her clients with a view to blackmail, but despite hundreds of enquiries no clue was found as to how she met her death. Two months later, 26-year-old Irene Lockwood (Sandra Russell), of Denbigh Road, Ealing, was found also on the Thames bank, at Duke's Meadows, Chiswick, only a few hundred yards from the former spot. A year or so previously a friend of hers, Vicki Pender, had been strangled in her flat at Adolphus Road, Finsbury Park, and Colin Fisher, an ex-paratrooper who lived with his wife and family at Leverstock Green, Hertfordshire, had been convicted and sentenced to life imprisonment. It was known that Vicki Pender had been concerned in the photograph-blackmail racket, and thus it was thought possible that Irene Lockwood, like Hannah Tailford, had met her death at the hands of one of the victims. The third body, that of Helen Barthelemy, 22, was found on 24th April behind Swyncombe Avenue, Brentford, which backs onto a recreation and sports ground. She lived in Talbot Road, off Church Road, Willesden, and plied her trade in the Notting Hill and Shepherd's Bush districts. By this time the police considered that there were no personal links between the killings, except that they were by the same hand. They were most probably, as in the case of Jack the Ripper, the outcome of casual encounters. Helen Barthelemy's body also was naked and, though there was no sign of actual violence to her face, four of her teeth were missing. The fourth killing occurred on 11th July when Mary Fleming, 30, was found, similarly unclothed, at the entrance to a private garage

in Berrymede Road, a cul-de-sac turning off Acton Lane, Chiswick. Mr George Head, who lived opposite, first saw the body
at about 5.30 in the morning. It was in a crouching position
and he mistook it for a tailor's dummy. Shortly afterwards a
report was received by the police from a man who, while motoring to work along Acton Lane, narrowly escaped being involved
in a serious accident when a van was driven furiously out of the
cul-de-sac. Mary Fleming lived in Lancaster Road, W11, and
walked the Notting Hill streets. When the body was examined
it was found that her false teeth were missing. November 25th
was the next date: Margaret McGowan was found, in similar
circumstances, in a car park in Hornton Street, a turning north
of Kensington High Street not far from the town hall. The
body was partly buried in foliage and debris and had evidently
been there for several days. On the day of her disappearance she
had been picked up in Portobello Road, with another girl, by
two men in separate cars. A rendezvous was made for later and
the girls paired off, but Margaret McGowan's car did not turn
up, and neither driver could be traced. The last body, that of
Bridget O'Hara, 28, was found behind a shed on the Heron
Trading Estate, Westfields Road, Acton W3, on 16th February
1965. She lived at Agate Road, between Goldhawk Road and
King Street, Hammersmith, and was last seen on the evening
of 11th January at the Shepherd's Bush Hotel. She, too, had been
killed some days before her body was discovered; and she, too,
had lost some of her teeth. In all six cases the bodies were naked,
the clothes had disappeared, and the cause of death was suffocation, though marks on the skin were slight. It was thought very
likely that the killer brought his victims in a van to a disused
warehouse on the trading estate, murdered them there, hid the
bodies under a transformer, and returned later in a van to dump
them elsewhere. In a full account of the case given in his book
Murder Was My Business (W. H. Allen, 1971) Ex-Detective
Assistant Commissioner John du Rose, who worked on the
Hammersmith murders, says that he knew the identity of Jack
the Stripper, but that the man committed suicide before any
arrest could be made.

To leave the district on a slightly less sordid note, we may
glance briefly at the grim story of the Hammersmith Ghost,
who, around the year 1820, terrified the inhabitants of the
village. For some time an unknown man had been dressing up

in white garments at night and scaring the women and children (and no doubt some of the men too) out of their wits. At length a hero called Francis Smith determined to put an end to such carryings-on, and lay the ghost. He walked the dark pathways with his gun until, one January night, he saw a white figure in Black Lion Lane. Bravely he challenged it, received no reply, fired—and killed an innocent bricklayer on his way to work clad in his customary clothing. Despite the fact that the jury wanted to return a verdict of manslaughter the judge considered it must necessarily be one of murder. The sentence, however, was of one year's imprisonment only. The Hammersmith Ghost was not seen again.

In Edinburgh, in 1926, a youth of 17, six feet tall, thickly built, and looking older than his years, was accused of killing his mother by shooting her behind the ear as she sat writing at her desk. There was considerable evidence against him—he had, for instance, been forging his mother's signature on cheques for large sums of money to cover expenses incurred at a palais de danse and similar places while supposedly studying at the university. In February of the following year, however, he was not found guilty, largely on account of the evidence for the defence from the famous expert witness Sir Bernard Spilsbury. Not found guilty—but not found not guilty either; the jury took advantage of the third alternative in Scottish law and returned a verdict of not proven. Had this compromise not been possible, a tragedy twenty-eight years later in Ealing, London, would have been averted.

John Donald Merrett served eight months for forgery and was then released. He later eloped with the 17-year-old daughter of an erstwhile friend of his mother, Mrs Mary Bonnar, who lived at that time in Hastings. A month later the girl, Vera, was back home and Merrett was in prison for obtaining goods by false pretences. At 21 he inherited—slightly above his deserts, we may think—£50,000 from his grandfather, about one-sixth of which he settled, under pressure no doubt, on his wife. The capital was to revert to him on her death. By this arrangement, that death was assured. He quickly got through the rest of the money and lived by various crooked activities, including blackmail and smuggling. He now called himself Ronald Chesney, grew a beard (unnoticeable today, but a rarity between the wars) and, suitably pirate-like, sported a single earring. After the war, which he spent in the R.N.V.R., becoming a lieutenant commander, he returned to both crime and prison, spending most of his time in Germany. Mrs Bonnar meanwhile, having awarded herself—on apparently doubtful but discreetly unquestioned grounds—the title of Lady Menzies, was running an old people's home in a large house, No 22 Montpelier Road, Ealing, helped by her daughter.

On 11th February 1954, the housemaid whose duty it was to call Lady Menzies saw that her bedroom was empty except for her dogs. Later she noticed that Mrs Chesney's room also was unoccupied. Thinking they were both looking after the residents, she made breakfast. A little later on two ambulancemen arrived with an inmate who was to stay in the homes. When there was still no sign of either Lady Menzies or her daughter the police were informed, and a proper search of the house was made. Vera Chesney was found first, lying dead in her bath in such a way that it might have seemed possible for her to have fallen in while washing her hair, and drowned; this theory was ruled out, however, when the body of Lady Menzies was discovered downstairs with signs of having been beaten to death after a fearful struggle. Chesney was known to have come over from Germany to see his wife a week or so before the murder, and to have returned later to the Continent. A man resembling him, looking as though he was wearing some sort of disguise, was seen near the house on the actual day of the murder, and when the police realized that Chesney and Merrett were one and the same, Interpol was alerted.

On 16th February Chesney was discovered shot dead in a wood near Cologne, his own gun by his side. His solicitor had received a letter declaring his innocence and indicating his intention to commit suicide. Various clues were found to link him with the murder and it was not difficult to reconstruct events. Having decided to recover his wife's capital for himself he had flown to England, entered the house secretly, and gone to his wife's room. For some time she had been addicted to gin, and it would not be difficult to make her drunk, drown her in the bath while she was in a stupor, and arrange things to make it appear she had fallen in. While creeping downstairs on his way out, however, he had been surprised by Lady Menzies, and instantly realized that he would now have to kill her also. Thus all his plans went awry. Some time before these events Chesney had confessed to a German woman that he killed his mother all those years ago. Had he suffered the extreme penalty for this crime, the later murders would never have been committed.

Just round the corner from Montpelier Road, to the north of the Princess Helena College, is Winscombe Crescent. Here in 1936 lived the Wheelers, often joined by their close friend Linford Derrick, a well-known tennis coach. On 5th August the latter walked into Ealing Police Station and announced, "I have killed my best friend." It appeared that for some time Arthur Wheeler had been suspicious—seemingly without any cause—that Derrick, who was separated from his own wife, was paying rather too much attention to Mrs Wheeler. At the time all three were sharing a holiday bungalow at Felpham, near Bognor Regis: at the beginning of August the two men came back to London for a few days for Wheeler to attend to some business. According to Derrick, on 4th August a furious quarrel suddenly broke out between them, with Wheeler hurling accusations at him. The following day Derrick went back to patch things up. Wheeler opened the door in his pyjamas with a police truncheon in his hand, and unwillingly admitted him. They went upstairs, and without warning Wheeler renewed his accusations, following them up this time with a violent physical attack. It was while trying to defend himself that Derrick accidently killed his friend. The police found Wheeler lying on the landing with a shirt fastened tightly round his neck, and several blows from the truncheon marking his head. The house had been disarranged in an amateurish attempt to suggest a burglary. Despite these potentially awkward points the defence, by J. D. Cassels and J. D. Casswell, succeeded in obtaining a verdict of manslaughter and—even more notably—in eliciting from the formidable Sir Bernard Spilsbury an admission that he had been mistaken on an important point. Derrick, who was clearly deeply regretful for what had happened, received a sentence of ten years.

We now move on to Turnham Green, scene of the battle of Brentford between Prince Rupert and the Roundheads during which the roar of the artillery—it was said—could be heard in the House of Lords, and of the activities of second-rate poet, painter and murderer Thomas Griffiths Wainewright. Linden House, Turnham Green was described in the 1820s as a handsome old mansion set in four acres of ground on the Great Western Road on the left-hand side of the road as you travel to Brentford, between Camden House and Bolton House. It belonged to a gentleman named Ralph Griffiths, LL.D. His daughter Ann married Thomas Wainewright of Chiswick, and died in 1797 giving birth to a son who was christened Thomas Griffiths Wainewright. When the boy's father also died his uncle, George Edward Griffiths, who had succeeded his own father Ralph as owner of Linden House, became his guardian. Young Thomas Griffiths spent much of his childhood there, meeting many distinguished writers and artists who visited the place.

Always vain and self-centred beyond the normal, he began his career with a short spell in the cavalry, mainly because of the nice smart uniform. Soon tiring of this, he left the army and started writing for the journals of the day, mainly on the subject of art. Despite Oscar Wilde's remark in his famous essay, "Pen, Pencil and Poison", that Wainewright showed "a simple, impassioned love of nature" much of his writing is flowery, facetious and boringly egotistical. Apart from writing he also painted and some of his pictures attained the eminence of a showing at the Royal Academy.

He married a Miss Frances Ward, daughter by a former marriage of Mrs Abercromby, who lived in Mortlake and had another two daughters, Helen and Madeleine, by her second husband. The young couple lived at 49 Great Marlborough Street in grand style, entertaining lavishly. Such extravagance and show on a tiny allowance (£200 a year) plus what he could make from his pen and pencil, soon landed him in grave financial difficulties. In 1826 he put the pen to criminal use, forging an order on the Bank of England for a transfer of stock. This particular piece of artistry earned him over £2,000. He then got himself and his wife invited to live at Linden House. The following year his uncle died mysteriously after making a will leaving the property to Thomas. His mother-in-law, with her two daughters, then arrived to share residence at Linden House—perhaps on his suggestion, perhaps on hers. Whoever made the decision, it was an unfortunate one for Mrs Abercromby, who died in convulsions after a severe attack of vomiting. Thomas gained nothing from her death, except the saving on her keep, and was now seriously in debt again, with the

Turnham Green tradesmen pressing him ever harder. He left Linden House and, with his wife and baby son, Helen and Madeleine, took apartments in 12 Conduit Street, London W. Here he persuaded Helen to insure her life for some £8,000, and to make a will leaving the money to her sister and appointing him as sole executor and trustee. Having seen to all this, Helen obligingly caught a chill and died—with vomiting and convulsions. A doctor from Hanover Square, also obligingly, diagnosed "abnormal pressure on the brain". His wife Frances now wisely left him and, accompanied by Madeleine and the baby, went to live in Pimlico. The insurance company refused to hand over any money on account of Helen's death, and Wainewright went to France. In Boulogne he met a friend of his from Norfolk, together with his pretty daughter. This gentleman was also short of money, and Wainewright advised him to insure his life and borrow on the policy. This the gentleman did, and died (with vomiting and convulsions) leaving Wainewright none the richer, but alone with the pretty daughter.

After a period on which history is vague he is found in a French prison, sentenced to six months on the ambiguous charge of being a "suspected person"—of what he was suspected was not stated, but he appears to have had on his person a quantity of strychnine. After he was freed, in June 1837, he somewhat rashly returned to London and took a room, under another name, in a Covent Garden hotel. Meanwhile the Bank of England had long discovered the forgery perpetrated on them, and the authorities were on the watch. Wainewright was recognized, in July, by a Bow Street Runner. Details of the actual arrest differ—some saying that the Runner saw Wainewright looking out of the hotel window, shouted, "That's Wainewright the forger!" and dashed wildly inside, others that he was taken while walking in Howland Street, a turning off Tottenham Court Road south of Fitzroy Square. Whatever the exact circumstances of his apprehension, he was tried, convicted of forgery, and sentenced to transportation for life. While in Newgate awaiting his removal to Hobart, Tasmania, he is said to have talked freely not only of the forgery but also of the poisonings (by strychnine, of course) for which he had escaped punishment. According to John Forster, Dickens was visiting Newgate with Macready the actor and others when the latter, who knew him well, exclaimed, "My God, there's Wainewright!" He was,

Forster says, shabby and dirty, with disordered hair. "He turned quickly round with a defiant stare . . . looking at once mean and fierce, and quite capable of the cowardly murders he had committed." Callous and facetious to the last, he is said to have declared, in answer to a shocked enquiry as to why he killed poor Helen Abercromby, "Upon my soul I don't know, unless it was because she had such thick ankles." Wainewright died of apoplexy in Hobart Town Hospital in 1852, a conceited, mean and totally unfeeling criminal. Apart from being the subject of Wilde's foolish and shallow essay, he is represented in Dickens' story "Hunted Down" and Bulwer Lytton's novel *Lucretia*.

Linden House was demolished in 1879. Its site is marked now by Linden Gardens, off the Chiswick High Road a short distance east of Turnham Green.

6

THE SMELL UNDER THE STAIRS
North-West: Regents Park, Camden Town, Kilburn, Hampstead

Until fairly recently Park Village East, a short road running off from the north-west corner of Regents Park, backed onto a basin of the Regents Canal—this is now drained, but the course can be followed. In November 1946 an unknown man murdered Mrs Olive Nixon, a 57-year-old widow, by hitting her over the head with a brick in a dark passage-way only a few yards from her home in the quiet road. No motive was apparent. In November 1956 a workman named Adam Ogilvie walked into Albany Police Station nearby and confessed to the ten-year-old crime, saying he had never been able to get it out of his mind. His reason for giving himself up after so long was that he had felt the same compulsion come over him since and was afraid that one day he would kill another woman. He had, in fact, attacked one in Torquay two months after the death of Mrs Nixon, in exactly the same way. At the trial he retracted his confession, saying he made it to prove his innocence to his wife, to whom he had pretended he was guilty of Mrs Nixon's death and would treat her in the same way if she did not stop quarrelling with him. As happened with Field and his retracted confession, however, Ogilvie knew too many unpublished details of the crime, and despite his statement that he had been told these by "a coloured man" the jury found him guilty. Fortunate, or cunning timing, however, saved Ogilvie; owing to the fact that the Homicide Bill was then being debated, he was reprieved.

Moving round the north of Regents Park we come to the approximate site of one of the most famous of all 'historical' crimes. On 17th October 1678 the body of Sir Edmund Berry (or Edmundbury) Godfrey was found in a ditch on the southern side of Primrose Hill, close to where the Regents Canal now runs. In those days the hill was open country, and the exact position of the corpse was described as two fields distant from Lower Chalcot Farmhouse. Lower and Upper Chalcot (or Chalcote, or Chalcott) Farms were on the Chalcot Estate, now commemorated in Chalk Farm. Godfrey was a man of substance and standing in the country, educated at Westminster School and Christ Church, Oxford. He was a successful wood dealer, a politician and a magistrate, knighted for his services in bringing criminals to justice during the Plague Year of 1665. On 12th October 1678 he left his house, at the river end of Northumberland Street, Charing Cross, to visit an address near St Clement Dane's. He did not return home and was not seen again until the discovery of his dead body, which had been run through by his own sword. He had also been strangled, which ruled out any idea of suicide.

In the previous September Titus Oates, ex-Catholic turned informer, liar and perjuror, had appeared before Godfrey in his capacity as magistrate, with two other men, bringing alleged news about the Popish Plot. Oates seems to have feared that, following a cross-examination by the Privy Council on treason charges he had made against a number of influential people, he might be in danger. He therefore wished to entrust a full account of his discoveries to Godfrey. The latter was known to have expressed a fear, some days earlier, that he himself might be under a threat, but he did not take any special precautions against possible attacks. In December 1678, several weeks after the discovery of the body, a man called Miles Prance, who was in detention for conspiracy, 'confessed' to the murder of Godfrey. His story was that as the magistrate passed Somerset House on his way from St Clement Dane's he was lured to a spot near the Watergate on the pretext of being needed to put a stop to a quarrel. There he was strangled and his body concealed for several days in various parts of Somerset House. Later it was carried in a sedan chair to Soho, transferred onto a horse, and taken to Primrose Hill where it was impaled on the sword and flung into a ditch. Three men were named as involved in the plot, Robert Green, Henry Berry and Lawrence Hill. These were arrested; there were apparently others, including two Catholic priests, who escaped. The three men were executed in 1679, but Prance's 'confession' was afterwards declared to be false and he pleaded guilty to perjury. A great outcry was raised against the Catholics, with evidence, statements, confessions and denials elicited by generally dubious means, but the real truth behind the murder will never now be known. Primrose Hill was earlier known as Greenberry Hill, though whether this has anything other than a chance connection with the leading conspirators is very doubtful. One thing is certain—after studying the story of the murder of Sir Edmund Berry Godfrey it is impossible to pass the little green hill rising so incongruously in the middle of London's cement without a slight shiver at the thought of the grim burden deposited at its foot on that long ago dark and deserted night.

Crossing Parkway, the short street from Regents Park to Camden Town, is Arlington Road where, on New Year's day 1926, 17-year-old Polly Edith Walker was discovered lying underneath her bed, clad in her nightdress, strangled with one of her own stockings. She lived in the flat with her mother, a charwoman who went out to work at 6 a.m., and was alone during that morning, sleeping off the effects of a party at which she had celebrated the arrival of what was to be, for her, so sadly brief a New Year. It was known that she had a lover, a street musician with the aristocratic name of Eugene de Vere. He was a French Canadian and had lost one leg as the result of an accident. De Vere was traced to Hitchin four days after the murder, and admitted his guilt. Polly, it appeared, had fallen for another man, and there had already been quarrels between them over this. Knowing that she would be alone in the house he had contrived to make his way in, and, in a fury of jealousy, killed her.

Continuing down Parkway we reach Camden Town Station. From here starts Camden Road, leading to the sites of three of the most famous murder cases of the early twentieth century: Phyllis Dimmock (the Wood Trial), Crippen and, across Hollo-way Road, Seddon. The last two come just outside the bounds of the present chapter, and before proceeding in search of Robert Wood we may go a few yards along the adjoining Kentish Town Road to a small thoroughfare linking it to Chalk Farm Road, called Hawley Crescent.

On the morning of 3rd January 1933 a man named Wynne,

whose address was No 30, found a hut in his yard burning strongly. Inside was a charred body and a note: "Goodbye all. No work, no money. Sam J. Furnace." Furnace was a builder to whom Mr Wynne had hired the shed. It soon became obvious that the fire had been started on purpose and at first glance the case looked like one of suicide. Very quickly, however, it was found that the dead man had been shot in the head. A coat was found nearby with a savings-bank book containing the name Walter Spatchett, a rent collector known to Furnace, who had not been seen since the previous day. Furnace was traced to Regents Park and thence to Southend. From there he wrote to a relative, obviously realizing by now (the B.B.C. had been called in to help the search) that his plan had failed. On being arrested, he claimed that he had shot Spatchett by accident. Furnace was never brought to trial—he succeeded in poisoning himself with hydrochloric acid the day after he was caught. It is clear that Furnace may have been influenced by A. A. Rouse, who in 1931 killed a man (whose identity is unknown to this day) and burnt the body in a car in an effort to fake his own death and escape from a morass of financial and amorous entanglements. However, in the case of Rouse (who lived in Buxted Road, Finchley) the plan was carefully thought out and only came to grief through a combination of ill chance and one unfortunate move. Furnace was apparently happily married, and though he owed money the amount was comparatively small. The motive for the killing may have been robbery (Spatchett was believed to have had some £40 on him) or may have resulted from some unknown trouble between the two men. The scheme, hurriedly thought up, was clumsy and doomed from the start.

Hawley Crescent is much changed now, with a firm of motor agents taking up most of one side, and commercial buildings and an open space on the other. Nothing remains to show where, some forty years ago, the builder with the bizarrely apposite name tried to erase his crime and his existence by means of fire.

The trial of Robert Wood for the murder of Phyllis (real name Emily) Dimmock in 1907 has never lost its interest for criminologists and has been written about several times, notably by Edward Marjoribanks in his life of Sir Edward Marshall Hall, and more recently by John Rowland in *Murder Mistaken*. The main points that have attracted the attention of students are three: the character of Robert Wood the accused, the magnificent defence by Marshall Hall, and the fact that this was the first occasion on which a person on trial for murder went into the witness-box to give evidence on his own behalf.

Wood lived with his father and half-brother at 12 Frederick Street, off Gray's Inn Road just north of the Royal Free Hospital. He worked at a glassware manufacturing firm, 58a Gray's Inn Road. He was a skilled artist (the sketches he made actually during the trial became famous) and had a good job as a designer. In 1907 he was 28 years of age, slightly built, good-looking in a rather pallid way, intelligent, cheerful and well liked. His general appearance was described by one witness as "shabby genteel". He had been carrying on a somewhat desultory affair (on his side, at any rate) with Ruby Young, who described herself—somewhat euphemistically—as an artist's model. At the time of the crime she was lodging in Finborough Road, Earl's Court—a street we shall meet more than once again. She was, it appears, accustomed to augmenting her earnings from artistic posings by less reputable means; Robert Wood knew of this but it does not seem to have worried him unduly. It may, indeed, have added a spice to their relationship, for Wood had another side to his shabby gentility, one which led him to enjoy the company of prostitutes—and led him also to the dock. He first met Ruby Young in 1904, when she was living in Liverpool Road, Islington, and one of their favourite haunts was the 'Rising Sun', 120 Euston Road, a pub that was to play a sinister part in his future.

On 12th September 1907 Phyllis Dimmock, a prostitute, was found lying naked on the bed of her room at 29 St Paul's Road, Camden Town, with her throat savagely cut. The body was discovered by Bertram Shaw, a night-shift worker on the railway who had been living with her as her husband. The room had been searched but nothing of value was missing. An album of postcards was lying on the floor with the contents scattered. The 'Rising Sun' was known to be one of Phyllis Dimmock's ports of call, and the police visited it to enquire whether she had been seen there on the evening of the murder. Soon they were led to Robert Roberts, a ship's cook. He had an alibi for the night in question, but told them that Phyllis had shown him a postcard signed "Alice", making an arrangement to meet her and decorated with a little drawing of a rising sun. This postcard, which was later found in her room by Bertram Shaw, was reproduced in the press, and seen by Ruby Young. She recognized Wood's writing. In recent weeks she had been worried about an apparent cooling off in his attentions to her. Despite her own activities she fiercely resented any links between him and other women. Before the card was seen by her, Wood had already asked her to say that she had been with him on certain days of the critical week. She now challenged him with having written the card and he admitted it, telling her a plausible, if rather improbable, story of his involvement with Phyllis Dimmock and asking her to help him. "Be true" was his rather strange, and constantly reiterated request. She agreed to be true, but could not resist telling her secret to a friend—from there it passed to a journalist, and so to the police.

Frightened and lonely, Ruby agreed to help the authorities. She arranged to meet Wood in Gray's Inn Road, and greeted him—by agreement—with a kiss. Apparently Wood suspected something was wrong and moved away, but Inspector Neill, who had been watching, immediately stepped up and detained him. When everything was gathered together at the trial a number of circumstances seemed to tell heavily against him, such as the fact that he was seen with Phyllis Dimmock at the 'Eagle' (a pub in Camden Road) late on the evening preceding the discovery of her body, and that early the following morning a man of similar size and walk was seen in St Paul's Road coming from the part near the house. Blackest of all was the fake alibi to which, not knowing Ruby Young had given him away, he adhered. Much of the evidence, however, was made to look much less impressive than it first appeared, by the brilliant defence put up by Marshall Hall, particularly the apparently damning suggestion of Wood's having been in the road the following morning. Above all, Wood's appearance in the witness-box told in his favour, though Marshall Hall, well aware of his client's over-confidence and a silly tendency to pose, was very worried as to whether he should put him there. Indeed, strictly speaking, Wood was very far from a 'good witness' in the accepted sense, and caused his counsel more than one moment of great anxiety, but his personality as a whole made a favourable impression and, following Hall's justly famous closing speech, he was acquitted. The verdict was universally popular. Ruby Young, who was—all in all—deserving of pity rather than fierce condemnation, had to be smuggled out of the Old Bailey disguised as a charwoman to escape the fury of the waiting crowd.

When John Rowland visited 29 St Paul's Road (now Agar Grove) for his book in 1963 he thought it might not be long before the rather drab old house and its neighbours disappeared. In 1972, however, it still stands, looking probably not much different from the time when Phyllis Dimmock was alive, despite the more modern blocks that have sprung up nearby. The brick wall concealing the railway almost opposite, which played an important part in the trial, also remains as it was. The 'Eagle', Camden Road, is now rebuilt, but the famous 'Rising Sun', with its passage-shaped bar and its splendidly ornamental Victorian decoration, retains all the atmosphere of the period; from the moment one glimpses the sign hanging outside only a small effort is needed to picture the slim young man in his shabby genteel Edwardian clothes entering to keep company with Ruby or his less reputable friends. The drama of Robert Wood and Ruby Young was played out against the buildings and in the streets of 1907 Bloomsbury and the West End. Their frequent meeting-place was, for some reason, a shoe shop (Phit-Eesi) in Southampton Row; a friend of Wood's who gave important evidence worked in a second-hand bookshop in Charing Cross Road; Ruby and Robert, during the time when he was pressing her to "be true" paid a visit to the Prince of Wales Theatre, Coventry Street, to see *Miss Hook of Holland*; they ate together in little cafés off Museum and Hart Streets; Ruby's fateful interview with Inspector Neill took place at Piccadilly Circus Underground Station (much different then from now); Wood was arrested in Gray's Inn Road. All these streets retain their identities if not altogether their appearance—except that Hart Street has become divided into Bloomsbury Way and Vernon Place—and it is not difficult to picture the figures of the two young people as they walked and worried over their problems in the smokier but less fume-choked London of 1907.

Three miles almost due west of Agar Grove is the junction of Kilburn High Road and Maida Vale. A turnpike once stood here, and Kilburn Priory marks roughly the grounds of a nunnery on which was afterwards built Kilburn Wells, a house where mineral water could be drunk from the spring. In the eighteenth century the place was also a favourite resort for music and dancing. Not all the district, however, was—or is—so salubrious. In 1958, in nearby Charteris Road, a 30-year-old prostitute, Veronica Murray, occupied an upstairs front bed-sitting room at No 58. Towards the end of December a friend, alarmed at the fact that she had not been seen since she went home in a taxi with a young man five days before, persuaded the landlord to break open the door. Veronica Murray was lying on her bed with her face smashed in (by an ornamental dumbbell, it was later ascertained) and her body savagely mutilated. The killer was obviously a dangerous sexual pervert, but apart from some fingerprints no clue was found as to his identity. As always in such cases where contacts are so frequent and so casual (Veronica Murray had had over one hundred convictions for soliciting), it proved impossible to trace any link and the usual "persons unknown" verdict was returned.

Ten months later the apartment in which George Sanders, the film actor, was staying at the Westbury Hotel, London, was broken into and a few items stolen. The fingerprints found matched those in Veronica Murray's flat. Late the next night, 10th October, Mrs Mabel Hill, who was separated from her husband and lived with her three children, was on her way home to Fulham from a visit to friends in Streatham when she was asked for a light by a young man as she changed trains at Leicester Square. They got into casual conversation and, despite her efforts to discourage him, he accompanied her to her home. This was a flat at No 5 Ismailia Road, Fulham, which then linked the tips of Wandsworth Bridge Road and Townmead Road just north of the bridge itself. Once there, he persuaded her to invite him in for a cup of coffee, made advances to her and, when she tried to put him off, assaulted her. He attempted first to rape her, then to strangle her with a stocking. She was found in the morning by her children in a distressed condition and had to spend several weeks in hospital. Fingerprints and other signs once again linked the man with the killing of Veronica Murray. A week later an elderly woman was attacked in her small house in Sloane Square; she managed to scream and the man ran off with a few insignificant articles. The fingerprints matched. On 1st November the same man burgled three Chelsea houses in one night, and on the 20th four more, in Jubilee Place and Markham Street.

Here the break came. A lighter stolen from one of the houses was of unusual design, and when the photograph of one similar was published in the press a soldier in the Welsh Guards stationed at Pirbright, Surrey, called the police with information that led to the apprehension of Drummer Michael Douglas Dowdall. Several of the items stolen from various houses were found in the camp, and eventually Dowdall made a statement admitting everything, including the brutal Charteris Road murder. An odd clue which, had its significance been understood at the time, might have saved the police a deal of trouble, had been left behind by Dowdall at George Sanders's hotel. Seeing a new pair of shoes in the corridor, he exchanged them for his own; on the left sole of the pair he abandoned someone had inserted nails to form the letters W.G. It was not realized until long afterwards that these initials stood for Welsh Guards. Dowdall was found to be suffering from diminished responsibility, convicted of manslaughter and sentenced to life imprisonment. He was 19 years of age.

Westwards across Queen's Park and the railway is Wrentham Avenue, a short road between Chamberlayne and Tiverton Roads, after which it relapses into anonymity as The Avenue. In 1904, in celebration of the British Empire at its mightiest, Wrentham Avenue was called Ladysmith Road. After that year an event that occurred in it caused local dismay to overcome patriotism, with a hasty change to it present name.

For some time a Mr William Dell, who rented part of a house in the street from Mr George Crossman, had been complaining about a nasty smell coming from a cupboard under the stairs. He was dissatisfied with Crossman's explanation that it came from a box of size gone bad—if that was the truth, why not get rid of the stuff? Dell took certain steps, and one day, as Crossman was arranging for the box to be carried from the house (smoking, as did Wainwright in similar circumstances, a large cigar), a policeman arrived evincing a certain curiosity in its contents. Crossman instantly rushed away down the street and, as his capture became imminent, snatched a razor from his pocket and cut his own throat, killing himself on the spot. The contents of the tin box proved to be the remains, embedded in cement, of Mrs Ellen Sampson, whom he had bigamously married more than a year previously, in January 1903. She was in fact the fifth of seven ladies who at one time or another—and often at the same time—had regarded themselves as Mrs Crossman. The first three apparently had had the legal right to do so. The fourth, whom he had bigamously wed a week before Mrs Sampson, had been sent away by him to stay for a short while with some friends, on the pretext that he had to go away on business. During the interval he brought home Mrs Crossman number five, murdered her almost at once, and then hid the body in an empty room. When number four returned home, refreshed from her holiday, he hid number five in her cement grave under the stairs. For almost a year all was quiet. Number four remained in Ladysmith Road, in unknowing company with number five, while Mr Crossman 'married' numbers six and seven, managing with expert dexterity to keep each apart from the others. He was then betrayed by Mr Dell's sense of smell. The incredible game—a sort of combination of chess and hide-and-seek, came to an end. The name of number four, incidentally, would have had a sinister ring in the ears of any student of crime gifted with a foreknowledge of eighteen years hence: it was Edith Thompson.

Changing its name halfway along to Belsize Avenue, Belsize Park links Finchley Road to Haverstock Hill on the way to Hampstead. Most of this area is built on the grounds of Belsize Manor, which traditionally belonged to the Dean and Chapter of Westminster since the reign of King Edgar, a century before the arrival of William the Conqueror. The manor stood roughly on the site of the present St Peter's Church. The Clerk to the Council under Henry VIII obtained the lease of "Old Belsize", rebuilt it and died there in 1568. It passed to Lord Wotten, then to the Earl of Chesterfield (who didn't like it), then, in the reign of King George I, to a retired sea-coal merchant named Povey. Following this, Belsize Manor (or House) opened as a place of public entertainment "with an uncommon solemnity of music and dancing". The last owners before its destruction in 1854 were a Roman Catholic family of bankers named Wright.

Nine years previous to this a Mr James Delarue, a musician, was murdered close by a corner of the grounds, in what was then a narrow lane leading from Chalk Farm to Hampstead— "a desolate spot, Belsize House being the only house nearby". Little is known of his murderer, named Hocker, but he was described as a man of excessive hypocrisy and cold-bloodedness. After the murder he went for a drink to the Swiss Tavern, Swiss

Cottage, then returned to the scene, asked the police what was amiss, felt the dead man's pulse, pronounced him dead, and paid bystanders some money to carry him away!

The means of killing was not stated, but Hocker's clothes were blood-stained and suspicion speedily fell on him. He attempted to put the blame on a friend, but was found guilty and executed. The motive was jealousy over Delarue's success-ful wooing of a young lady of Hampstead, whom he was presumably journeying to see when he met his death.

Turning off Haverstock Hill to the east is Upper Park Road. In 1933 Dr Angelos Zemenides lived at No 23, known as the head of the Cypriot colony in London. Among a number of apparently somewhat questionable activities (said to include helping foreign prostitutes to come to England by acquiring British citizenship through a nominal marriage), was that of finding suitable girls for his compatriots to marry. In March 1933 a 20-year-old pastrycook, Theodosius Petrou, was tried for his murder. It transpired that he had given Dr Zemenides a sum of money slightly in excess of £10 to come up with a suitable spouse, adding the request that she should be a girl with a dowry so that he could send financial aid to his poor relations in Cyprus. When the deal, perhaps not altogether surprisingly, fell through Petrou asked for his money back. Dr Zemenides said £9 was spent—gone, presumably, for ever. The famous ballistics expert, Robert Churchill, demonstrated that the bullets could have come from a gun sold previously to Petrou, but the evidence as a whole was inconclusive. The still dowerless pastry-cook was found not guilty, and the case remains unsolved.

Within a year of each other two murders were committed in the same unlikely, quiet, rather old-fashioned Hampstead Street known as South Hill Park, which pokes up into the southern part of the Heath and resembles on the map, in con-junction with South Hill Park Gardens, a frying-pan or tennis-racket with a bent handle. In 1954 the ground and first floors of No 11 South Hill Park were inhabited by a Greek Cypriot named Stavros Christofi, who worked as a waiter in a West End restaurant, his German wife Hella, their three children and his mother, Mrs Styllou Christofi. Stavros and Hella Christofi had been married for about fifteen years when, in 1953, his mother came from Cyprus to stay with them. Her intention was to make enough money in England to pay off a mortgage on property she owned. Mrs Christofi was an uneducated—indeed an illiterate—woman, but she managed to find employment with a ladies belt manufacturer at 3 Helena Road, Willesden. The domestic arrangement, however, was not a success. From the start Hella and her mother-in-law, from widely differing backgrounds, failed to hit it off together. Finally it was decided to bring what was becoming an intolerable situation to an end. Hella was shortly going to Germany with the children, and on her return Mrs Christofi would depart for Cyprus. All was settled with no apparent ill will on either side.

Around midnight on 28th July 1954 Mr John Young, who lived at 15 South Hill Park, saw a fire burning in the garden of No 11. He called out once or twice in case of trouble, then jumped the fence into the next garden to see that everything was all right. He smelt paraffin and saw what he thought was a tailor's wax dummy on the ground with flames all around it. As he watched, a woman came through the french windows to stir the fire, and the sight reassured him. An hour or so later a restaurant owner and his wife on their way home in their car were stopped by an excited woman crying, in broken English, "Please come—fire—three children sleeping!" They ran to the house and found the almost naked body of Hella Christofi in the back garden, near the windows. It was charred and smelt of paraffin. Mrs Christofi said she had smelt burning and come down. "Threw water. No good. She was dead." The skull, however, was fractured, and marks of strangling were on the throat. Charged with murder, Mrs Christofi refused to plead insanity, and was in fact declared sane by three examining doctors. It was revealed afterwards that thirty years previously she had been tried in Cyprus for the murder of her own mother-in-law by forcing a piece of burning wood down her throat. She was acquitted on that occasion—on this, however, the fiendishly cruel woman was found guilty, and executed.

The 'Magdala' public house curves round towards the lower end of South Hill Park. In the roadway outside, a little under a year after the events just related, Ruth Ellis shot her lover dead and earned the dubious distinction of being the last woman to be hanged in Britain. It was the climax and conclusion of a two-year relationship—a dreary, hysterical catalogue of off-again on-again quarrels, reconciliations, alternative affairs on both sides, set against backgrounds of small tawdry clubs, fringe motor-racing, cheap superficial sophistication, drinks and drives —all seeming strangely embalmed in its period of the fifties.

Ruth Ellis and David Blakely, whom she was later to kill, first met in 1953 at Carroll's Club (formerly called the Court Club), 58 Duke Street, off Oxford Street, of which she was then a hostess. Born Ruth Neilson, she married a North Country dentist, George Ellis, in 1950, but the marriage broke up a year or so later. Ruth and her two children (one of them illegitimate before the marriage), went to live with her parents at 11 Lucien Road, Tooting Bec. The owner of the club, however, a man of unsavoury reputation known as Morris Conley, arranged for her to go and live in Flat 4, Gilbert Court, Oxford Street, a building owned by his wife, in which he installed a number of his hostesses at high rents. She met Blakely for the second time when she had transferred her managerial activities to another club, the 'Little', 37 Brompton Road, Knightsbridge. They became lovers, and two months later, on 11th November 1953, Blakely publicly announced his engagement to a Yorkshire girl, Mary Dawson. This, according to Ruth's evidence, did not prevent him offering to marry Ruth also. She on her part, in a half-hearted attempt to break the relationship, left the Little Club and went to live with a company director, Desmond Cussen, at his flat, No 20 Goodwood Court, Devonshire Street. Blakely, however, clung on, so in February 1955 she left Cussen's flat and moved with her former lover to a furnished room at 44 Egerton Gardens, South Kensington, off the Brompton Road. This new arrangement did not last long, the tedious jealousies and quarrels flared again.

At the beginning of April she suffered a miscarriage, terminating a pregnancy which might or might not have been the result of her intimacy with Blakely. On the morning of 8th April, which was Good Friday, Blakely, worn out by the constant rows (which the presence in the single room of her young son made even less tolerable), went off to 29 Tanza Road, Hampstead, close to South Hill Park, the home of his close friends Anthony and Carole Findlater. He had told Ruth he would return in the evening, but did not do so. Instead, he told the Findlaters he couldn't stand it any longer, and must get away from his eternally squabbling and hard-drinking mistress. When it was suggested he should just up and leave her he replied, "You don't know her, you don't know what she's capable of." There

followed two days of furious telephoning from the now frequently intoxicated Ruth, and of scenes created by her in the
middle of the night outside the Tanza Road flat. When Blakely
prudently remained indoors she even made two attacks on his
car parked outside, and the police had to be called to control
her. On the evening of Easter Sunday she put her son to bed,
picked up a revolver, hailed a taxi and once more returned to
Tanza Road. This, at least, was one of her accounts. The story
of the gun and her final journey to Hampstead has alternate
versions. At one time she said the gun had been given to her
two years previously—this the police disbelieved. After her
trial and sentence she said it had been given to her just before
the murder by a man (the name was not mentioned) who made
her drunk and then drove her to Hampstead to kill Blakely.
Whatever the truth—and the whole story is a squalid morass
of lies and deceit—the outcome, for both Blakely and Ellis, was
the same.

As she arrived at Tanza Road, Blakely and a friend, Clive
Gunnell, left in the former's car to drive the few yards to the
'Magdala' for some beer. Gunnell came out of the pub first and
waited by the passenger door. A moment later he heard a cry
and two shots. He went round to the back of the car and saw
Blakely on the ground and Ruth Ellis shooting him in the
back.

The hysterical outcries of indignation at the death sentence
imposed on Ruth Ellis were in sharp contrast to the silence in
the case of Mrs Christofi. Public indignation and sympathy,
as Sir Richard Jackson comments in this connection, are highly
selective. The synthetically attractive face of Ruth Ellis had
looked out from countless newspapers. Mrs Christofi had less
appeal. Ruth Ellis shot her lover twice (putting on her rarely
worn spectacles to do so), fired two more bullets into him as he
lay on the ground, then two more at random (one of which
wounded a passer-by in the hand), then went on clicking the
weapon to make sure she had used all the contents. She never
denied her purpose (her answer to the one question put to her
in cross-examination was, "When I shot him I intended to kill
him"), nor pleaded insanity. A gun is a great equalizer of sexes,
and in a hand of a woman like Ruth Ellis was obviously as
dangerous as in that of any man. She appears to have expressed
no remorse at any time for what she did, and to have remained

bitter—even vindictive—to the end.* She told a visitor she didn't mind hanging but didn't see why the Findlaters should get away with it. Mrs Gladys Yule, the passer-by who was shot in the hand by Ruth Ellis while going along to the 'Magdala' with her husband for an evening drink, wrote afterwards, "Don't let us make Ruth Ellis into a national heroine. I stood petrified and watched her kill David Blakely in cold blood, even putting two bullets into him as he lay bleeding to death on the ground. . . . She might easily have killed an innocent passer-by, a complete stranger. As it is, I have a partly crippled right hand for life for which there is no compensation."

From the heights of Hampstead to the depths of Golders Green. In his seven-room maisonette above a greengrocer's shop in Finchley Road, across the way from Golders Green Station, Donald Hume on 4th October 1949 stabbed Stanley Setty to death with a Nazi S.S. dagger. He then took the car keys from the dead man's pocket and returned his car to its garage in Cambridge Terrace Mews, Regents Park. The next day, contriving to avoid both his wife (who had been away the previous evening) and a charwoman, he cut up the body and made it into three parcels which he weighted with small pieces of brick. With two of these he drove in a hired car to Elstree aerodrome, going along Dagger Lane on the way. He told someone at the aerodrome that he was going to Southend, but in reality dropped his cargo into the English Channel. The next day he brought in a decorator to paint over the bloodstains and also got the man (who must have been of a singularly incurious disposition) to carry the third parcel into the car. Later he remarked on the squelching noises it made as they lugged it downstairs. From there on he followed the same procedure, but this time he misjudged his whereabouts. In addition the weights broke loose, and the package floated until it was washed up near Burnham-on-Crouch, where it was found by a man in a punt shooting wildfowl. Fingerprints identified the remains as those of Setty, who had already been reported missing, and £5 notes known to have been on the dead man when he disappeared led the police to Hume. In the maisonette was a left-luggage ticket for Golders Green

---

* Though she did ask that after her execution some flowers should be placed on the grave of the man she had deliberately and with malice aforethought killed.

Station. This produced a blood-stained trunk in which Hume had temporarily stowed the body. All these details came to light from Hume's own published 'confession'. The jury at his trial failed to agree on a verdict—a second jury was directed to find him not guilty on a murder charge, and he admitted to being an accessory after the fact, receiving a sentence of twelve years' imprisonment. The 'confession', which appeared in the *Sunday Pictorial* after his release, also revealed as a complete invention an elaborate story he had made up of being approached by three gangsters, Greeny, Mac and the Boy, and persuaded, or threatened, to get rid of three mysterious packages on their behalf.

Long before this climax Hume's career might have been described mildly as chequered. He seems to have been born with what he himself admitted to be a chip on the shoulder—a grudge against everything and everybody. After a pre-war record of hooliganism and petty crime he joined the R.A.F. in 1939, developed meningitis, and was invalided out in 1941. For a few years he was engaged in a number of enterprises legal and illegal, and at one time was prospering quite considerably, running—among other things—a firm called Little Atom Electrical Products in Hay, Herefordshire—the little country town noted for its incongruous associations with the enchanting diarist Francis Kilvert and the less enchanting poisoner Herbert Armstrong. Later things began to go wrong, and money became scarce. In 1948, when he was married and living in the Finchley Road apartment, he met, at the Hollywood Club, Marble Arch, Stanley Setty (real name Sulman Seti, of Baghdad), and the two set up a racket illegally acquiring and selling cars, with associated sidelines such as forging petrol coupons. It was an uneasy partnership, and mutual trust seems to have been noticeable by its absence. With each partner knowing something of the other's character this was, of course, only reasonable and right. The trivial spark which ignited the fatal row was, according to Hume, Setty's rudeness to Hume's dog. He kicked it.

After his release Hume committed bank robberies in England and Switzerland. In the course of the latter attempt, in January 1959, he shot and killed a taxi-driver and would have been lynched by the furious crowd had the police not quickly arrested him. He was found guilty and received a life sentence of hard labour. In Switzerland, it seems, such a sentence—in certain cases at any rate—means what it says.

7

"NEARER MY GOD TO THEE"
North London: Islington, Highgate, Muswell Hill, Southgate

Islington Green is a small triangular patch formed by the junction of Essex Road and Upper Street, where formerly stood the famous Collins' Music Hall. A year after the conviction of Frederick Field for the murder of Beatrice Sutton (see page 58) a crime with oddly similar features occurred in the warehouse of Hardings, Furnishers, No 22 the Green. On 14th May 1937 the firm received word from one of their employees, Frederick Murphy, living at 57a Colebrooke Row nearby, that he had discovered a dead woman in the cellar of their premises. The police arrived, to find Murphy gone. The body was identified as that of Rosina Field, a prostitute, living apart from her husband, who was in the habit of taking a room nightly at 13 Duncan Terrace and last stayed there on the 11th. The following day Murphy walked into Poplar Police Station, with bloodstains on his clothes, declaring that he was completely innocent and desired to clear himself. He made a long statement concerning his movements on the night of the murder: most of these were progressions from pub to pub, in loyal celebration of the Coronation of King George VI. The 'Fox', 151 the 'Green', and the 'Queen's Head', Queen's Head Street, were among those listed. However, Murphy had been seen entering the warehouse between 10.30 and 10.45 that evening, with Rosina Field, and detail after detail of his elaborate alibi proved false. He was charged.

It was revealed later that Murphy had been accused of murder before—that of Katherine Peck, interestingly if puzzlingly known as Carbolic Kate. He had been seen with her outside an

Aldgate pub, and later she was found in the street with her throat cut. Murphy had disappeared, but two men informed the police that he had told them he was responsible for her death. His photo was published in the newspapers and some weeks later he turned up at Bethnal Green Police Station denying all knowledge of the crime. He was charged, but at his trial one of the two men failed to appear and could not be traced. The only remaining evidence, his alleged confession to the other man, was considered insufficient to convict and Murphy was acquitted. He proceeded to accuse his accuser of perjury and taking bribes, and worked himself up into a fine state of righteous indignation, bringing things to a climax by breaking a window of the Home Office itself, for which piece of impertinence he spent a fortnight in prison. For the murder of Rosina Field he was sentenced to death.

Moving west to Camden Road and then turning northwards we pass on our left the address better known, perhaps, than any other to the student of crime—39 Hilldrop Crescent, home of Hawley Harvey Crippen. This particular house is now rebuilt and modern blocks are destroying the symmetry of the crescent, but adjoining houses still remain much as they were to outside view. They are large, dignified, slightly despondent-looking semi-detached dwellings, with half-basements and a flight of some dozen steps to the front door. Mr and Mrs Crippen lived in the half-basement and ground floor of No 39, leaving the others almost empty. The idea when they moved in had been to take lodgers.

The story of the little American doctor (he obtained a medical degree at the Hospital College, Cleveland, Ohio), his music-hall artist wife Belle Elmore, and his typist mistress Ethel le Neve is too well-known and too often told to need recounting in full here. Long before the fateful year of 1910 Cora Crippen (his wife's non-professional name: she had been christened Kunigunda Makamotski) had become bored with and contemptuous of her small, pebble-eyed, insignificant husband. Unwisely, she made no attempt to conceal either the boredom or the contempt.

Crippen was involved in various minor medicinal undertakings. His main job was as agent for Munyon's Remedies, first in Shaftesbury Avenue and then in Albion House, 61 New Oxford Street, but he was also connected with less successful enterprises—the Sovereign Remedy Company, The Drouet Institute, the Aural Clinic Company. Around 1909 he became a partner in the Yale Tooth Specialists, whose office also was in Albion House. Some time previously he had met 20-year-old Ethel le Neve, who was working for the Drouet Institute—when that business collapsed she became Crippen's secretary at Albion House. She was living in lodgings at 80 Constantine Road, Hampstead, and her life was probably as lonely as his. They became lovers in the true sense of the word, and the one bright feature in an otherwise dark and sordid story is the deep affection between them, and Crippen's concern, right up to the end, for the welfare of his mistress.

In the middle of January 1910 he ordered five grains of hyoscin hydrobromide from Messrs Lewis and Burrows' New Oxford Street shop. At the end of that month Belle Elmore was seen alive for the last time, by her friends Mr and Mrs Martinetti who dined at Hilldrop Crescent. Crippen explained her disappearance by saying first that she had gone to America and later that she had died there. Meanwhile, however, he behaved with extraordinary lack of circumspection with regard to Ethel le Neve—dressing her in Mrs Crippen's jewellery and later actually taking her into the house. Suspicious friends informed the police, but nothing was discovered until one day, after several interviews, Chief Detective Inspector Dew paid a last, more or less routine, call—and found both Crippen and Miss le Neve gone. A more rigorous search of the house was then made, revealing portions of a woman's body buried in the cellar wrapped in a piece of pyjama jacket. The head was missing, and was never found. Crippen and Miss le Neve were now on the liner *Montrose* bound for Quebec, posing as father and son. The astute Captain Kendall noticed the strangely affectionate nature of their behaviour, the fact that the boy's trousers fitted oddly on the supposedly masculine behind, and a number of other points—even down to the fact that father, though not wearing spectacles, had red marks on each side of his nose indicating that he had recently done so. For the first time, police were notified by wireless of the captain's suspicions. They crossed the Atlantic on a faster boat and were awaiting 'Mr and Master Robinson' on the further shore.

Throughout the trial Crippen, who must have realized the hopelessness of his own situation, thought only of how best to protect Ethel le Neve. After her acquittal she went to Canada.

Later she returned to England, married, settled in the Home Counties, and brought up two children. How much she knew of the real situation can only be conjectured—but the rest of her life, one may surely hope, was happy in its obscurity.

Towards the northern end of Camden Road, Parkhurst Road splits away from it and crosses Holloway Road to become the Seven Sisters Road, named after an old circle of seven elm trees. On 14th December 1959 a fight flared up outside Gray's Dancing Academy between two local gangs of toughs, the Angel Mob and the Finsbury Park Lot. Two of the leaders faced each other, one with an axe, the second with a carving knife. At that moment P.C. Summers came up and made his way into the excited mob. He took hold of one of the biggest and started to take him to the police station; a moment later he fell to the ground stabbed in the back. The gangs ran off, so did the bystanders. Only three young girls remained to try to help the dying man, until a passing motorist called the police. Suspicion fell on a scaffolder named Ronald Marwood, and this deepened when he disappeared. Several weeks later he went to the Caledonian Road Police Station and confessed to the killing, saying he didn't know why he did it. At the trial he retracted the confession saying it was a forgery by the police. He was nevertheless found guilty and sentenced to death. In a vehement, not to say violent campaign for the reprieve of this tough, knife-wielding killer great emphasis was laid on his 'youthfulness'—Marwood was 25 and over six feet in height! As Sir Richard Jackson remarks in his comments on the case,* no mention was made of the fact that Marwood's victim, P.C. Summers, was only 23.

Leading off Hornsey Road a little north of the Seven Sisters is Tollington Park, not very different in appearance—despite new blocks and schools here and there—from the days when it was not merely a respectable address but—at least for an insurance superintendent—indicative of a definite step up in the world. Such a position was held in 1910 by Mr Frederick Henry Seddon from Lancashire. He lived at No 63, with elegant red-and-yellow brickwork, fourteen rooms, a half-basement, an area, and a few neat steps to the smart front door. He certainly got all he could out of (or rather, put all he could into) this fairly large house. Apart from his own family of a wife and five child-

* *Occupied with Crime.*

ren (aged from one to 17 years), he managed to accommodate an office (for which he charged his firm rent), his elderly father, a servant—and a tenant on the top floor who was to bring him to his doom. Though there is no evidence that Seddon actually ill-treated his wife or family (indeed, the one moving moment of his trial was when, on her acquittal, he kissed her goodbye), he seems to have been a cold, humourless and overbearing man. He had, however, one great love in his life—one warm spot in his chilly heart—and that was for money. It was the affection of the true miser, the delight in physically handling coins (real gold, of course, in those less synthetic days), making up accounts, planning this and that devious method of finishing up a penny the richer.

His tenant arrived on 25th July 1910. She was Miss Eliza Mary Barrow, a shabby, dirty, ill-mannered old woman with extremely unpleasant, not to say disgusting, personal habits, but also with £200 in gold in a cash-box, a small amount of property and various investments. With her came an orphan boy of about 9, whom she made to sleep in the same bed as herself even when she was ill, and a married couple who were friends of her own. The latter, however, stayed only a few days; according to Seddon he turned them out on Miss Barrow's instructions. It was not long before Seddon had his fingers firmly in his tenant's financial pies. In return for annuities, she made over to him most of her stock and the leasehold of a public house in Camden Town called the 'Buck's Head', together with that of a barber shop next to it. The trouble with annuities, however, is that the income has to keep on being paid. So Miss Barrow fell very ill, and then died: of epidemic diarrhoea and general exhaustion, said the doctor who signed the certificate. She was buried, very quickly, in Islington Cemetery. Unpleasant though she had been, however, Miss Barrow was not without friends, and Seddon's neglect to inform them of her condition and his generally off-hand treatment caused both offence and surprise. These rapidly turned to suspicion when it was revealed that all that was left of Miss Barrow's worldly goods was about £10. After all, she could not have taken it with her, and it seemed strange that everything should fall out so very conveniently for her financial adviser. Various incidents, combined with Seddon's behaviour, determined the friends to call in the police. Miss Barrow's body was exhumed and found to contain a large amount of arsenic. Seddon was arrested in Tollington Park, in the street itself, exclaiming in outraged propriety that such a thing had never happened in his family before.

The evidence against him, which included a very doubtful allegation that he had sent his daughter to a chemist's shop at 103 Tollington Park to buy arsenic, was not very strong, and it is generally considered that it was his cold and callous performance in the witness-box as much as anything else that decided the jury on his guilt. From the time of his arrest he preserved his chilly imperturbability, protesting violently on only two occasions—once against an allegation that he had made a remark that seemed to implicate his wife. The second incident that aroused his anger was a suggestion that he had been seen counting Miss Barrow's money immediately after she died. "I am not a degenerate! That would make out that I am a greedy, inhuman monster! . . . The suggestion is scandalous!" he cried, then rather spoilt the effect by adding that he would have had all day to count the cash. Seddon was a freemason, a fact which is generally held to have been responsible for the famous scene after the verdict when, asked if he had anything to say, he declared his innocence "before the Great Architect of the Universe"—so greatly upsetting Mr Justice Bucknill, a fellow mason, that he was barely able to speak the final words.

Seddon maintained his coolness to the last. One final incident roused him. On hearing that his property, including a motor-car of which he was intensely proud, had been auctioned for a paltry sum, he exclaimed, in disgust and despair, "That's done it!"

Waterlow Road, No 19, is a bright, tidy street of solid red-brick little houses, joining Archway Road to Highgate Hill just north of Whittington Hospital. In 1914 it was known as Bismarck Road, and the reasons for a change of name during the years that followed might seem obvious. There was, however, cause nearer home for blotting out the past, for it was at No 14 Bismarck Road that the appalling George Joseph (Brides-in-the-Bath) Smith drowned his last 'wife'.

Smith was born in 1872 at 92 Roman Road, Bethnal Green. At the age of 9 he was sent to a reformatory, which he left at 16. At 18 he served his first term of imprisonment, at 19 his second, at 24 his third, for theft, larceny and receiving; and so it went on. During a brief period of honesty he opened a barber's shop in Leicester and married (against her family's wishes) Miss Beatrice Thornhill, under the name of Mr and Mrs Love. The new business failed; the old businesses, with their inevitable consequences, revived. His wife proved an apt pupil and soon turned criminal also, taking a post as a maid and stealing from her employers. They parted after about two years and she—luckily for herself—went to Canada. With Mrs Love out of the way Smith 'married' his second dupe, at St George's, Hanover Square. He was now starting on what was to be his main career—tricking women out of their savings, and later their lives. His one true romance, if such a thing is conceivable, was born in 1908 when he won the heart of Edith Pegler, who had advertised for a post as housekeeper, and settled her down in Bristol.

The incredible financial and marital complications of the following years demand more space than we have available here to unravel in detail, and in any case do not touch very closely on London. Smith's first known murder-by-bath took place on Saturday 13th July 1912 in Herne Bay, the victim's name being Bessie Mundy. For his sinister purpose he bought a zinc bath on 8th July for £1 17s. 6d. (beating the price down from £2), took it to the house he had rented on a yearly tenancy, and returned it to the shop, after Miss Mundy had been found dead in it, on the 15th. The next victim was Alice Burnham, 'married' on 4th November 1913, drowned on 12th December. This second unfortunate accident took place in lodgings at Blackpool. It was to his landlady here, Mrs Crossley, that he made his famous retort, when she and her husband protested at his intention to give his wife a pauper's funeral, "When they're dead they're done with." Despite a verdict of accidental death, the astute Lancashire landlady noted on a card of Smith's, "Wife died in bath. We shall see him again." In September 1914, as Britain braced itself for the recently declared war, Smith was in Bournemouth, where he met Alice Reavil, 'married' her and took her to furnished rooms at 8 Hafer Road, Battersea Rise, London. There, a few days later, he abandoned her, taking with him everything she possessed except the clothes she stood up in—and her life. Alice Reavil, had she known it, was fortunate.

Towards the end of the year he was back in Bristol with Edith Pegler. In between his various activities he would dash back to this accommodating but surely somewhat gullible lady for rest and relaxation. Very soon, however, he told her he felt restless and would "have a run round again before Christmas with another young fellow he had met in Clifton". The meeting had, in actual fact, been with Miss Margaret Lofty, 38-year-old daughter of a deceased clergyman. Apparently he caught her on the rebound from an unhappy love affair and very soon, as John Lloyd, won her lonely heart. They were 'married' in Bath (ominous name) on 17th December and left that day for London. They went first to 16 Orchard Road, Highgate, but here encountered a snag. 'Mr Lloyd' had already called a few days previously to inspect the rooms—and the bath. Mrs Heiss, the landlady, said afterwards, "I did not like the way he asked about the bath." Apparently he "measured it with his eyes", then said it was a bit small but "I daresay it is large enough for some-one to lie in." Mrs Heiss (who was a German when it was an awkward time to be one, and had had trouble with undesirable lodgers before) was so put off by his manner that when he returned on the 17th she would not let him in, saying the rooms were not ready. After making a bit of a scene, Smith-Lloyd was persuaded to leave—influenced perhaps by the presence of a detective-sergeant who had helped Mrs Heiss in such difficulties before. He went off in a rage and so, at last, reached 14 Bismarck Road, where there was a furnished room to let.

Having enquired about the bath and received a satisfactory reply, Smith took the room and settled in with his bride. The remainder of that day and the next were taken up with necessary financial formalities (wills, etc.), and with a visit to Dr Bates at 30 Archway Road. In each case Smith took his prospective victim to a doctor beforehand, to whom she obediently complained about her health, thus facilitating the issue of a certificate when the need arose. On the evening of the 18th, about 7.30, Mrs Lloyd took a hot bath. A few moments later, after Miss Blatch the landlady had heard sounds of splashing and a sigh, the harmonium in the front parlour suddenly pealed forth—Smith was accompanying himself singing "Nearer My God, to Thee." Then he went out to buy some tomatoes—in each case he had made a similar excursion to get something for supper. A minute or two after his return, the distracted husband found his newly-wed bride dead in her bath. At the inquest Smith was exonerated, and doubtless commiserated with. Reports of the death, however, appeared in the press and were seen not only by a relative of Alice Burnham but also by the Crossleys in Blackpool. They wrote to the police.

Once planted, suspicions flowered rapidly. Smith was arrested and charged in the first instance with causing a false entry to be made in the Bath marriage register. He was remanded at Bow Street and three weeks later, after intensive police work, charged with murder.

Of all Marshall Hall's cases as defence counsel this must have been the one which presented him with the smallest hope. Throughout the summing-up Smith interrupted violently, telling the judge to "hang me and have done with it". "It is a disgrace to a Christian country!" he cried. "I am not a murderer—though I may be a bit peculiar"—surely the understatement of the century. He was hanged at Maidstone, in a state of collapse, on 13th August 1915.

Agar Grove (St Paul's Road), 1907; Hilldrop Crescent, 1910; Tollington Park, 1912; Waterlow (Bismarck) Road, 1914; within seven years and within this small section occurred four of the most notorious murders in London's criminal history.

Millfield Lane was, and still is, a narrow thoroughfare winding through Ken Wood and alongside Highgate Ponds. In 1814, on 4th October, Elizabeth Buchanon, known also as Elizabeth Dobbins, a washerwoman, was found dead in Millfield Farm, a cottage in the Lane. Her 'husband' (they were in fact unmarried but had lived together for many years) worked for the Hampstead Water Company, and came home to find her lying on the kitchen floor with savage head wounds caused by a poker which was covered in blood and bent from the force of the blows.

Before he knew what had happened, a workman on a job nearby had detained a stranger he had seen creeping furtively away with two bundles as if making off with the proceeds of a robbery. The bundles were found to contain clothing from Elizabeth Buchanon's wash. The detained man, one Thomas Sharpe, told an unlikely story of having bought the bundles from a gipsy, but several other witnesses had seen him near the cottage, and no-one had caught sight of any gipsies. Sharpe, who already had a police record, was swiftly found guilty and executed for the brutal murder of a washerwoman.

Moving north across the Archway Road, we come to Muswell Hill and a short, dignified thoroughfare leading off Queens

Avenue and Fortis Green known by the rather curious name of Tetherdown. In 1896 its most imposing house was Muswell Lodge, set in its own grounds on the west side of the street and inhabited by a retired engineer named Smith, 80 years old, a miser and a recluse. Despite highly ingenious devices against illegal entry, the house was broken into during the night of 13th–14th February. Smith's body was discovered the next morning by the gardener. It was lying in the kitchen amidst evidence of a violent struggle. He had been killed by blows on the head of tremendous force and then wrapped in a red cloth. Several windows showed signs of attempted forcing, and one leading to the kitchen had finally given way. Beside the body was one of the strangest and most bizarre clues ever found in a commonplace murder and robbery case—a clue that more than any other sealed the fate of the men involved—a child's toy lantern. Suspicion was soon directed towards two men already known to the police, Albert Milsom and Henry Fowler, both of whom had disappeared from their usual haunts. A stolen bank-note was traced to one of them, and an unusual piece of jewellery belonging to Smith—a gold trinket in the shape of a human leg—was pawned in Swindon by a man later identified as Fowler. Final confirmation came from the toy lantern. Police called with it at Milsom's home, 133 Southam Street, North Kensington, and his 16-year-old brother-in-law claimed it as his own, indicating a number of distinguishing marks. The men were traced to Bath and arrested there in April. They were a strangely contrasted pair—Milsom sly and meagrely built, Fowler a hulking tough. At first both denied any knowledge of the crime, but before very long Milsom confessed and the usual procedure was followed—each criminal blaming the other. Apart from the Clue of the Toy Lantern, the case is famous for the violent outburst as the jury returned with their verdict, when Fowler flung himself across the dock onto Milsom and very nearly succeeded in anticipating the executioner. Several warders joined in a general mêlée for a considerable time before he was secured.

Muswell Lodge is gone now; its site was roughly on the corner of Burlington Road. Schools and playing-fields replace the grounds. The two men were supposed to have escaped from the back of the lodge, through nearby Coldfall Woods.

About three miles north of Tetherdown, Wade's Hill, South-gate, leads from the green near Winchmore Station to Green

Dragon Lane. On 14th February 1948, fifty-two years to the day after the crime of Milsom and Fowler, P.C. Nathaniel Edgar was on special plain-clothes patrol duty on account of a number of recent burglaries in the Southgate area. In the early evening two passers-by heard shots and the sound of running footsteps along Broadfields Avenue. Edgar was found dying at the entrance of 112 Wade's Hill. He was able to whisper the name of his murderer, which he had also managed to scribble in his notebook, together with the identity number. The man, Donald George Thomas, a deserter from the army, was traced through the publication of the photograph of a married woman with whom he was living in Stockwell. He was arrested while in bed, and a gun was found beneath his pillow. Thomas, aged 23, had been good at both work and games at his school, but when called up in 1945 he deserted, and spent some time in detention. He was tried and convicted, but as the trial took place during the five-year suspension period he was not executed, but imprisoned for life. P.C. Edgar, who met his death at Thomas's hands, was 33, a married man with a family.

8

THE DEATHS OF PUBLIC MEN
South-West, North of the River: Westminster, Pimlico, Knightsbridge, South Kensington, Fulham, Chelsea

Two names for ever linked with the murder of public men for private reasons are John Bellingham and Daniel M'Naghten (though the latter killed the wrong man). The dates were 1812 and 1843. In the first case the culprit was executed, in the second he was committed to an asylum. Both were, even at the time, widely regarded as insane—it being rather touchingly assumed that no-one in his right mind could want to do away with a politician.

John Bellingham was a merchant of about 40 whose home was in Liverpool, though for some time before the murder he himself had been living in lodgings in London. Several years previously, while in Russia on business, he had been imprisoned on a charge of dishonesty. On his release he complained to the British Ambassador in St Petersburg, Lord Leveson-Gower, protesting that the charge had been entirely false. Despite the fact that Bellingham had a right to expect a demand for reparation, or at least an enquiry, the ambassador showed complete lack of interest, and in fact Bellingham was sentenced to a second term. On his return to England, with his affairs in a bad way as a result, he took rooms at 9 New Millman Street (now the northern part of Millman Street) and determined to seek restitution. He approached ministers, government officials, Members of Parliament, even the Prince Regent himself, only to be met with the same polite indifference, and passed from one to the other with bland, ruthless, civil-servant courtesy. He became a well-known figure haunting the law courts and government buildings, whiling away his waiting hours in the European Museum, King Street, St James's, the site of which is now occupied by Christie's. He wrote constantly to his wife, whenever there seemed to be the smallest gleam of hope. Among those whom he approached was General Isaac Gascoigne, M.P. for Liverpool, the only man to show any interest in his case. He advised Bellingham to communicate with the Prime Minister, the Right-Honourable Spencer Perceval, who was also Chancellor of the Exchequer. Here, too, however, the unfortunate merchant came face to face with a blank wall of urbanity, and was at last driven to despair.

On the afternoon of 11th May 1812 he waited in the lobby of the House of Commons, and, as the Prime Minister passed through, shot him through the heart. He made no attempt to escape, collapsing on a nearby seat, protesting his sorrow and declaring it was against the minister and not the man that his desperate act had been directed. His trial lasted one day only. An appeal for time to bring witnesses from Liverpool to testify as to Bellingham's mental instability was refused. After a passionate statement of the wrongs he had suffered he was swiftly sentenced and executed, one week after his crime.

Less is known of the motives, if any, that influenced Daniel M'Naghten (variously spelt McNaughton, McNaghten), who in 1843 shot Edward Drummond, the Prime Minister's secretary, in mistake for Sir Robert Peel. The killing took place in Parliament Street. M'Naghten was a wood-turner from Glasgow who lodged at 7 Poplar Row, Newington, where his landlady described him as sullen and reserved. He appeared to have made quite a lot of money, and the reasons for his grudge against Peel are unexplained. He was found insane and sent to Bethlehem Hospital. The case gave form to the famous M'Naghten Rules, for many years accepted as the valid definition of insanity in law.

We may mention briefly here two attempts at royal assassination that occurred in Constitution Hill at an interval of almost exactly a century. In 1840 Edward Oxford, 18, fired at Queen Victoria and Prince Albert as they drove along the route from Buckingham Palace. He was found to be insane and committed to an asylum, where he lived for many years. Previously he had worked as a barman in various public houses. At the time of the attempt he was at the 'Hog in the Pound' which still stands, rebuilt but bearing the same name, at the point where South Molton and Davies Streets converge on Oxford Street.

Nearly one hundred years later, in July 1936, George Andrew McMahon flourished a revolver at King Edward VIII during a state drive up Constitution Hill. He said he had been employed by a mysterious foreign power to kill the monarch for £150. It was considered that he was a paranoiac, with no real intention of shooting the King, and he received twelve months hard labour.

In 1681 on the south-west corner of Pall Mall East, not far from what is now Waterloo Place, a Mr Thomas Thynne was "most barbarously shot with a musketoon in his coach", and died the following day. His murderer, by proxy, was Count Könings- mark. Mr Thynne was engaged to marry a wealthy heiress, Lady Elizabeth Ogle, whom the Count wanted for himself. He therefore made use of a contemporary Murder Inc., hiring "three ruffians" to commit his crime for him. Having fired their musketoon, however, they were speedily caught, tried, convicted and hanged on the spot where the murder was committed. The Count escaped punishment, it was reported "by favour of a corrupt jury".

Caxton Hall, Westminster, might seem an unlikely setting for murder, but on 13th March 1940 one occurred, for vaguely political motives, in the Tudor Room. Sir Percy Sykes had just finished delivering a lecture on Afghanistan, at which the Secretary of State for India took the chair. Among those on the rostrum was Sir Michael O'Dwyer. As the meeting was breaking up six shots were fired. Two struck Sir Michael, killing him instantly. A man rushed to the exit door but was grabbed by a woman and held until he could be disarmed. He was an Indian by the name of Udham Singh, soldier, deserter, trafficker in illegal weapons, general agitator and trouble-maker. He was apparently consumed with hatred for the British and made a hysterical speech at his trial. "I didn't mean to kill," he de- clared when charged. "I just did it to protest."

Another politically inspired murder occurred in 1922 outside 36 Eaton Place, where, on 22nd June, Reginald Dunn and Joseph O'Sullivan shot Field-Marshal Sir Henry Wilson on the doorstep of his home. Sir Henry, then M.P. for North Down, Ulster, had recently returned from Belfast where he had been adviser to the Northern Ireland government on methods of deal- ing with bomb outrages caused by Southern Republic terrorists.

As he collapsed dying on the pavement the two men ran off and were eventually captured in Ebury Street, where they narrowly escaped lynching at the hands of a furious crowd.

From political murder and assassination we return now to those committed for less exalted reasons. On the south side of Victoria Street, leading into Vauxhall Bridge Road, is Rochester Row, well-known for its police station. Almost exactly opposite this, at No 86, an office was rented in 1927 by Mr John Robinson. On 6th May of that year a trunk was deposited at Charing Cross Station left-luggage department. It was of the wicker-work type, covered with black American cloth, and thus by no means airtight. After lying around for a while unclaimed it began to give off a most offensive smell. The police were sent for, and the trunk opened. It contained a woman's body divided into five parts by an unskilled hand. From laundry marks on the clothing the body was identified as Mrs Minnie Bonati, wife of an Italian waiter. She was 36 and had been for some years separated from her husband and earning her living by various dubious means. The last time she was seen alive was when she visited the Chelsea Relieving Officer on 4th May. The trunk was traced to a second-hand dealer in Brixton. There, for a few days, the trail ended. Then, after details had appeared in the press, a taxi-driver went to the police to say that on 6th May he had just dropped a fare in Rochester Row when he was hailed by a man standing rather furtively in a block of offices just opposite the Police Station. He was asked to help lift a heavy trunk onto the cab and then drive his passenger to Charing Cross Station. All tenants in the block were interviewed by the police, except one who was missing. His name was John Robinson, and he had told the landlord he was leaving as he had no money left to pay the rent. Robinson's wife was traced to the Greyhound Hotel, Hammersmith. Robinson, it appeared, though not an altogether satisfactory husband, kept in touch with her. He had an appointment to meet her at the Elephant and Castle—and there he met the police as well. He was questioned but released for lack of any solid evidence against him. This was on its way, however. In addition to its other contents, a duster had been found in the trunk. This, when washed, revealed the printed words The Greyhound. Faced with this new factor, Robinson broke down and confessed. On 4th May, he said, Minnie Bonati had accosted him in

Victoria. He took her to the office, and she demanded money. When he said he had none, she attacked him. He struck her in self-defence, and she fell. He then left the office, and returned later fully expecting to find her gone. Instead, he found her dead. On 5th May he bought a chef's knife in a shop in Victoria Street (the same shop at which Patrick Mahon had bought the cook's knife and saw to dismember Emily Kaye—see page 215). After his grisly work across the road from the police station, he had buried the knife under a tree in Clapham Common.

Tachbrook Street, Pimlico, is a longish, dullish street joining Vauxhall Bridge Road to Lupus and Bessborough Streets. In 1928 an army bandsman, William John Holmyard lived at No 39 with his father. Next door, at No 37, lived his grandfather William—an elderly but vigorous 72. Both houses still stand today, but are very dilapidated and presumably due soon to disappear. In the early dark of a December afternoon, 1928, old William Holmyard was seen outside his own house clinging to the railings, with blood pouring down his head. He died three days later from a broken skull. His grandson had already been arrested on a charge of assault, and this was now changed to one of murder. His plea was that the blows were struck in self-defence. He went to see his grandfather because he was seeking his help in finding a job, but the old man, who was in a very bad mood, first abused him and then attacked him with a chair. Young Holmyard grabbed the nearest thing to hand to defend himself—a pair of tongs. He had no intention, he said, of seriously injuring his grandfather, nor did he realize he had done so. The old man was much stronger physically than the fraily-built young one and, as Holmyard's counsel pointed out "youth has as much right to defend itself as old age". Despite a good general reputation, and the fact that he seemed to have no motive for murder, Holmyard was found guilty and executed. His defence was conducted "with conspicuous ability", in the words of the judge Sir Travers Humphreys, by Miss Venetia Stephenson—the first occasion on which a woman barrister had led in a murder trial.

"Now that she has been found not guilty she should, in the interests of science, tell us how she did it." Sir James Paget's remark on hearing of the acquittal of Adelaide Bartlett has become as famous (whether he actually made it or not) as the Pimlico Mystery itself. The case has become so linked with

Claverton Street—the short, unusually wide road from Lupus Street to Grosvenor Road and the river—that it is surprising to realize that the people concerned were only in residence there for a bare three months. On 3rd October 1885 Edwin and Adelaide Bartlett moved into two adjoining rooms on the first floor of No 85, the "drawing-room floor" as the respectable landlady Mrs Doggett called it; on 1st January 1886 Edwin was dead—from poison by chloroform.

Adelaide, born in Orléans in 1855, was said to be the natural daughter of an Englishman of "good social position". This certainly seemed to be borne out by her maiden name—Adelaide Blanche de la Tremouille. Almost nothing is known of her early life—not even the identity of her mother—but at the age of 19 she was married, by a financial arrangement with her father, to a man she had met only once before, Edwin Bartlett. He was some ten years older than she, the owner of a small but successful chain of grocery shops in London suburbs. The marriage took place in Croydon. Immediately afterwards her husband, whose passion for learning exceeded that for the more earthy joys of marital life, sent her off to boarding-school at Stoke Newington, and two years later to a finishing school in Belgium. Duly educated to his satisfaction, she was permitted to return home and set up house at No 1 Station Road, Herne Hill, one of Edwin's shops. She seems to have accepted this somewhat strange beginning to married life with equanimity if not with enthusiasm, and outwardly their delayed existence together was a happy one, in spite of a strained relationship with her father-in-law, who came to live with them after his wife's death. A child was stillborn, the sad fruit of what was, according to Adelaide, the only occasion the marriage was consummated. Edwin Bartlett thought a man should have two wives; one for companionship, the other, in his own words, "for use". Adelaide, willingly or not, belonged to the former category. 'Use' was not for her—though certain evidence at the end of the trial raised some doubts as to this.

About 1883 the couple moved to another of the shops, this time in Lordship Lane, near Dulwich Park, leaving the old man behind, to Adelaide's presumed relief. From there they moved again to The Cottage, Phipps Bridge, Merton—which was then a village about two miles from Wimbledon. There they attended the Wesleyan chapel and met the minister, 27-year-old George

Dyson, noted—apart from his preaching—for the beauty of his heavy, silky black moustache. A close friendship developed between the three of them, and Edwin further indulged his passion for education by arranging that the clergyman should give Adelaide lessons in a variety of subjects while he himself was away at his grocery business. The Reverend Dyson jumped at the chance and paid regular tutorial visits—apparently without finding a need for any text-books, but always with Edwin's full knowledge and consent. While on holiday with his wife at Dover, Edwin paid Mr Dyson's fares to come and see them, and later made a will leaving everything to Adelaide unconditionally and appointing Dyson as one of the executors. This, as it happened, healed a rather sore spot for Adelaide as it replaced a will stipulating she would not inherit if she remarried.

October 1885 and Claverton Street now arrived. Dyson had already been transferred to a larger chapel, in the Upper Richmond Road, and was now living at 18 Parkfields. Adelaide's courses in further education were thus able to continue without undue inconvenience to anyone. The whole triangular situation, in fact, became curiouser and curiouser, Edwin declaring that he had decided, when the time came for him to die, to 'give' Adelaide to Dyson, and encouraging them to get into practice by kissing each other in his presence.

It was shortly after their arrival in Claverton Street that Edwin, who had hitherto been an unusually healthy man (except for trouble with his teeth), became ill. Adelaide, to all appearances, nursed him devotedly, and sent Dyson around the chemists' shops to buy chloroform which, she said, soothed his pain. The obliging clergyman scurried about picking up ounces of the stuff in High Street, Putney, Upper Richmond Road and Wimbledon; and pouring it from his small bottles into one large one. This he gave to Adelaide. All in vain. On 31st December Edwin died. Stirred up mainly by old Mr Bartlett, who never lost his dislike of Adelaide, suspicions were aroused, and a post-mortem called for. In a panic, Dyson threw away his chloroform bottles under some bushes on Wandsworth Common. The pleasant relationship between him and Adelaide was finally broken in an angry scene at a friend's house, during which Dyson cried out in agony that he was a ruined man. Chloroform was said to be the cause of death, and both he and Adelaide were arrested. At the start of the trial Dyson was released, the prosecution announcing that they had no case against him: at the end of it, following a brilliant defence by Edward Clarke, Adelaide Bartlett was acquitted, though with an unusual qualification. "We have well considered the evidence," said the foreman of the jury, "and although we think there are circumstances of grave suspicion attaching to the prisoner, we do not think there is sufficient evidence to show how, or by whom, the chloroform was administered." Sir James Paget uttered his witticism, and Adelaide Bartlett disappeared into an obscurity from which she never again emerged.

Claverton Street today is shorn of its former pleasant dignity. Almost all the three-storied, porticoed and cellared houses have gone, replaced by featureless blocks of flats. Though it survived the war by several years, No 85 is now among those destroyed. Its site, however, can be fairly accurately placed. A short distance up from the river on the left-hand side is a pillar-box— only recently replacing one that still showed the letters 'V.R.' and had received Adelaide's letters to her George. A few yards before the pillar-box is reached the traveller passes the spot where three or four steps led Edwin and Adelaide to the heavy front door of No 85, and to all that awaited them there.

We now move north to Knightsbridge—receiving its name, according to tradition, from a quarrel between two knights who fought it out on a bridge which then spanned the West Bourn. On less speculative ground, it was for a long time the last village before one arrived in London, and hence something of a boundary for highwaymen. Evelyn refers in 1699 to the many robberies between London and Kensington, and in 1687 thieves murdered Mr Thomas Ridge of Portsmouth "almost at Knightsbridge". In 1744 a footpad was shot dead a little west of the bridge.

While on the subject of highwaymen we may digress briefly to note that, somewhat surprisingly, the most notorious spot was Finchley Common, with Hounslow Heath as chief rival and Epping close behind. It was in Epping Forest that Dick Turpin progressed from thief to murderer, killing a steward of one of the keepers named Thomas Morris. The glamourizing and Black Bessing of Turpin is one of the minor curiosities of historical distortion. He was in reality a mean, cowardly, stupid and cruel robber and murderer, with nothing worthy and little interesting about him. The son of a farmer, he was apprenticed to a butcher in Whitechapel, and noted early on for his general boorishness and brutality. He married a girl from East Ham and soon began his thieving career by stealing cattle and cutting them up for sale. His reputation for gallantry has no basis in fact. When working with King, a fellow highwayman, he held up two young women. It was King, not Turpin, who remarked that it was a pity to rob two such pretty girls. Turpin merely grabbed the money they had just received for the sale of their corn, and made off.

On Hounslow Heath in October 1738 one George Price strangled his wife with the thong of his whip within sight of the gallows, dying of gaol fever in Newgate before he could be brought to trial. Jack Sheppard, as noted, was captured on Finchley Common, which was the haunt also of Claude Duval, Will Holloway, Turpin and others. The Earl of Minto, delayed until sunset in starting a journey, decided to wait until the following day, remarking to his wife, "I shall not trust my throat on Finchley Common after dark." One of the latest recorded murders by highwaymen was that of a Mr Steele as late as 1806.

Returning to modern Knightsbridge, we turn down William Street, just before the branch with Brompton Road, to William Mews. In 1932 this quiet backwater grabbed the headlines as the setting of a quarrel—or climax to a series of quarrels—that landed a woman in the dock and a man in his grave. Mrs Elvira Barney, at 27, was possessed, it appeared, of more money than sense. At her trial her defence counsel, Sir Patrick Hastings, described her as "a spoilt child of fortune" who had "drifted into an atmosphere of idle luxury". She had separated from her husband and was living in a converted maisonette over a garage at 21 William Mews, then known as Williams Mews, not far from her parents' house in Belgrave Square. Here she was in the habit of giving rowdy parties which on more than one occasion brought complaints from other inhabitants of the mews, even leading to the police being called. For some time she had been carrying on an affair with William Scott Stephen, by all accounts a singularly characterless young man of 24. It was a relationship which in the course of time had dwindled from a mutual attraction to a desperate and rather pathetic possessiveness on the part of an already coarsening and ageing woman.

On the night of 30th May 1932 there was a party which broke up earlier than usual, and Mrs Barney and Stephen went on to the Café de Paris, returning together afterwards to the mews. In the early hours of the 31st the long-suffering neighbours heard Mrs Barney screaming that she would shoot someone, and then the sound of a gun being fired. Mrs Barney herself telephoned for a doctor, who found Stephen dead in the flat with a revolver beside him, surrounded by bottles and glasses of gin. The defence was that she had been threatening to commit suicide, Stephen had tried to get the gun, and in the struggle it had gone off. The words heard by a witness, "I will shoot you" *could* have been "I will shoot"—meaning herself. The trial was notable for the skill of Sir Patrick Hastings in putting forward this defence, and in particular his handling of that formidable pair of experts, Spilsbury and Churchill. Despite such additional hurdles as an earlier shooting incident in which Mrs Barney was involved, he secured an acquittal. It was an achievement that might have cost him his life. Shortly after the trial he was motoring in France when a car drove furiously round a corner on a steep hill, on the wrong side of the road, missing him by inches. The driver, as Sir Patrick's chauffeur exclaimed in high indignation, was Mrs Barney.

William Mews, a private cul-de-sac, is now largely rebuilt with neat little houses and garages, and a small block of flats. One or two of the older buildings remain, however, and much of the atmosphere is preserved.

For three of its sides the nearby Lowndes Square also retains much of its earlier air of gracious dignity, though sadly threatened by a circular monstrosity which is being erected, with no thought of fitness or harmony, on its fourth. In 1922, while it was still unspoilt, the quiet square was the setting for a peculiarly bizarre and horrible murder. Ernest Albert Walker was a footman in the service of a Colonel Trotter, an inhabitant of the square who was away at the time. Late on a day in April a police constable in Tonbridge was approached by a young man who announced that he had killed someone in London earlier in the evening. When the police broke into the Lowndes Square address given to them they found Raymond Davis, a district messenger boy from Sloane Street, lying dead in a gas-filled room. He had been hit on the head by an iron bar which was wrapped in an umbrella cover, and a length of rope with a noose at one end was by his body. There was also a letter from Walker to the butler describing how he had first tried to commit suicide with one of the guns in Colonel Trotter's possession but lost his nerve. He had then sent for the messenger boy and deliberately tortured and killed him. Walker had never met Davis, and did not even know his name. Later the police discovered a list, written on a sheet of black-edged notepaper, giving himself detailed numbered points to be followed in the course of the torture and eventual murder—a course he had followed almost exactly: "(1) Ring up Sloane Street messenger office for boy, (2) Wait at front door, (3) Invite him in, (4) Bring him downstairs, (5) Ask him to sit down, (6) Hit him on the head, (7) Put him in the safe, (8) Keep him tied up, (9) At 10.30 torture, (10) Prepare for end, (11) Sit down, turn gas on, (12) Put gas light out, (13) Sit down, shut window." At the trial it was revealed that Walker's family had a history of hereditary insanity, and that he himself from an early age had suffered from fits. His mother had died three months before the murder, and in his letter to the butler he wrote that he could not live without her. The obvious verdict of guilty but insane was returned and Walker was sent to Broadmoor. He was 17.

At the Sloane Street junction with Knightsbridge, Brompton Road branches off to the south-west. About half a dozen turnings along on the left is Beaufort Gardens. Our concern is with No 5. On 30th November 1946 John Mudie, a 35-year-old barman at the Reigate Hill Hotel, Reigate, was found dead in a chalk pit at Woldingham. He had been strangled: a cord was tied loosely round his neck, on which there was a deep mark. He was identified by a card in his pocket. A pickaxe and a piece of polishing rag nearby were traced to 5 Beaufort Gardens. These discoveries were the beginning of one of the oddest and most complicated cases of the period.

In 1922 the Minister of Justice for New South Wales was Thomas Ley, then about 40 years of age, an active if not wholly reputable figure in Australian public life. He seems to have been an efficient but unlikeable man, and charges of share-pushing and bribery—together with suspicions of even more dubious operations—put an end to his public career. In 1929 he came to England, followed shortly afterwards by Mrs Brook, widow of an Australian J.P. (he had died from bee-stings), who had for some years been Ley's mistress. With her came her daughter, who later married a man named Barron and rented a flat at 3 Homefield Road, Wimbledon. During part of the war years Ley and Mrs Brook lived at 16 Knightsbridge Court, Sloane Street. When the tenancy expired she took a room in West Cromwell Road while he went to his club. A little later, while Mrs Barron was away in hospital, Ley suggested that Mrs Brook should stay in the Wimbledon flat and look after Mr Barron. In June 1946, a year after this arrangement, he suddenly rang her up in the middle of the night and accused her (a woman nearer 70 than 60) of having sexual relations with her son-in-law. This outburst seems to have been the first occasion on which the madness that undoubtedly lay beneath his bland exterior showed itself on the surface. Ley, at this time an enormously obese and physically unprepossessing man, had always been of an intensely possessive nature, though physical intimacy between him and Mrs Brook had ceased long before the present explosion. Ley then questioned Mrs Evans, landlady of 3 Homefield Road, about the men lodging there, among whom was John Mudie, working as barman at the 'Dog and Fox', High Street, Wimbledon. For absolutely no reason whatsoever (Mudie had only spoken to Mrs Brook once, when he passed her on the stairs) Ley fixed on this harmless young man as the one who was carrying on with his ex-mistress. At two-thirty in the morning of 19th June he drove to Wimbledon in a hired car and removed the bewildered and distressed Mrs Brook to West Cromwell Road. He then worked out a tortuous and pointless plot to test his suspicions, sending Mudie some cheques which required Mrs Brook's endorsement and asking him to obtain this from her. Mudie, as bewildered as she had been, returned the cheques through Mr Barron senior, father of Mrs Brook's son-in-law, who took them to the offices of Connaught Properties, a firm of which Ley and Mrs Brook were co-directors, wisely insisting on a receipt. Ley had meanwhile instructed his solicitors to demand the return of the cheques from Mudie. He found that the latter had now gone to a new job in Reigate and went down there to see him—the only time, apparently, the two men ever met before the murder. Ley insisted on Mudie accompanying him to Mr Barron to have his story verified, and then apologized—as well he might. This fantastic series of events, deriving from a 65-year-old man's suspicions that his 65-year-old ex-mistress was having an affair with a 35-year-old barman to whom she had scarcely spoken, would be almost comic were it not for its appalling consequences.

While all this was going on, Ley had been getting together an incongruous group of people to encompass Mudie's death. He was now living in Beaufort Gardens, a wide, dignified cul-de-sac of large five-storey houses, with a row of full-grown trees down its centre, where he was converting No 5 into flats. At the Royal Hotel, Woburn Place, he contacted, through the hall porter, a car-hirer named John Buckingham, and arranged a meeting with him and another man, John Smith, a joiner who was working on the Beaufort Gardens conversion. There he spun another fantastic web of fantasy, saying that Mudie was a blackmailer whom he was anxious to lure to London and compel to sign a paper promising not to molest Mrs Brook any further. Buckingham had a friend named Mrs Bruce, and she was brought in to make friends with Mudie in Reigate and ask him to come to Beaufort Gardens one evening and act as barman at a party she was giving. Buckingham's son was recruited to pick Mudie up on the date in question and drive him and Mrs Bruce to Beaufort Gardens while Ley, Smith and Buckingham senior waited in the house. There was no shortage of money to finance these elaborate plans, unfortunately, and all went as arranged. When Mudie arrived at No 5, Mrs Bruce opened the door of the house, then made some excuse to rejoin young Buckingham. She closed the door behind Mudie, and the two of them went for a drink to the 'Crown and Sceptre', 132 Brompton Road, a pub just across the way. Buckingham senior joined them only a few moments later, and Mudie was now shut inside the house with Ley and Smith. The date was 28th November. Two days later his body was found in the Woldingham chalk pit.

At the trial Buckingham, who turned King's evidence, said that he and Smith had thrown a blanket over Mudie's head and tied him up, and he had then been given £200 and told to leave the house and keep out of Ley's way. Thirty pounds of this sum was to be passed on to Mrs Bruce, who seems to have been completely ignorant of the true purpose behind the plan. Not the least fantastic part of this whole fantastic case was the evidence given for the defence by a man named Robert Cruikshank. He said that on the night of 28th November he had called at 5 Beaufort Gardens to see if he could persuade Ley (whom he had never met) to give him some money so that he could go to Australia. He could get no reply at the front door, so tried the basement and found it open. Thinking there might be something of value around to which he could help himself, he went in—and saw someone tied to a chair. He had only a momentary glimpse of this alarming sight by his lighter, which then went out and wouldn't come on again. He pulled on the rope securing the man to see if he could free him, then his nerve snapped and he ran out of the house, and made his way to Sloane Square. In pulling on the rope, he hinted, he might have caused Mudie's death. Cruikshank was an ex-convict with a bad record, and his story helped the defence not at all. The judge, Lord Chief Justice Goddard, suggested in no uncertain terms that it might have been inspired by less than altruistic motives. "It is not uncommon, you know, that people of bad character come and tell these various stories," he said in his summing-up. . . . "If an ex-convict of that description sees a man in trouble, who, according to the evidence, has been willing to give £300 to one, £200 to another, might he not have thought that if he, finding that man in trouble, comes forward and tells some story that might help him afterwards, he might also be a recipient of this man's bounty?"

Ley and Smith were sentenced to death, but Ley's insanity was clear and he went to Broadmoor, where he died a month later; Smith, as a lesser light, escaped execution himself for this reason, receiving penal servitude for life. The luckiest person in the whole affair was probably young Mr Barron. Around the time that Ley was suspicious of him he received an invitation supposedly from Mrs Brook asking him to tea with her at Beaufort Gardens. Sensing something a little odd, he consulted his father, who advised him not to go near the place. It came out that Mrs Brook had never made any such arrangement; she was, in fact, living in West Cromwell Road. One can only surmise what might have been awaiting Mr Barron at No 5 Beaufort Gardens.

The Imperial Institute, built on the site of the exhibition grounds south of the Royal Albert Hall, was opened by Queen Victoria in 1893. In 1909, occupied by London University, it was the scene of an Indian political murder similar to that at Caxton Hall thirty years or so later. Sir Curzon Wyllie, who for many years had worked in India and was noted for his interest in the welfare of Indian students, was honorary treasurer of an organization formed to help and advise them, known as the National Indian Association. On 1st July he attended a concert given in aid of the association and was about to leave when he was shot four times at point-blank range by Madar Lal Dhingra, a 25-year-old student at University College. On trial, the murderer declared that his act was inspired by patriotic fervour, because the British had no right to pollute the sacred soil of India.

Turning down Exhibition Road and crossing Cromwell Road —named after one of Oliver's sons who lived there—we reach, via Thurloe Street, South Kensington Underground station, and its telephone kiosks. At the beginning of July 1959 the flat of Mrs Verne Schieffman, Roland House, Roland Gardens, South Kensington, was broken into while she was away, the intruder taking her passport in addition to a number of valuables. A day or two later she received a letter demanding $500 in return for certain alleged incriminating photos and documents which the writer said he had collected about her. Knowing she had done nothing whatever to lay herself open to blackmail she got in touch with the police. As a result, when a stranger rang her up on 12th July and demanded to know whether she was prepared to pay up she pretended to agree to do so and, in accordance with a prepared plan, arranged for further calls to be traced. One came the following morning, instructing her to withdraw the money from the bank and await further calls. When the third call came that same afternoon she kept the man talking while, through the help of a neighbour, Chelsea police traced its origin. Two detective sergeants drove to a telephone kiosk at South Kensington station and took hold of its occupant. He broke away as they led him to a car, and ran to nearby Onslow Square. The police followed in a taxi and saw him run into the entrance hall of No 105, a block of flats. Here he was found hiding behind a pillar, arrested, and made to sit on a window-sill while one of the men, detective-sergeant Sandford, rang for the porter. While the other officer's attention was momentarily distracted, the man whipped out a gun and shot him. He then escaped into the square. The murdered policeman died within minutes. The detectives had in their possession a black notebook which the man had had in his hand while telephoning, fingerprints on the window-sill, and of course an excellent description. After a remarkably short period—as a result of reports from the general public, from the underworld around Soho, from an air-terminal hotel, and finally from Interpol, the killer was identified. His name was Gunther Podola, a 30-year-old German who had crossed to Canada in 1952, been deported back in 1958 after imprisonment for housebreaking, and arrived in England a couple of months before the murder. Podola's photograph was broadcast in the newspapers, and on the same day it was reported that a man resembling him was living—or rather hiding, for he had not been out since his arrival—in room 15 of the Claremont House Hotel, 95 Queen's Gate, only a couple of minutes' walk from Onslow Square. He had taken the room under the name of Paul Camay. Police went to the door of the room and, when their demand to open up resulted in silence followed by a dangerous-sounding click like the cocking of a gun, broke in and secured Podola after a struggle. He proved, in fact, to have no gun on him and the sound was that of the door being unlocked.

Podola, who had received a severe gash over the left eye, was taken to St Stephen's Hospital, Fulham, for treatment, and later appeared on trial at the Old Bailey. There was, of course, no question as to whether he had fired the shot, the crucial point at issue was his state of mind and his fitness to plead. His defence, Frederick Lawton, Q.C., submitted that he was suffering from amnesia, remembering nothing before 17th July, the day after his arrest. The prosecution countered this with the assertion that the loss of memory was feigned. After hearing doctors, psychiatrists and neurologists on either side the jury decided that the amnesia was not genuine. Podola, now pleading not guilty to a charge of murder, staged a remarkable recovery of memory in order to attempt an alibi. He was, however, convicted after two days.

Shortly after Podola's arrest sensational charges were made against the police, accusing them of brutality in their treatment of the accused. These were firmly denied: not only were the medical witnesses for the defence satisfied that he had suffered no physical ill-treatment once he was secured, but his own counsel stated specifically that "there is no evidence of any kind that any violence was done to Podola at Chelsea Police Station. Indeed, such evidence as exists points the other way."

The murderer's brief odyssey is easily traced from South Kensington station to one of the two internal pillars in the hall of 105 Onslow Square and thence the few hundred yards to Claremont House Hotel, now undergoing reconstruction. For the microscopically curious, the telephone kiosk down the steps in the underground station still, at the moment of writing, bears the number it did when he used it—2355.

Onslow Square, incidentally, was not always as quiet and dignified as it is now—it marks the site of a lunatic asylum and its grounds, and years later was the centre of indignant protests against the noise caused by the early motor-omnibuses.

Because of the sensational circumstances of the case the name of Podola is widely remembered to this day: not so widely remembered is the name of the man he murdered—Detective-Sergeant Raymond Purdy.

Among the residents of the eminently respectable Onslow Court Hotel, Queen's Gate (almost apposite Claremont House) was numbered, in the closing year of the Second World War, a man of about 35, pleasantly mannered and well liked by his eminently respectable fellow guests—many of them elderly ladies in comfortable circumstances. His name was John George Haigh. He had recently, it was understood, set up in business on his own—something to do with engineering—with a room in London at 38 Queen's Gate Terrace, an office address in Eccleston Square, Victoria, and a basement at 79 Gloucester Road. At the latter address he stored several petrol drums and carboys of acid. He appeared to be prospering, in his quiet modest way; the eminently respectable residents were in happy ignorance of the fact that before his arrival in their midst he had spent much of his time in prison for theft and fraud of various kinds, that his claims to be a university graduate with a degree of B.Sc. were false, that in fact he was an habitual and potentially dangerous criminal. Murder, it could be said, was on his doorstep.

Haigh's first known victim was a former employer, a young man named Donald McSwan who was living with his parents in Claverton Street (of Adelaide Bartlett memory). McSwan owned various properties, and at the time was wondering how he could 'disappear' to avoid being called-up for military service. Haigh took advantage of this fortunate combination of circumstances, invited McSwan to the basement in Gloucester Road, killed him by hitting him on the head with a cosh, and then in truth caused him to disappear by dissolving his body in sulphuric acid—pouring the result down the drain. He then forged letters (at which he was brilliant) to McSwan's parents to make it appear their son was in Scotland. In July 1945 he persuaded the old couple to come to the basement, probably for a supposed meeting with their son, and murdered them also, disposing of their bodies by the same means. At his leisure he thereafter set about a complicated process of forgery in order to obtain possession of the McSwan properties and securities. The proceeds seem to have lasted him until about the autumn of 1947.

At this time he became acquainted with Dr Archibald Henderson and his wife who were advertising the sale of their house, No 22 Ladbroke Square. They became friendly first at Ladbroke Square and later, when this house was sold, at 16 Dawes Road, Fulham, where they took a flat above a dolls shop. On 12th February 1948 Haigh made up some story which caused Dr Henderson to accompany him to his Crawley 'factory'—and there carried out the same procedure as in Gloucester Road. The following day he brought Mrs Henderson down on the pretext that her husband was ill, and she suffered the same fate. By cunning lies and further expert forgery he contrived to quieten all suspicions as to their disappearance—and also to take over their estate. In a long letter supposed to be from Mrs Henderson to her brother he concocted a story that she and the doctor were leaving for South Africa to start a new life. It was estimated that he received some £7,000 from the result of his labours in this connection.

Meanwhile he had become friendly with one of the ladies at the 'Onslow Court', Mrs Olivia Durand-Deacon, a widow. Over lunch at the hotel in February 1949 she happened to show him a box of artificial finger-nails, and wondered whether he would be interested in a scheme for manufacturing and marketing them. Haigh was certainly interested in something about Mrs Durand-Deacon, and a few days later he drove her to Crawley to look over his factory. There he shot her, and disposed of her body by the method he was now using with almost unimaginative regularity. A day or two later he was showing kindly anxiety over Mrs Durand-Deacon's absence from the hotel. In this, however, he had been forestalled. A friend of hers of some strength of character, Mrs Constance Lane, had become anxious already and, what was more, determined to do something about it. With Mrs Lane firmly accompanying him, Haigh went to Chelsea Police Station to report the lady's disappearance. During this brief period he was selling various pieces of Mrs Durand-Deacon's jewellery to pay pressing debts, for it had not taken him long to get through the proceeds raised from Dr and Mrs Henderson.

It was the beginning of his end. Despite a smooth story of Mrs Durand-Deacon failing to keep an appointment at the Army and Navy Stores the day after the Crawley arrangement suspicions began to sprout, and then to grow. Eventually the police went to have a look at the Crawley workshop. Despite all Haigh's efforts at dissolution, a few remnants of Mrs Durand-Deacon were found—a grim mixture, indeed, including some plastic dentures, three gallstones, a lipstick container cap, small pieces of human bone, a red plastic handle from a handbag, and—most conclusive of all—a partially-eroded but recognizable left foot.

Charged with her murder, Haigh confessed to everything, including the earlier killings, and made a desperate attempt to be labelled insane. He told lurid stories of drinking the blood of his victims and put on some notable performances in prison. The jury, however, returned a verdict of guilty, requiring a mere fifteen minutes to do so, and Haigh was executed at Wandsworth on 10th August 1949.

The Onslow Court Hotel had one more, totally unexpected, link with John George Haigh. The judge at his trial was Sir Travers Humphreys. When his wife died in 1953, Sir Travers gave up his house in Ealing and moved into a quiet, comfortable hotel—the 'Onslow Court'. It was a pure coincidence, he had long forgotten its association with one of his most famous cases. No 79 Gloucester Road is almost exactly opposite the Tube station—standing out among the shops as the only building with a basement. It now houses St Anthony's School of English —recognized by the Ministry of Education—but it may be that late at night, or during a power cut, a shadowy figure may be imagined moving silently among the carboys of acid, intent on its gruesome work.

Gloucester Road Tube station itself was the scene of a still unsolved murder on 24th May 1957. An elderly Polish countess, Teresa Lubienska, was returning by Underground from a party at the house of a compatriot in Florence Road, Ealing, to her own home in Cornwall Gardens, Kensington, at about 10.20 p.m. She was travelling alone, though there were several other passengers in the same coach. At Gloucester Road station she alighted, and a minute or two later staggered into the lift moaning, "Bandits, bandits!" She was the only occupant of the lift except for the attendant and for a moment he had no suspicion that anything was wrong—until he noticed that blood was oozing from her clothes. When the lift reached the street she was rushed to St Mary's Hospital. On the way she murmured that someone stabbed her as she was walking along the platform, but she was unable to give further information and died before the hospital was reached. It was found that she had indeed been stabbed several times. Countess Lubienska was known to have been closely involved with the Polish Resistance movement during the war; the Germans trapped her and she was sent to Auschwitz and Ravensbrück. At the time of her death she was still active on behalf of Polish ex-political prisoners, and one theory was that she may have been killed from political motives. Detective Assistant Commissioner Du Rose, however, after four years of investigation inclined to the less colourful view that the Countess, a stickler for civilized behaviour, may have reprimanded some 'Teddy boys' who were creating a disturbance, whereupon one of them attacked her with a penknife. It appeared that she was in the habit of using the word "bandits" to describe any exhibition of bad manners. Du Rose also described attempts to solve the problem of how a killer could escape unseen in a Tube station, reconstructing the crime with the help of two colleagues. They proved that a man could have stabbed the Countess by the lift, then raced up the emergency stairs, beating its arrival by thirteen seconds in which to vanish along Gloucester Road.

The original Earls Court Village was bounded by the present Cromwell Road–Earls Court Road–Hogarth Road triangle. Continuing to the end of Earls Court Road, and turning right along the Old Brompton Road brings us, on our left, to Finborough Road. This lengthy but in no way unusual thoroughfare, which still retains many of its Victorian stucco buildings, features in three of the cases discussed here. In 1907, as we have seen, Ruby Young lodged in it during the trial of Robert Wood. Two later murders, in 1922 and 1948, occurred almost next door to each

other, at No 13a and No 17, at the Fulham Road end close
to the corner with Redcliffe Place.

Ronald True, born in 1891, was mentally unstable from an
early age. He led an incredible life of fraud, robbery, impersona-
tion, drug addiction and fantasy until his arrest in 1922 for the
murder of prostitute Olive Young. His mother was 16 when he
was born, his father only a year older. Eleven years later the
former married a wealthy man, so that young Ronald was
brought up with every material advantage. Despite this, he
proved erratic and unmanageable, a compulsive liar and possessed of an ominous streak of cruelty. At the age of 18 he was
sent abroad to try his hand at various jobs in New Zealand, the
Argentine, Canada and Mexico, but every attempt to help him
settle to some form of work was a failure. During the First
World War he joined the R.F.C. and suffered two bad crashes
while in training. This greatly increased his mental instability
and generally unpredictable behaviour. Nevertheless he must
have had a remarkably persuasive manner, for his boastful and
completely false stories of heroic war exploits were widely believed. Around 1917 he married an actress, Frances Roberts,
and shortly afterwards went to America to work in a flying
school, leaving his wife in England. This project failed like all
the others, and he arrived back in England without any money
and hopelessly addicted to morphia. His wife by this time was
expecting a baby. He failed again in another job on the Gold
Coast, and once more sought the support of his long-suffering
family. By now, however, they had had enough—they gave him
an allowance, and let him go his way. Attempts to cure his
drug addiction proved useless. He began to have hallucinations,
to talk of another Ronald True who exactly resembled him and
was determined to harm him—a sort of real-life Jekyll and
Hyde. All this while he was living it up in London, astonishingly
successful in passing dud cheques, avoiding paying hotel bills,
and carrying off other petty frauds. He patronized exclusive
dance clubs such as Murray's, and often slept—when not in
high-class hotels—at the Savoy Turkish Baths, representing
himself as Major True and getting away with a minimum of
payment.

Some time in 1922 he met Gertrude Yates, once a shopgirl and
now a prostitute calling herself Olive Young, who lived at 13a
Finborough Road, a basement flat. She must have done fairly

well at her trade for she had money in the savings bank and employed a daily woman to come and clean the flat and cook for her. Though at first she tried to avoid True (he had stolen £5 from her handbag on his first visit to the flat), he seemed to have overcome her reluctance. On Sunday 5th March she admitted him to spend the night there. Early on the Monday morning he made her a cup of tea, and while she drinking it, killed her with blows on the head from a rolling-pin. He then drank his own tea, carried the body into the bathroom, dressed himself and gathered up any money and jewellery he could find. For some strange reason, though he had plenty of time to do all this and leave the place, he was still in the flat when the daily woman, Mrs Emily Steel, arrived at nine o'clock. Mrs Steel knew him, and they cheerfully passed the time of day, True suggesting that her mistress should not be disturbed as she was sound asleep. He then left the flat—with discovery of his crime inevitable within minutes.

During the hours that followed he pawned Olive Young's jewellery (redeeming at the same time his own watch and cigarette-case), spent her money on some new clothes for himself, and cancelled an arrangement he had made for a hired car to pick him up in Finborough Road at 11 a.m. He met a friend, James Armstrong, and went with him in another car to Feltham, where they examined some internal combustion engines in which they were interested. They then had tea in Croydon and returned to London for dinner, after which they went to the Hammersmith Palace of Varieties for the evening show. Meanwhile Olive Young's body had been discovered almost immediately by Mrs Steel, and the police summoned. They tracked their quarry without trouble, and True was quietly apprehended as he sat in a box at the theatre. He was found guilty and sentenced to death. An appeal was dismissed. The Home Secretary, however, ordered a further medical examination, and as a result he was committed to Broadmoor.

A macabre meeting occurred between True and Henry Jacoby (see page 72) while they were both in Brixton prison hospital for observation. In some way True managed to gain admittance to Jacoby's ward and loudly welcomed him into the "murderers' club"—for which, he declared, only those who killed outright were eligible. True died in 1951.

Two doors along Finborough Road, at No 17, on 6th May

1948, Winifred Virginia Mulholland was found lying head downwards across the area steps. Her shoes were missing, and she had been battered to death by two heavy instruments of different shapes. Her body had then been thrown down to make the killing appear an accident. Cyril Epton, a 41-year-old engineer, who had recently lost his wife, lived in a flat above, in which were found a blood-stained hammer and flat-iron, both of which could have caused the injuries, and both of which bore his fingerprints. Epton was sentenced to death, but the execution was not carried out as his crime took place shortly after the question of the suspension of the death penalty had been discussed in Parliament.

Finally, before crossing the river, we move briefly to Chelsea and the year 1771, when it was a fairly large village about three miles from London, separated from the city by open spaces to the east of Sloane Street known as the Five Fields. At about ten o'clock on a Saturday evening in that year, as the Sabbath ended, a group of Jewish youths gathered in the Fields and some of them, led by Levi Weil, Asher Weil, Jacob Lazarus and Solomon Porter, proceeded along the King's Road (so named after Charles II who used this route to Hampton Court), bent on mischief. They forced their way into the farmhouse of a Mrs Hutchings. She was a muscular countrywoman and fought them energetically, but eventually they overpowered her, secured her by tying her petticoats over her head, roped her two maid-servants together back to back, and proceeded to ransack the place. In doing so, they entered a room where two farmhands, John Slow and William Stone, were sleeping soundly after a healthy day's work. The men woke up (somewhat tardily, one might think), and in the ensuing fight John Slow was killed. For several months the gang escaped arrest, until a German Jew named Isaacs gave them away in order to obtain the ransom money. The four murderers were anathematized by the Synagogue and executed at Tyburn on 9th December of the same year.

9

A SHOT THROUGH EACH EYE
South-West, South of the River: Battersea, Wandsworth, Brixton, Balham, Wimbledon

Crossing the river by Battersea Bridge we arrive at the site of a curious unsolved mystery that occurred in 1910. On the north side of Prince of Wales Drive (formerly Prince of Wales Road), at the corner of Rosenau Road, is a small row of houses called Clifton Gardens. For ten years up to 1910 the first floor of No 17, which was let off in flats, had been occupied by Mr Thomas Weldon Anderson and his mistress. He was an actor whose stage name was Atherstone. She worked as 'teacher of expression' at the Academy of Dramatic Art. Though separated from his wife, he was devoted to their two sons, and there appeared to be no family ill-feeling. Towards the end of May he had had a quarrel with the lady with whom he was living and he was at present staying away from home. On the evening of 16th June his 17-year-old son was having dinner at Clifton Gardens with Anderson's mistress, whom he looked on as his mother. During the evening they heard a sound like two shots being fired. Looking out of a back window, they saw a figure climbing over the wall of an adjoining house.

Some time later Anderson's dead body was discovered outside the door of the ground-floor flat, which was empty. He had been shot twice at close quarters after what had evidently been a violent struggle. He was wearing carpet slippers, and his outdoor shoes were found on the mantelpiece in one of the empty rooms. In his pocket was a strip of insulating cable about eighteen inches long, wrapped in brown paper. No explanation was forthcoming of his presence in the unoccupied flat, nor of the purpose of the cable, let alone the peculiar disposition of his footwear.

Turning down Latchmere Road we come to Lavender Hill, already mentioned in connection with Steinie Morrison. A little further along is a house associated with a railway murder popularly known as the Merstham Tunnel mystery. In 1905 young Mary Sophia Money, an early example of a career girl, lived on her own at No 245, working in a dairy. At about seven o'clock on the evening of 24th September she mentioned to an acquaintance in a sweetshop that she was going to Victoria Station; earlier in the day she had told somebody else she was just going for a walk. That night she was found lying on the railway line in Merstham Tunnel, just before Redhill. Her body was severely mangled, and the obvious explanation was that she had either fallen or been pushed from a moving train. A railway guard reported having seen a girl whose appearance matched Miss Money's on a train with a man at East Croydon at about 9.30 p.m., and a signalman saw a man and a woman struggling together in a compartment as the train passed Purley Oaks, a couple of stations beyond. Miss Money was not known to have any men friends at all, and no-one could explain how she might have been persuaded to go to Victoria and then on to a Brighton train. Some suspicion fell on her brother—a dairyman who two years later was to shoot his two mistresses, his three children and finally himself—but nothing conclusive ever came to light.

Clapham Common, which also had important connections with Steinie Morrison, was the scene of a particularly vicious crime involving a gang of Teddy boys in 1953. John Beckley, a 17-year-old engineering apprentice, and his friend Matthew Chandler, a bank clerk, had been listening to the band playing in the central stand, and after the programme finished had been unwise enough to make some joking remark about the group of youths loitering near. The gang instantly fell on the pair, beating and kicking them. Someone shouted, "Get the knives out!" Beckley and Chandler ran to the road and jumped on a bus, only to be dragged off as it slowed down at a request stop. Both were slashed and stabbed. Chandler, badly wounded, managed to scramble back on the bus, but Beckley fell dying on the pavement. Six members of the gang were arrested—

four were found guilty of assault. The other two, 16-year-old Ronald Coleman and 20-year-old John Michael Davies, were tried for murder. The jury were unable to agree, and charges against Coleman were dropped. Davies, a labourer who lived at Turret Grove, Clapham, was eventually found guilty and sentenced to death. Appeals to both the Courts and to the House of Lords were dismissed, but Davies was ultimately reprieved and his sentence commuted to penal servitude for life. A feature of the case noted in the press was the reluctance of other passengers on the bus to give evidence. A secretary, Miss Mary Frayling, was almost alone in coming forward to help the police bring the murderer to justice.

Bay Tree Road, Brixton, is a small curving thoroughfare that links Acre Lane to Brixton Hill. On 9th May 1923 a number of people in the road saw a cab-driver struggling with a man. Shots were fired, the driver fell to the ground, the man disappeared. On the spot was found an unusual ebony walking-stick—it had a gold knob in which was inserted a gold pencil case. The dead man was identified as Jacob Dickey—he had no known criminal associates. The stick was traced to James, or Eddie, Vivian, a known crook, who was living at the time with a prostitute in Charlwood Street, Pimlico. Vivian, however, said that the stick had been in the possession of a friend of his, Alexander Mason, another man with a criminal record. Mason was charged with murder, and himself accused Vivian of having fired the fatal shot. Mason's story was that Vivian shot Dickey. He himself was frightened and ran, escaping across the back garden of 23 Acre Lane, climbing the walls to No 15 and then terrorizing a woman into allowing him to pass through. Certain evidence on the walls pointed to the possible truth of this. The motive for the crime, whoever was responsible, was presumably robbery, though this never became clear. Mason was convicted and sentenced to death, but later reprieved.

We now continue down Brixton Hill, Streatham Hill and Streatham High Road, turning left along Kingscourt Road to Bedford Hill. To our right after we have crossed Tooting Common stood 'The Priory'. 'Stands' is, I suppose, the correct word, for it is still there—decrepit, dilapidated, cracking, left in half repair, shorn of its grounds and its famous tree, hidden behind other houses—no longer even a shadow of the attractive example of Victorian pseudo-Gothic it once was. As I write, it is on the

list of protected buildings, but even its very existence is in
doubt for the future. One can only hope that the destroyers will
not once more have their way, and that, rather than face final
demolition and vanish for ever, this delightful little house will
have something of its former personality and appearance restored
to it. Few famous murder cases are more closely associated with
their setting than the Balham Mystery, or the Death of Charles
Bravo. So many accounts have already been written, so many
solutions suggested, that we shall, as in similar cases, deal with
it fairly briefly here.

Florence Campbell was the eldest daughter of a country
gentleman residing at Buscot Park, Berkshire, with a town house
at 37 Lowndes Square. In 1864 she married a Captain Ricardo
and could expect to look forward to a brilliant and happy social
life. Ricardo had a country home at Hockham Hall, Norfolk,
and a town one at 24 Chester Square, London. Ricardo, however,
was a drunkard, and gradually the brightness faded from the
marital skies. On Florence's mother's advice he went for treatment to a Dr Gully, who by reputation combined physic and
hypnotism to miraculous effect. He failed with Ricardo—but
Florence was certainly impressed.

Things went from bad to worse with the young couple, until
in 1871 Ricardo died in *delirium tremens*, leaving Florence some
£40,000. Her friendship with Dr Gully had meanwhile grown
to an intimacy so close as to cause considerable scandal and
family concern. Shortly after her widowhood she took a detached
house in Leigham Court Road, Streatham. After a joint trip to
Italy, Dr Gully took one opposite. Florence then engaged Mrs
Jane Cannon Cox, a 43-year-old Anglo-Indian widow, as her
companion. Mrs Cox, a plain woman viewing the world through
formidable spectacles, soon became an intimate member of the
circle, or triangle. About 1873 Florence moved again, into the
roomier and delightful 'Priory'. Along came Dr Gully into a
house half-way along the same road, which he named Orwell
Lodge after his Malvern home. They met as frequently as ever,
though their relationship may have become less close.

In December 1874 Mrs Cox went to call on friends, Mr and
Mrs Joseph Bravo, who lived at 2 Palace Green, close behind
Kensington Palace. Florence went to collect her, and there met
Charles Bravo for the first time. Very slightly younger than
Florence, he had been born at 39 Upper Charlotte Street (now

Charlotte Street) near Tottenham Court Road, and was now a barrister with chambers at 1 Essex Court, Temple. In character he appeared to be a strange mixture of extreme high spirits and deep gloom, of pomposity and unassuming friendliness, of conceit and disarming modesty. When he was seen to be paying attentions to the attractive Mrs Ricardo, he was, inevitably, accused of chasing her for her fortune. Nevertheless, their friendship ripened, each confessing former peccadilloes to the other, and Florence promising to discard Dr Gully. On 7th December 1875 they were married; on 21st April 1876 Charles was dead, poisoned by antimony.

On the afternoon of 18th April he had returned to the Balham countryside from his chambers and gone out to exercise his horse—returning in a somewhat distressed state saying that the animal had bolted with him. However, he ate a hearty dinner in the company of Florence and Mrs Cox, and drank his customary number of glasses of burgundy. (They all seem to have been fairly heavy drinkers and Florence eventually succombed to alcoholism less than three years after the tragedy.) At this time Florence had recently been unwell and Charles was sleeping in a separate room. The two women retired early—and at about ten o'clock Charles was heard crying for help. Throughout his three-day-long agony he never uttered either explanation or accusation, though both have been proffered freely ever since. There were two inquests. The first, held at the 'Priory', was a brief, discreet affair resulting in an open verdict, with a hint from the coroner that it may have been *felo de se*. The point was made during it that the only form in which the antimony could have been administered was tartar emetic.

The second inquest was held as a result of a rising tide—a tidal wave, in fact—of rumours and suspicions. A fierce and probing light was shone on Florence's former relations with Dr Gully, Mrs Cox was reported as having been in danger of dismissal by Bravo and thus losing her livelihood—all three, it seemed, would have liked Charles out of the way. The most mysterious figure undoubtedly was Mrs Cox. At both inquests she said Charles had told her he had taken poison—on the second occasion she added the words "for Dr Gully". This second inquest resulted in a finding "that Mr Charles Delaunay Turner Bravo did not commit suicide; that he did not meet his death by misadventure; that he was wilfully murdered by the

administration of tartar emetic; but there is not sufficient
evidence to fix the guilt upon any person or persons"—hardly
a happy outcome for anyone concerned. The truth is never likely
to be known now, but the fascination of conjecture will continue for long enough. In setting, characters and events it is
the classic Victorian murder puzzle, as Wallace is the classic
murder puzzle of the 1920s.*

The shooting of P.C. Gutteridge by Browne and Kennedy in
1927 sent a wave of horror through the whole country which
is remembered to this day. Not only were armed criminals a
rarity in those times, but the cold-blooded killing of a policeman in the execution of his duty was regarded everywhere as
among the most inexcusable of outrages, and its punishment
with the utmost severity looked on as a plain obligation owed
by society to those whom it engages to protect it. Frederick Guy
Browne, 36, was a criminal with a number of minor convictions
and a later spell of four years penal servitude for dealing in
stolen cars. On his release in April 1927 he converted a shed in
Northcote Road, Clapham, into garages and started up again
transforming and re-selling stolen vehicles. He was a coarse
brute of great physical strength and vile temper, and was known
to carry a loaded gun around with him. While in prison his
outbursts of violence lost him all remission of time. In Dartmoor
he met William Kennedy, a weaker specimen of sneak thief (he
stole bicycles where Browne stole cars), who also, however, had
been found in possession of a loaded revolver. The two afterwards set up a criminal partnership in the Northcote Road
address, Kennedy living over the garage itself while Browne
moved to 33a Sisters Avenue, Lavender Hill. The garage they
christened the 'Globe'.

On 26th September 1927 the two crooks decided to add
another car to their stock. They went to Billericay, Essex, and
chanced on the bungalow of Dr Edward Lovell. When the
occupants were asleep they forced the garage door, pushed the
car into the road and drove off, avoiding the main thorough-
fares and sticking to the unfrequented country lanes. Their
way took them to Stapleford Abbots, near How Green. There

* *The Balham Mystery, or the Bravo Poisoning Case* was issued in
seven weekly penny parts in 1876. Three excellent full-length studies,
with varying solutions, are John Williams, *Suddenly at the Priory*,
Heinemann, 1957; Yseult Bridges, *How Charles Bravo Died*, Jarrolds,
1956; and Elizabeth Jenkins, *Doctor Gully*, Michael Joseph, 1972.

P.C. Gutteridge, who lived in Stapleford Abbots and was on night patrol, became suspicious of a car creeping along the lonely by-roads, and signalled the driver to stop. He was found early the next morning by a motor engineer, shot dead, with a pencil in his hand and his notebook and helmet beside him. His police whistle hung loosely from the pocket. A trail of blood led from the road to the spot where he was lying. P.C. Gutteridge had been shot through the head and, as he lay dying, the murderer had bent down and shot him again through each eye.

At 7.30 the same morning a car was found abandoned in a gravelled passageway between two houses in Foxley Road, Brixton. It was traced to Dr Lovell. Marks on a damaged fender looked like those made by the bark of a tree. There was blood on the running-board, and a cartridge case on the floor. Various tests, including mileage calculations, enabled the police to link the car with the murder, but for some months that was as far as they got. Then Browne was arrested, following a crash in Sheffield, for the theft of another car and the Globe garage searched. Besides other stolen vehicles the police found several weapons, and also cartridges of the type that killed P.C. Gutteridge. Browne was detained and a hunt began for Kennedy, who had fled to Liverpool. When arrested he pulled out a gun, pressed it against the officer's body and pressed the trigger— but he had forgotten to release the safety catch. Once secured he promptly poured out a full version of what had occurred on 26th September. He stated that when the policeman began to put the customary questions as to where they had come from, had he a licence and so on he, Kennedy, gave the correct car number. As Gutteridge was about to write it in his notebook Browne fired two shots. Gutteridge fell. They went over to where he lay on the road, groaning, his eyes open. Browne bent down and, according to Kennedy, said, "What are you looking at me like that for?" He then sent bullets into both eyes. At the trial precautions were taken against a repetition of the Milsom-Fowler attack, but Browne treated with contemptuous indifference the fellow criminal who had given him away. He was executed at Pentonville, Kennedy at Wandsworth. It was suggested later that Browne shot P.C. Gutteridge's eyes out because he thought his own image might be imprinted on the retinae and give him away. It is difficult to see how this imbecilic supposition—even if it were sincerely held—could in any way excuse the callousness of his revolting act.

The lengthy Trinity Road passes through Wandsworth Common to Tooting Bec. At No 345 is the County Arms Hotel, and nearby is a block of flats called Chesham Court. On the ground floor, at No 14, lived Miss Elizabeth Ivatt, Vice Principal of Whitelands Training College for Women Teachers, Putney, until her retirement and, in 1959, 88 years of age. She was by this time bedridden, and with her lived Miss Phyllis Squire, some twenty years younger, as her companion. To start with Miss Squire had her Tuesdays free, but it became increasingly difficult to leave Miss Ivatt for any time at all—already nurses were on duty to look after her at night. An advertisement for a "pensioner" to fill the vacant day was therefore placed in the window of a nearby newsagent, and meanwhile Miss Ivatt's nephew and his wife sat in on Tuesdays with her. On 25th August, while they were there, a man called to enquire whether a younger woman would be suitable for the post, and it was arranged that she could come for an interview the following day. Nobody turned up. On the next Saturday afternoon neighbours noticed a man walking along a passage to the street, and a little later saw smoke coming from Miss Ivatt's flat. They could not get any response so called the fire brigade, who broke open the door. Both women were found in Miss Ivatt's room, killed by savage blows on the head. Miss Squire's body, which was lying on the floor, was also badly burned. Nothing of value appeared to be missing, but a broken chair gave some indication of the violence of the attack. The police issued a description of Tuesday's caller, given to them by Miss Ivatt's nephew who had at the time noticed something strange in his manner. Enquiries led to Ronald Benson, a 35-year-old unemployed man, who was seen a couple of days later on Wandsworth Common. He was unable to account satisfactorily for his movements during the Saturday afternoon and said he could have been responsible for the killings because he was really two persons and his other self might have done it. Later he told Inspector John Du Rose that Miss Ivatt and her companion were in the bedroom and gave him a cup of tea, but when he asked them for money they refused. He then "went mad and hit the old lady". It became obvious that Benson was mentally abnormal. He had in fact been so for many years, suffering in addition from epileptic fits after being blasted from his bicycle by a bomb during the war. He had already made two attempts at suicide. At the Old Bailey he was found unfit to plead and sent to Broadmoor.

The first train murder in which the victim was a woman occurred in 1897 on the line from Hounslow to Waterloo. On 11th February Elizabeth Camp, working as a barmaid in East London and due to be married in a month's time, paid afternoon visits to her two sisters, one at Hammersmith and the other at Hounslow. She left the latter station on the 7.42 p.m. train to Waterloo to meet her fiancé. At the terminus there was no sign of her, and later that evening her body was discovered by a cleaner, half hidden under the seat in a compartment that bore signs of a violent struggle. A puzzling feature of the case was the celerity with which the murder must have been committed. The longest interval between stations was about four minutes—Vauxhall to Waterloo. The murder weapon, however —a heavy pestle, bloodstained and bearing hairs that matched those of Miss Camp—was found by the rails on the Putney side of Wandsworth Station, thus showing that the assault must have occurred before the latter was reached. The murderer was never found, nor was it discovered how, in what must have been a severely bloodstained condition, he managed to escape observation—unless he was able to jump from the train as it slowed down on approaching the station at Wandsworth.

Wimbledon is probably best known, criminally speaking, for Dr Lamson's iniquity in a private school in 1881—at least until the brutal abduction of Mrs Mackay from her home at 20 Arthur Road some ninety years later. George Henry Lamson, born in 1850, began his medical career in France at the age of 21 during the Siege of Paris, and continued it afterwards in the Balkans as an army surgeon. There he became addicted to the morphine which was to prove his downfall. He married a Miss John, who brought him a modest sum of money, and came into a further £700 from the death of his brother-in-law Herbert John. He was now back in England where he bought a practice in Bournemouth. This, however, failed—as did various other projects including an attempt to start up in America. In order to support his family and keep himself supplied with drugs it was imperative that he should find some way of obtaining money quickly. Among the inmates of Blenheim House Private School in 1881 was his wife's second brother, Percy John, an

18-year-old boy with a deformed spine, who was doomed to spend his life in a wheelchair. In three years time, when he became 21, Percy John would come into several thousand pounds, but if he died earlier half the amount would go to Mrs Lamson, and through her, of course, to the doctor.

A purchase of aconitine by Lamson was followed by Percy's severe illness while on a summer holiday in Shanklin—but he recovered. Following this episode Lamson made another trip to America, but was back again by November, staying at Nelson's Hotel, Great Portland Street. From there he wrote a letter to Percy at Blenheim House saying he would be dropping in to see him before taking a trip to France (his real intention being to receive news of the boy's death there with every sign of appropriate grief). Acting out his part as the thoughtful elder brother-in-law, he arrived at the school bearing a cake from which he personally cut a slice and handed it to his crippled relative who had been wheeled into the dining-room for tea. The headmaster also was present, but does not seem to have been offered any cake. Lamson, in sight of the headmaster, poured some sugar from the tea-table into a capsule and jokingly gave it to Percy John to swallow, remarking that he should show what a "swell pill-taker" he was—which the boy obligingly did. He bade Percy an affectionate farewell at about 7.30. Shortly afterwards Percy John was taken violently ill, and he died later the same evening.

Poison was naturally suspected, though there was at that time no means of detecting aconitine. The firm from whom Lamson had bought his supply read about the case in the newspapers, however, and got in touch with the police. On 8th December Lamson took a step which has proved a murderer's undoing in more than one instance—he went to the police of his own accord and said he wanted to straighten things out. The straightening out resulted in his own conviction. It was hinted afterwards that he may also have been responsible for the death of Herbert John, but though he confessed to the murder at Blenheim House he declared himself innocent of any others. He was hanged in 1882, at the age of 32, despite attempts to have him certified as insane. It is difficult to see how he could ever have expected to get away with his poisoned slice of cake—but perhaps to his drug-wrecked mind it appeared to be a brilliant solution of his problems. The night before the murder he spent some hours with a medical student friend. They visited the recently opened Comedy Theatre in Panton Street (to see a comic opera, *La Mascotte*), then went for a meal to Stone's Chop House, almost opposite, where Lamson tried in vain to cash a cheque—he managed to do so later at the 'Eyre Arms', St John's Wood, because the student knew the landlord. With the proceeds he bought, among other things, the cake. During the course of the evening he told the medical student he was afraid his young brother-in-law "poor Percy" would not last long—words he repeated to the headmaster on his departure. In this instance, at any rate, he spoke truth.

Blenheim House School was in St George's Road, which turns southward from Wimbledon Hill Road almost opposite the Underground station. The houses it comprised, numbers 1 and 2, still stand.

Somerset Road leads east from Wimbledon Common and winds confusingly before passing by the All England Lawn Tennis Ground to Church Road. Here, during the night of 13th July 1938, a van-driver employed by a boot repair firm in St Pancras killed a prostitute known as Irish Rose (her real name was Rose Atkins), stabbing her with a cobbler's knife, beating her on the head with a starting-handle and finally running the van wheels over her body. He then returned the van to the firm's garage, stole about £30 and fled. The body was discovered the following morning. A friend of the dead woman remembered seeing her the previous evening talking to a man in a green van, and the police were able to identify the make of tyre-marks found on the road. When two days later the firm reported that one of its drivers had disappeared with a sum of money the police checked the van he had been using. It was green, and the tyres matched. There were marks of blood on it, and in the garage was a blood-stained knife. After a hunt lasting several days the man was found hiding on the Isle of Sheppey. His name was George Brain, living—somewhat unsuitably—in Paradise Road, Richmond. He confessed to having killed her, saying she was blackmailing him. He was to have been married in a week's time.

10

CREAM COUNTRY
South-East (1): Lambeth,
Southwark, Camberwell

In the war year of 1942 Waterloo Bridge was still unfinished
and not yet open to the public. At about midnight on 19th–20th
February the night-watchman heard sounds of a quarrel between
a man and a woman coming from the centre of the bridge.
Together with a nearby shopkeeper he went to investigate, and
found a Canadian soldier, somewhat the worse for drink, standing by the parapet. They escorted him from the forbidden
territory, then went back again and picked up a woman's scarf
from the ground. It was impossible to see anything else in the
deep gloom of the blackout. Half an hour later a 47-year-old
Canadian private named Joseph McKinstry went into Waterloo
Station to try to obtain a pass for sleeping accommodation at a
Y.M.C.A. hostel. He was carrying a woman's handbag which,
he explained to an enquiring constable, belonged to a girl he
had picked up in a pub. A difference of opinion in the street
afterwards led to the girl hitting him on the head with the bag;
when he grabbed it to defend himself she let go and ran off—a
not altogether probable story. In those days of identity cards a
policeman's routine work was often simplified—the name on
the card in the bag was Peggy Richards.

In the early morning, as soon as it was light enough to see,
the shopkeeper went back onto the bridge and peered over. The
body of a woman was lying on the edge of the river below. It
was identified as that of Peggy Richards, a prostitute living in
Deptford. From the nature of various bruises and fractures it
appeared that she had been forced over the side of the bridge,
and there were also signs of an attempt to strangle her. On being

questioned McKinstry enlarged his story to some extent. He now stated that he met Peggy Richards while he was in a pub with a friend and that the bag-wielding incident had taken place later—after he had twice paid for her services rendered—on the bridge itself. McKinstry was tried for murder at the Old Bailey, but was acquitted on the grounds that there was no proof it was he himself who attacked her; it might well have been a later client who happened to come along after he had left the bridge. The case remained open.

Once over Waterloo Bridge we are plunged almost at once into what might be called Cream country. Among the more puzzling and less pleasing multi murderers Thomas Neill Cream's place is a high one. In some ways his career south of the river paralleled that of the unknown Ripper north of it, and in fact suggestions have been put forward that he himself *was* Jack the Ripper—though comparisons of the time schedules make this impossible. Considering Cream's appearance—the front part of his head bald, the back covered with sketchy brown hair through which the scalp could be seen, a thick moustache, a decided squint peering through gold-wired spectacles, limbs perpetually on the twitch, teeth ceaselessly chewing tobacco, "a very hairy man"—it seems strange that he should have had so much ease in gaining the confidence of the women he murdered. It was, perhaps, the influence of the clothes he habitually wore, which were smart and fashionable, crowned by a tall silk hat—or occasionally a flat-topped hard felt one. Men on the whole found him repulsive. His conversation endlessly centred on his exploits with women and his language about them, according to an article published after his execution, was "far from tolerable or agreeable". He carried around a number of pornographic postcards which he displayed at the slightest opportunity, and was fond of extolling the aphrodisiac qualities of the pills he took, which he said contained strychnine, morphia and cocaine. "Indeed," the article concludes, "he was exceedingly vicious, and his tastes and habits were of the most depraved order."

Cream was born at 61 Wellington Lane, Glasgow, in 1850. He emigrated with his family to Canada four years later, studied medicine at the McGill University and obtained a degree in 1876, impressing his tutors by his essay on the uses of chloroform. At this time he was already suspected of indulging in petty frauds, illegial abortions and other criminal activities, though nothing was firmly brought home to him. In 1876 he spent a short period at St Thomas's Hospital in London, and later received further honours from the Royal College of Physicians and Surgeons at Edinburgh. He then returned to Canada and later went to Chicago, where he was arrested on a charge of murder by abortion, but acquitted through lack of evidence. A poisoning charge in 1881, however, resulted in a verdict of guilty of murder in the second degree and imprisonment at Joliet "for life". This was later reduced to seventeen years and he was released, with full remission for good conduct, in 1891. In October of that year he returned to London and stayed, as Dr Neill, at Anderton's Hotel, Fleet Street. Shortly afterwards he entered the country of his future exploits by removing to 103 Lambeth Palace Road, close against St Thomas's Hospital.

On 6th October, the day after his arrival, he picked up Elizabeth Masters, a prostitute, in Ludgate Circus, stood her a drink at the 'King Lud', then went to her lodgings at 9 Orient Buildings, Hercules Road, not far from his own address. After a reasonable interval they emerged again and visited the Canterbury Music Hall which was a few minutes walk away, in Westminster Bridge Road. There they met a friend of Elizabeth's, Elizabeth May, had a drink at the bar, went across the river again to the 'King Lud', had a few more and then parted. Elizabeth Masters was perhaps fortunate in meeting Cream before he really got started, and, by surviving, she was able to furnish the programme of a typical evening's entertainment in his company. On 9th October she received a letter saying the Doctor would pay her a visit in the afternoon. Together with her friend she sat in the room in Orient Buildings, waiting. They saw him approaching down the street, but he then stopped and spoke to another member of their profession named Matilda Clover. The two Elizabeth's decided to see what he was up to. They went out and followed Cream and Clover to the corner of Hercules Road and Lambeth Road. Matilda opened the door of No 27 Lambeth Road, where she lodged, and went in. Cream followed, and that was the end of Elizabeth's appointment.

A day or so later Cream went to a chemist's in 22 Parliament Street and bought some *nux vomica* and some gelatine capsules, signing his correct name, "M.D.", and address. This was his first purchase of the scheduled poison, which was available only on the production of a suitable name and address. On the 13th occurred a murder which, though it was not brought home to Cream, seems almost certainly the first in his remarkable series. Ellen Donworth, aged 19, who lived at 8 Duke Street, off Stamford Street, collapsed suddenly in the Waterloo Road opposite the 'Wellington' public house. She was in great agony from something she had taken, but managed to gasp that a cross-eyed man in a tall silk hat had met her in the York Hotel, Waterloo Road, and given her a drink from a bottle with some "white stuff" in it. She was dead before a hospital was reached; the cause was found to be strychnine poisoning. Ellen's death caused a certain excitement, but in that dark and dismal neighbourhood it was a less than nine-day wonder.

On the 20th occurred the death for which Cream was to pay the penalty. The victim was Matilda Clover, the girl with whom he had been seen by the two Elizabeths a few days previously. She was known to have made an appointment "with a gentleman" outside the 'Canterbury' at 7 p.m., and later she brought him back to her house. It was described as "a house of ill-fame— a wretched place", the hall of which was lit by a dim oil lamp. The servant who let them in, Lucy Rose, glimpsed a tall, broad man of about 40 with a heavy moustache and a tall silk hat. The visitor left at ten o'clock. At three in the morning Matilda Clover was screaming in agony, at 8.30 she died. A doctor had been treating her for alcoholism, and he signed a certificate giving *delirium tremens* and syncope as the cause of death.

Around this time Cream picked up a woman who had an even narrower escape than Elizabeth Masters, and who was to play an important part in securing his conviction. Her name was Louisa Harvey, she said. In actual fact it was Louisa Harris, but she was living with a labourer named Harvey in Townshend Road, St John's Wood, and used his surname for the sake of 'appearances'. She gave an account of her association with Cream to a magistrate during the hearing. She met him ("a very hairy man who wore gold-rimmed glasses and had very Peculiar eyes") in the promenade of the Alhambra Music Hall, Leicester Square, and made an appointment for later in the evening outside St James's Hall, Regent Street. They spent the night together at a hotel in Berwick Street, off Oxford Street. The following night they met again at Charing Cross Underground station, had a drink at the 'Northumberland' and walked back to the Embankment. There he gave her two capsules to take, but she didn't like the look of them. So she only pretended to swallow them, and later threw them over the wall. He left her there, arranging to meet her again at the Oxford Music Hall, but he never turned up. Three weeks later, after she had moved to Stamford Street—a dreary thoroughfare running from Waterloo to Blackfriars Road and later to be the scene of a double murder by Cream—she encountered him by chance in Piccadilly Circus. Without recognizing her, he took her for a drink at the 'Regent', in Air Street. When she asked him if he did not remember who she was, and told him her name, he squinted at her in astonishment for a second, then hurried away—leaving her none the wiser but a good deal luckier than she knew.

There was now a short intermission. The deaths of Ellen Donworth and Matilda Clover were forgotten—except by the police—and Cream returned to America and Canada for six months. We may fill this interval by mentioning one of the oddest habits of this excessively odd man, who was clearly more than a little mad. He followed up each of his murders with an accusatory letter to the person least likely to have committed it. These contained either threats or suggestions for help—all with a view to his own financial bentfit. They were to become important links in the chain of evidence against him as they all contained knowledge of details revealed—at the time of writing—only to the police. The first letter, following Ellen Donworth's death, was to the coroner, offering the services of one "A. O'Brien, detective", who would bring the murderer to justice for the sum of £300,000—no pay if not successful. Later he wrote to F. W. D. Smith, M.P., a member of the well-known stationers W. H. Smith and Son, enclosing a copy of an "incriminating letter" purporting to prove his responsibility for the woman's death and suggesting that he get in touch with "a barrister, H. Bayne", who would be able to save him from the consequences. After Matilda Clover's death he wrote first to Countess Russell, accusing her husband, then to Dr William Broadbent, a well-known and highly respected medical man in Portman Square. The latter was asked to pay £2,500 to a Mr M. Malone to secure his silence on the matter. While in Quebec he ordered from a printer five hundred circulars to be handed to visitors at the Metropole Hotel, London, notifying them that the poisoner of Ellen Donworth was employed by the hotel and that their lives were in danger—"Yours respectfully, W. H. Murray". This incredible document, however, was never distributed.

At the beginning of April 1892 Cream was back in London, staying first at Edward's Hotel, Euston Square, and then in his old lodgings in Lambeth Palace Road. Early on the morning of the 12th a police constable patrolling Stamford Street noticed Emma Shrivell, an 18-year-old streetwalker, standing at the door of No 118, where she lived with her friend Alice Marsh. She was saying good-bye to a man of about 45 who sported a large moustache and a tall silk hat, and wore gold-framed glasses. Under an hour later the same constable was called back to the house to find both girls shrieking in agonizing convulsions. They were rushed to St Thomas's Hospital, one dying on the way and the other a few hours later. The cause of death was strychnine poisoning. In May Cream went to another prostitute's lodgings, in North Street, Kennington Road, and showed her some pills and a concoction he called "The American Drink". Without realizing her wisdom she showed no interest in either and he did not press the matter. This failure seems to have discouraged him and is generally held to have been his last attempt at murder.

Meanwhile the police still had little enough to go on, but Cream was by now doing his best to incriminate himself. He talked with reckless freedom to a friend of his named Haynes, an engineer who shared with Cream an interest in photography and had at one time been a private enquiry agent employed by the Government. After the deaths of the two girls in Stamford Street, Cream wrote to a Dr Joseph Harper accusing his son, a medical student also lodging at 103 Lambeth Palace Road, of responsibility for the murders, but enclosing for some unknown reason a newspaper cutting about another of his killings, that of Ellen Donworth. Through his rash confidences to Haynes (who was very soon passing everything on to the authorities), he put the police on to the track of Louisa Harvey. He even suggested himself that Matilda Clover's body should be exhumed and analysed—as it very shortly was. Inevitably the death-wish that this behaviour seeemed to indicate was granted. Cream was arrested in the first place for the blackmail of Dr Harper. Later he was charged with the murder of Matilda Clover. He was executed in Newgate on 15th November 1892.

The motives underlying the crimes of Neill Cream are surely among the least comprehensible to any normal person. There was certainly no high moral indignation against the profession of prostitution, and it can only be assumed that he derived some kind of vicarious sadistic satisfaction from inflicting agonizing deaths on women without watching the results. He never admitted his guilt, but was supposed to have muttered the words, "I am Jack the . . ." as the trap fell. If he did indeed make the remark it was probably from the same sort of gleeful, malicious exhibitionism that underlay so many of his actions.

As in the case of the Ripper, little is left of the atmosphere or settings in which the appalling Dr Cream tracked down his unfortunate victims. The Lambeth Palace Road and Lambeth Road houses are gone, so is 118 Stamford Street, though at the moment Nos 61–123 can be seen on the opposite side. Duke Street, leading off Stamford Street towards the river, is now Duchy Street; North Street, joining Hercules Road to Kennington Road, is Cosser Street. Still to be seen in Hercules Road are Orient Buildings, from which the two Elizabeth's watched Cream's first, fated meeting with Matilda Clover.

Adjacent to Cream country, joining Blackfriars Road to Southwark Bridge Road, is Union Street, centre of the culminating wickednesses of another candidate for Jack the Ripper, George Chapman. Despite the fact that much of his time was spent in Whitechapel, however, and that elaborate timetables have been drawn up to show how it was physically possible for Chapman to have committed the Ripper murders, there is no binding evidence that he did so, and, as Colin Wilson points out in his *Encyclopedia of Murder*, it is very unlikely that a sadistic killer like Jack would be content to turn from actual mutilation to Chapman's method, which was poison. Chapman was not arrested until 1902, when Jack the Ripper was assumed by the authorities to have been dead for some years.

George Chapman's real name was Severin Klosowski. He was born in Poland in 1865 and spent his early working life as a barber-surgeon. It was a combination customary in England also at that time, indicating a certain proficiency in the simpler type of 'operations' such as blood-letting, corn-cutting or wart removals. He arrived in Britain around 1888, after a short spell in the Russian army, and stayed at 54 Cranbrook Street, Green

Street, by Victoria Park. Green Street is now known as Roman Road, and Cranbrook Street itself has been swallowed up in the Cranbrook Estate. Chapman obtained a job as a barber at 89 Whitechapel High Street. It has also been stated that he worked for a time in George Yard, scene of a Ripper murder. Later he moved to another shop, at 5 West Green Road, Tottenham, then set up on his own at 518 High Road, Tottenham. This venture failed and he was back in employment, first in Rushton and Rivington Streets, Shoreditch, then in Church Lane, Leytonstone. During this period, in 1889, he married a Polish woman, Lucy Baderski, whom he met at a club for his countrymen in St John's Square, Clerkenwell. They lived first at Cable Street, then Greenfield Street, off Commercial Road—at the corner of which Mr Wainwright had picked up Alice Day during his extraordinary cab drive with the remains of his mistress.

Mr and Mrs Klosowski (as he was still called), then went to America. She returned alone following a quarrel. Matters were patched up for a while when he himself came back to England, but the marriage finally disintegrated and he went to live with a woman named Annie Chapman—a coincidental link with the Ripper, this being the same name as that of one of his victims. Chapman took his mistress's surname, and never again recognized that of Klosowski. It was after he parted from Annie that he committed the first of his known murders. While in lodgings at Leytonstone he met Mrs Mary Spink, a woman whose husband had left her. One day she and Chapman simply went out together and returned saying they were married. They set up a hairdressing business in Hastings, but it was a failure. Chapman now changed occupations and took the lease of the Prince of Wales Tavern, Bartholomew Square, near City Road. Not long after he moved in there Mrs Spink (as she still was in reality, of course) became ill with stomach pains and constant vomiting. She died on Christmas Day 1897, the doctor ascribing her death to phthisis. Chapman then engaged a barmaid, Bessie Taylor, and after going out with her to get 'married', lived with her as his wife. He moved from Bartholomew Square to a pub at Bishops Stortford, and then to the Monument Tavern, Union Street, Borough. He seems to have been as restless a publican as he was a barber. In Union Street Bessie soon fell ill and died after much vomiting and diarrhoea—according to the doctor's certificate the cause of death was exhaustion from these two activities. A touching verse was composed (possibly by the bereaved husband) for her grave:

> Farewell, my friends, fond and dear,
> Weep not for me one single tear:
> For all that was and could be done,
> You plainly see my time was come.

Chapman then took on another barmaid, Maud Marsh (the surname, it will be remembered, of one of Neill Cream's victims), and, very much against the will of her parents, 'married' her. By professed religion Chapman was a Roman Catholic, and according to this somewhat gullible girl the ceremony took place in a "Roman Catholic room" in Bishopsgate. Soon after, Chapman was on the move again, leaving the 'Monument' for the 'Crown', 213 Borough High Street. There Maud Marsh, who had already followed custom by falling ill, died with much the same symptoms. This time, however, Chapman had Maud's watchful and angry parents to contend with. They came from their home in Croydon with their own doctor, who passed on certain fears to the one who had attended the dead girl. As a result the latter took the strange step of performing a private and totally unauthorized autopsy. The analyst to whom he sent the sample reported the presence of arsenic, and Chapman was arrested on 25th October 1902. The bodies of Mrs Spink and Bessie Taylor were exhumed, and antimony was discovered. It was then confirmed that antimony and not arsenic was the cause also of Maud Marsh's death. Chapman, who was identified as having bought tartar emetic while in Hastings, was found guilty of the murder of Maud Marsh, and was executed at Wandsworth in April 1903. The underlying reasons for Chapman's callous acts is obscure. He was known to have treated women brutally on occasions. That he was also a compulsive liar, a boaster, and a typical mixture of cunning and stupidity is clear from a study of his trial. But on the darker recesses of that shadowed mind little light is thrown.

Most of the streets where Chapman walked can be trodden still, though the buildings may have gone. Bartholomew Square, however, once reached from City Road by way of Leage Street and Mitchell Street, will have finally succumbed to redevelopment by the time this book appears. A street sign still encouragingly states "Leading to Bartholomew Square", but leads in fact only to a muddy expanse of building works, and is sternly countermanded by the words "No Trespassers".

In 1837, while living at the long vanished Carpenters Buildings, Lambeth, James Greenacre put to death Hannah Brown, his betrothed, cut her in pieces, and hid them in various parts of London, managing in some ingenious way to conceal the trunk under the flagstones by a toll-bar, the 'Pineapple', Edgware Road. In defence of his action he said that she had pretended to own a certain amount of property and had laughed at him when he discovered this to be false. So he hit her on the head with a silk-roller. It is recorded that hundreds of people slept on the steps of St Sepulchre's Church, Newgate, the night before the hanging. His last words to his executioner, on beholding the hissing multitude, were, "Don't leave me long in this concourse."

That unpleasant pair, the Mannings, lived during 1849 in a small house in Minver (alternatively spelt Miniver) Place, Bermondsey, which at that time led off from near the middle of Western road and consisted of a number of neat two-storey villas. Their own was No 3. Of Maria Manning her defence counsel, Serjeant Ballantine, was to write: "Although she was my client I suspect she was the power that really originated the deed of blood." She was a Swiss with the aristocratic maiden name of de Roux, and on emigrating to England became employed as lady's maid to the Duchess of Sutherland. While there she made the acquaintance (presumably on her days off) of an ex-railway employee, Frederick George Manning, who had been sacked on account of the considerable amounts of property that vanished from the trains on which he worked. After her marriage she left the Duchess and he became landlord of an inn at Taunton, but was dismissed under similar suspicions as those held by the railway company. He then opened a beershop in Hackney.

Maria for some time had had another gentleman friend, Patrick O'Connor—as may be surmized, an Irishman—who was fairly comfortably off and had a good job with the Customs authorities. It seemed to have been an amicable triangular set-up, though Mr Manning got a bit annoyed when Maria went so far as to run off with most of his furniture and set herself up in a room paid for by Mr O'Connor. He persuaded his wife to abandon such unconventional behaviour and return to him, and they moved together to Minver Place. Mr O'Connor continued to be a regular, not to say an intimate, visitor, and doubtless found the arrangement an agreeable change from his lodgings at 21 Greenwood Street, Mile End. This street has disappeared but was then near Adelina Grove, Sidney Street.

The Mannings also enjoyed the more permanent company of a medical-student lodger. Though he apparently gave no sign of it, the young man must have been somewhat surprised by his landlord's constant enquiries as to the effects of chloroform, shotguns, blows on the skull and other lethal matters, and also by his wanting to know what the chances were of a murderer being admitted to Heaven. In August 1849 this pliable and obliging person was sent off by the Mannings to enjoy a short holiday. Left alone in the house, the pair bought a crowbar, a shovel and a sackful of lime, and invited Mr O'Connor to a meal. They then shot him through the head (Mrs Manning), hit him with a blunt instrument (Mr Manning) and together buried him under the stone kitchen floor. Next day Mrs Manning called at Greenwood Street and took away jewellery, money and share certificates belonging to O'Connor, some of which were sold by her husband. Mrs Manning then left him once again, this time taking away everything she could lay her hands on, and the presumably finally disillusioned man went off himself a couple of days later. The whole business was singularly stupid as well as revolting. O'Connor was missed almost at once, both at work and at his lodgings, and enquiries were immediately made at Minver Place. When the house was found empty it was thoroughly searched, the body brought to light, and a hue and cry started. Mrs Manning was found in Edinburgh, Mr Manning in St Helier. They met again, in icy silence, at Horse-monger Lane Prison. Mr Manning agreed with Serjeant Ballantine, putting most of the blame on his wife, but both were hanged outside the prison on 13th November—the lady in a new dress of black satin.

The Mannings are probably best remembered for the vivid description by Charles Dickens of the crowd's behaviour at their public execution, which he attended—his indignation being directed not so much at the ordained punishment for a disgusting crime as at the idea of such punishment being turned into a public spectacle.

On 20th October 1818 Robert Dean, a young clockmaker's assistant, went to the Watch House of St Andrew, Holborn, and said that he was the murderer four days previously of Mary Albert, a little girl who lived in Jacques Court, Thomas Street, Elephant and Castle. He had been visiting the child's mother, whom he knew, and had then left with a friend and walked up London Road to the Surrey Theatre, Great Surrey Street (now Blackfriars Road), where they parted. Dean returned, led the child out to Jacques Court under the pretext of buying her an apple and cut her throat with a kitchen knife he had taken from the house. Mrs Albert found her staggering about the court with blood pouring from the wound. Dean's reason for this appalling act, as he stated it, is extraordinary. There was a girl living in Church Row, Aldgate, with whom he was deeply in love, but he had been forbidden to see her again by her father, following a quarrel. At first he contemplated suicide, then decided to kill her first. While playing with the little girl in Jacques Court it suddenly occurred to him that killing an innocent child would not be so great a crime in the eyes of Heaven as murdering an older person with all her sins upon her. Despite this story, and the fact that he went through his trial in an apparent stupor, Dean was regarded as sane and executed, his last words being a loud cry to those assembled, "God bless you all!"

Thomas Street and its courts stood just behind the start of New Kent Road from Elephant and Castle circle. Few places have undergone more drastic alteration, but Meadow Row, into which it led, is still there at the time of writing. The Surrey Theatre, to which the wretched young man walked with his friend just before the murder, stood on the corner of Blackfriars Road at St George's Circus until 1935, though the building he himself saw was burnt down in January 1865 during a pantomime transformation scene. It was rebuilt the following year. The site is marked now by part of the Royal Eye Hospital.

Exactly ninety years later the body of another small girl, Marie Ellen Bailes, was found murdered in the same way, within minutes of the scene of the earlier tragedy. She had left the St John's Roman Catholic School in Islington, where she was a pupil, on the afternoon of 30th May 1908 but never arrived at her home close by. Early the following morning a man entered a public lavatory at the corner of St George's Road, Elephant and Castle, and left a large parcel behind him when he went out. The attendant noticed something nervous in the man's behaviour, and when he did not return, opened the wrapping, to find that it contained the body of a child who had been dead for several hours. Her throat was cut, but she had not been sexually assaulted. The man was never found.

Turning off Kennington Lane almost opposite Oval Way is St Oswald's Place. On the night of 14th April 1941, a policeman walking the blacked-out streets saw smoke and flames coming from the cellar of a Baptist chapel that had been partially destroyed by bombs. A man was standing agitatedly close by. The fire was quickly extinguished by the brigade, but the police were to remember that the man had not reported it, even though he was on fire-watching duty (admittedly at another building) at the time. His name was Harry Dobkin, a Russian-born Jew of about 50 who had been engaged by a firm of solicitors to keep watch for incendiaries falling on a small building near the chapel. He made his headquarters a blitzed house, No 302 Kennington Lane, where during the intervals between patrols he would rest in an old armchair. Nothing more suspicious was found at the time, but over a year later, in July 1942, a woman's scorched body was found beneath the chapel by a workman. Sufficient of the flesh remained for Dr Keith Simpson, the Home Office pathologist, to determine that death had been due to strangulation and that she was not, as had been at first assumed, the victim of an air-raid.

It was then recalled that Dobkin's wife Rachel, from whom he was separated, had been reported missing on 12th April 1941. They were married many years ago but it had been a failure from the start, and after a very brief stay at Brady Buildings, Bethnal Green, Dobkin had gone off on his own to live at No 1 Nathaniel Buildings, Flower and Dean Street, Whitechapel. A son was born to Mrs Dobkin and she rigorously and constantly applied for maintenance. Long after the child was old enough to earn its own living she followed and hounded her husband, making scenes in public and even causing him to be sent to prison on several occasions for failing to meet payment dates. It was also suspected that she was blackmailing him over some past misdemeanour. Dobkin told the police that he had last seen her on 11th April 1941, and that they had parted on quite good terms. This, it seems, was almost certainly untrue.

The probability is that she came to see him on or before the night of the 14th demanding more 'maintenance'—or perhaps even seeking a reconciliation—and that in a rage he killed her, deliberately or by accident. He then hid the body in the crypt of the chapel. The nightly bombing of London had eased off, but with the likelihood of a sharp raid at any time (and the massive assaults of 19th April and 10th May were not far ahead) there was always a chance that a fortunate bit of bomb damage would conceal an individual crime. The Luftwaffe failed to co-operate, however, and Dobkin paid the penalty. It is impossible, on reading the trial, to avoid feeling that, though it does not excuse what he did, he was—and had been for a long time—a sorely provoked man.

Chester Way links Kennington Lane and Kennington Road just before they cross each other. One hundred years ago it was known as Chester Street. At the end of August 1867 a Mrs Hills, living at No 53, heard cries of, "Murder!" and, "Police!" coming from a neighbour. A boy named Roberts ran out and said his mother had killed his small brother and sister and was about to kill herself. Mrs Hills rushed into the house and found a girl of 9 and a boy of 7 with their throats cut, and their mother lying on the floor. She had gashed herself in the upper arm, and died soon afterwards. There was a family history of insanity and she had been depressed for a considerable time over some imagined wrong. It was considered certain that the killings were premeditated as she had waited until some lodgers had left the house before doing anything. Even so, the verdict that she had wilfully murdered her children before killing herself while of unsound mind seems somewhat contradictory in logic, however correct in law.

Wyndham Road joins Camberwell Road to New Camberwell Road, and during the early years of this century No 22 was a successful little grocer's shop in a busy neighbourhood, run by John Darby and his wife Beatrice, both under 30 years of age. A week or two before Christmas 1902 customers were surprised to see the windows shuttered and a notice on the door stating that the business had been sold. It was true that the Darbys had been advertising for a buyer, but this seemed somewhat precipitate, and fears were aroused that the young couple had most unexpectedly committed the unforgivable sin of running off with the Christmas Club money. The police were informed, but the

owners had disappeared without trace and there was not much
to be done. There the matter might have rested for long enough,
but a few weeks later another grocer who was advertising a
sale was violently attacked, and the police arrested a man named
Edgar Edwards, an apparently gentle and courteous individual
who lived at 89 Church Road, Leyton. There they found some
office stationery bearing the name and address of the Darbys
on it. Remembering the vanished couple, they made a thorough
search, not only of the house but of the garden. There they
found, buried in sacks, the dismembered remains of Mr and Mrs
Darby and the body of their baby, which had been strangled.
They had also seen, without at the time realizing it, practically
every movable article, down to the smallest kitchen utensils,
which the Darbys had possessed in their little shop-and-house
dwelling.

It transpired at the trial that Edwards had called at 22 Wyndham Road in answer to the advertisement carrying a heavy
window-sash weight hidden in paper. Once inside, he had killed
the couple and their child, shut the shop, hung up the notice,
and gone off home with all the available cash, including the
club money. Later he returned accompanied by a horse and cart
and, with a cool rashness that amazes even when one knows of
the insanity in his family, proceeded to strip the entire place
bare, actually accepting help from watchers willing to earn a
shilling or two carrying the stuff out. In one of the loads went
the unfortunate previous occupiers. Had Edwards not been
foolish enough as to repeat the experiment he would very likely
have got away with it. Despite the family history of mental
abnormality he was found guilty and sentenced to death. He
showed a fine sense of the drama of the English judicial processes,
remarking as the judge was about to deliver sentence that it was
just like being on the stage. Edwards had the doubtful distinction
of being described as a "hot 'un" by fellow murderer George
Chapman, who was awaiting his fate at the same time.

Kennington Common was not one of the major highwaymen
haunts, but before leaving the district we may note the execution
thereon of Jeremiah Lewis Avershaw, known for villainies on
this and other open spaces, in 1795. He was sitting drinking in
the Three Brewers Inn, Southwark, when two officers came to
arrest him. On seeing them he at once drew his gun and fired,
killing one and seriously wounding the other. He was secured,

tried and found guilty, but after the verdict a technical hitch was discovered in the conduct of the trial, rendering the conviction void: with commendably swift resourcefulness, however, the prosecution brought forward on the spot one of his previous murders, for which he was sentenced forthwith. He remained violent throughout the short period of life left to him, spending his quieter moments drawing pictures of his crimes on the cell walls. His execution took place on the common in 1795. During the final preparations he stood with a flower between his teeth, nodding to friends in the crowd, exchanging ribaldries, and cursing the officials—behaving generally, in fact, with gay abandon or callous indifference, according to where one's sympathies lay. Fifty years or so later the open space was enclosed and made into an ornamental park.

11

"A GREAT RECKONING IN A LITTLE ROOM"

South-East (2): Deptford, Blackheath, Eltham, Norwood, Penge

We now move farther afield, to Deptford—scene of the most famous of literary murders. Neither the settings, nor the details, nor the motives that brought about the death of 29-year-old Christopher Marlowe are ever likely to be cleared up now. According to the generally accepted story, from the coroner's record, four men—Marlowe, Ingram Frizer (or according to some sources Francis Archer—apparently an early misreading), Nicholas Skeres and Robert Poley—gathered at the house of a Mrs Eleanor Bull at about 10 a.m. on 30th May 1593. They passed the day together, dined and walked in the garden until 6 p.m., then returned to an upper room for supper. After the meal a quarrel broke out over the reckoning, weapons were drawn, and Marlowe was slain by a stab above his eye from Ingram Frizer. The latter was a servant of Sir Francis Walsingham, Marlowe's patron; Poley was a spy; Skeres a cheat and a gaolbird—both he and Poley had worked on the breaking up of the Babington Plot. All three appear to have been pretty disreputable characters. Theories have been advanced ever since, suggesting that the killing was not so simple and unpremeditated a matter as was officially stated. The coroner, it has been said, was influenced by "certain powers" not to enquire too closely into the circumstances. It is strange, for instance, that there is no record of Eleanor Bull being called in evidence. On 12th May, eighteen days earlier, Thomas Kyd the dramatist had been arrested on charges of atheism and seditious libel. He did not wholly deny the charges but said he had had the "atheistic papers" from Marlowe, though these were not in the latter's handwriting. Kyd, it seems, thought that Marlowe had been responsible for the arrest. Marlowe himself was apprehended on 18th May. He was not imprisoned, but was ordered to remain within certain bounds. There had been other accusations of "foulest blasphemies" against him, notably on 29th May, the day before his death, by one Richard Baines, who said that all men in Christianity should endeavour to stop the mouth of so dangerous a member. Here may be grounds for suspecting some kind of motive, and there were hints of other political reasons. None of this, however, can be more than speculation now.

The status of the building itself is uncertain. Dr S. A. Tannenbaum in his study *The Assassination of Christopher Marlowe* refers to it as a "cheap tavern"—other sources, including local history records and the coroner's report, call it a "house". It may well have been just that, a private house. Richard Bull, Eleanor's husband, is described as a "gentleman" and may have been of some standing locally. Eleanor Bull is referred to as a widow, so perhaps she was in reduced circumstances after her husband's death, and turned the house into an inn. Its size is, of course, unknown. Its most likely situation was on Deptford Strand, near the river, beyond St Nicholas Church. An entry in the parish register of St Nicholas and St Paul records the burial on 1st June 1593 of Christopher Marlow [*sic*], "slaine by Ffrancis Archer". Much more we are never likely to discover.

On 27th March 1905, occurred a fairly commonplace crime which, however, pointed to new methods both of detection and the avoidance of detection. A fingerprint (to be exact, a thumbprint) was used for the first time in England as a means of identification; and the criminals wore stocking masks. The victims were a Mr and Mrs Farrow, both elderly, who managed a chandler's shop at 34 High Street, Deptford. On the morning in question a boy assistant found the place shut up and called the owner. He broke in through a window, and found Farrow downstairs and his wife in bed, both savagely beaten about the head. A cashbox had been forced open. On the inside was a clear thumb-print, which the police photographed. Also found were two black silk masks made from stockings which, it was learnt later, belonged to Mrs Farrow. From this precaution it was considered that the criminals may have been local men who feared they would be recognized if their victims recovered, or if they were surprised before they got away. Among local known criminals approached in the course of routine enquiries were two young brothers, Alfred and Albert Stratton, both with records for housebreaking. Alfred lived with his mistress in Brookmill Road, Albert lodged at 67 Knott Street (now Creekside). When questioned, Alfred's mistress admitted that he had been out during the night in question and had later destroyed some clothing. Both brothers were arrested, and the print on the cashbox matched Alfred's thumb. Though this new form of evidence was regarded with some caution by the judge (there were of course other factors to support it), there is no doubt as to the importance of its share in securing a verdict and in opening the door to the acceptance of fingerprint identification in the future.

Leading east out of Greenwich Park is St John's Park, Blackheath, scene of the final exploit of Charles Peace. After his career of infamy in the north, culminating in the murder of Albert Dyson at Banner Cross, Sheffield, on 29th November 1876, Peace vanished completely and was seen no more in those parts. In 1877 a gentleman of about 60 took up residence at No 5 Evelina Road, Peckham. The respectable Victorian inhabitants of that respectable Victorian neighbourhood found Mr Thompson very much to their liking: a regular churchgoer, an accomplished violinist, the life of many a genteel party, a friend to the various dumb animals and birds he sheltered. He was clever in scientific matters, too, working with a neighbour, Mr Henry Brion, on an invention for raising wrecked ships by replacing the water in them with air and gas. The one slightly odd thing about this amiable newcomer was the extreme darkness of his complexion, but a man is not to be judged by the colour of his skin. There was a Mrs Thompson (there were, in fact, two ladies with equal claims to the name, the second posing as a servant), who took affectionate care of the elderly gentleman, in particular seeing that he was not disturbed during his night's rest. He often slept till noon.

At about two o'clock on the morning of 10th October 1878, P.C. Edward Robinson, on patrol duty round Blackheath, noticed a light at the back of No 2 St John's Park, a large, solid, dignified house in which lived Mr J. A. Burness. The policeman quietly summoned a colleague and they watched together. After a short while a figure emerged from the house and crept down the garden. When Robinson approached him the man fired two shots, crying, "Keep back or by God I'll shoot you!" This was followed up by three more shots as the constable pounced, the last one wounding him in the arm. When the prisoner appeared on remand he said he was John Ward. Owing to his colour he was taken for a half-caste, and for a few days nothing further was discovered about him. Then he made his first, incredibly stupid mistake. He obtained permission to write to his neighbour Henry Brion, requesting him to come to Newgate and "help an unfortunate man, John Ward, who is in trouble through drink and family unhappiness". Doubtless very curious about this mysterious plea, Brion went, and found himself confronting his erstwhile friend and fellow inventor. In a very short time the secret of the double alias was out—to the utter consternation and furious anger of the fooled residents of Evelina Road. The dark complexion paled rapidly when the supply of walnut juice was no longer available. Mrs Thompson, who had explained her husband's absence by saying he had taken a short trip for business reasons, fled. The rest of the villa ménage also scattered, but all were soon traced. Peace was sentenced at the Old Bailey to life imprisonment, then sent to Leeds to be tried for the murder of Dyson. It was on this journey that he made his sensational bid for freedom by jumping, still handcuffed, from the compartment window while the train was travelling at speed. He was hanged in February, 1879, described by Marwood the executioner as, "professionally speaking, one of the best subjects I ever handled".

Blackheath was another open space noted for its highwaymen, and travellers would gather together on the edge at dark to avoid venturing across it alone. On Shooters Hill a gallows was left standing, hopefully to deter wicked men from evil deeds. On one occasion as he travelled by Samuel Pepys remarked on "the man that hangs upon Shooters Hill, and a filthy sight it was to see how his flesh is shrunk".

Turning up north-west from Rochester Way a little distance from Shooters Hill is a short road known today as Brook Lane. In 1936 it still appeared on the map as Kidbrooke Lane (not to be confused with the present day Kidbrooke Lane off Well Hall Lane) and one hundred years ago it was a lane in reality, a lovers lane, in fact, bounded by trees and ditches and hedgerows, and through it ran the little Kid Brook. In the early hours of 27th April 1871 a patrolling constable saw a young girl crawling along the lane sobbing, "Oh my poor head, my poor head!" She had been appallingly beaten, her face was gashed and one of her eyes was actually hanging out of its socket. She was taken, barely alive, to a doctor in Eltham and thence to Guy's Hospital, where she died very shortly afterwards, able only to mutter, "Save me," followed by a name no-one could understand. For a few days she remained unidentified, then a Mr and Mrs Trott, who lived in Deptford, became worried about the whereabouts of their niece. The girl had recently disappeared from her lodgings with a Mrs Hamilton at No 12 Ashburnham Road (now Ashburnham Place) Greenwich. Reading of the discovery in the newspapers they went to the police, and later recognized the pitiful remains. The girl was Jane Clouson—she had been battered to death within a few days of her seventeenth birthday.

At 15 Jane had gone into service with the Pook family. Ebenezer Pook ran a local printing firm and lived with his wife and two grown-up sons, Thomas and Edmund, at 3 London Street, Greenwich, now Greenwich High Road and completely rebuilt. Edmund Pook was 20 years of age, suffered from epileptic fits and was known as an avid girl-chaser. He used to carry a whistle around to summon any young woman he fancied. Jane was a pretty girl and inevitably attracted his attention. On his part it was just another casual affair, but Jane was naturally flattered by the condescension of the master's son towards the servant-girl. Equally naturally, she became pregnant.

On 13th April 1871 Mrs Pook suddenly dismissed her—after nearly two years, saying she was not doing her work properly. More probably, she had just discovered Jane's relationship with her son. Through a friend, Jane found a room with Mrs Hamilton. During the next few days, frantic with worry, she confided her troubles to her kindly landlady, to another friend, Jane Prosser, and in particular to her cousin Charlotte Trott. A couple of days before the murder she suddenly appeared more cheerful, telling Charlotte that Edmund was arranging to send her away for a few weeks and eventually to marry her. Charlotte, she said, was not to worry if nothing was heard of her for a while. On the 26th she went to Deptford with Mrs

Hamilton, probably to do some shopping. She left the landlady in Douglas Street (now Douglas Way), saying she had to meet Edmund at Crooms Hill, Greenwich Park. None of her friends saw her alive again.

Edmund Pook was charged. The evidence against him seemed incontrovertible. He was identified as having bought a particular kind of hammer—with an axe-type blade on one side—that fitted the girl's wounds; he was seen leaving Kidbrooke Lane the night of the murder covered with mud; blood was found on his clothing; Charlotte made known the story she had heard from Jane. The defence was a blank denial of everything: the blood and mud were accounted for by nose-bleeds and fits, and a cut wrist; he was nowhere near Kidbrooke Lane at the time, but in Lewisham. His mother declared, with shocked *hauteur*, that her son would never so demean himself as to become intimate with a servant-girl.

Edmund was acquitted, largely because (*a*) the judge, Chief Justice Bovill, would not allow Charlotte Trott to tell Jane's story because it was hearsay, and (*b*) the trial took place before the time when the accused might feel compelled to go into the witness-box and thus lay himself open to cross-examination. In his summing-up the judge said that much of the evidence was circumstantial and that many of the statements made by witnesses were clearly unreliable. In those days public indignation was more likely to be roused on behalf of the victim than of the criminal. Edmund's guilt—acquittal or not—stared them in the face. Crowds demonstrated outside the Pook residence. Eventually a deliberately libellous pamphlet was issued by a wealthy merchant who was determined to air what he considered to be a gross miscarriage of justice and the escape of a brutal killer from the consequences of his deed. The family could not avoid bringing a case against him, which meant that this time Edmund had to undergo cross-examination. He scraped through somehow, but the damages awarded were so paltry as to seem a clear comment on the true opinions held by the jury. Further lawsuits followed, bringing little credit to anyone, and the case remains—officially—unsolved.

Another Eltham murder—also of a young girl—occurred fifty years later, in 1918, when the body of 16-year-old Nellie True was found on the common not far from Well Hall Road. She had been sexually assaulted and strangled after a violent struggle. Nellie True lived with her family in Well Hall and worked as a clerk at the Woolwich Arsenal not far away. On Saturday 9th February she left home to change her library book at Plumstead. When she had not returned by midnight her father informed the police, who discovered her body early the next morning. It was ascertained that she had in fact visited the library, and she must have been killed some time between leaving it and two o'clock the following day. Beside her handbag and library book the police found an army badge in the shape of a tiger, and a bone overcoat button with a piece of metal in its holes instead of the usual thread. Photographs of both objects appeared in the press, and an employee in the Hewsom Manufacturing Company of Newman Street, Oxford Street, which made aeroplane parts, recognized the tiger. It was a copy of an obsolete badge of the Leicester Regiment which a workmate named David Greenwood had been in the habit of wearing on his overcoat lapel. The day after the murder the badge was missing. This disappearance, coupled with the fact that Greenwood's house actually backed onto the common close to the spot where Nellie True's body was found, aroused some natural curiosity in the firm. Greenwood said he had sold the badge to "a man on a tram", but agreed with a general suggestion that in the circumstances he would be wise to get in touch with the police. It was proved later that the piece of wire found in the button was of a kind specially manufactured by the Hewsom Company; all the buttons were missing from Greenwood's overcoat after the murder. It transpired that he himself had cut off those that remained. Greenwood (who had been discharged from the R.A.M.C. suffering from neurasthenia and heart trouble following shellshock) was found guilty with a recommendation to mercy. His appeal was dismissed, but he was later reprieved. Sir Travers Humphreys, who prosecuted, was fond of posing the question : if Greenwood had used thread instead of wire to secure one of his overcoat buttons, would there have been enough circumstantial evidence to convict him?

In 1929 Mrs East, wife of an auctioneer in the City, was found murdered in a train between Eltham and Kidbrooke Stations. The killer was never found, though cries for help were heard by passengers in adjoining compartments. The case illustrated once more the need for communication between such compartments.

   Though motives for murder often seem inadequate, few surely are less understandable than that which impelled Louisa Jane Taylor on her tortuous course in August 1882. Naylor's Cottages, Plumstead, long vanished now, was the setting. In No 3 lived 85-year-old William Tregillis and his slightly younger wife, inhabiting two rooms. Both were physically healthy, though Mr Tregillis was not quite so bright mentally as when he pursued his career as a Customs official, and had in fact recently spent a few months in an asylum. The old couple had only been installed in Naylor's Cottages for about three weeks when they were visited by Mrs Louisa Taylor, a woman of 37 whose husband—a former friend of Mr Tregillis—had died a few months previously. She must have been a remarkably persuasive woman for in a very short time she had not only moved in with them, but was sleeping in the back room with Mrs Tregillis while the old man was moved out to pass his nights alone in the front one. The new arrangement had not been in force for long before Mrs Tregillis's hitherto sturdy constitution began to crack up. She fell ill with much vomiting and shivering which the doctor, named Smith, put down to ague and general senility. Mr Tregillis seems to have accepted everything, including his wife's unusual state of ill health, with stoical equanimity at first, but even he was somewhat astonished when Mrs Taylor began to make unmistakable physical advances to him (he was, after all, not far off 90) and even suggested an elopement. His surprise increased when she showed him a will she had made in his favour, together with a letter addressed to herself saying she had been left £500 and could draw it whenever she pleased. The inference seemed to be that he should share and eventually inherit her fortune. The will, however, mysteriously disappeared from the cupboard in which he placed it.
   The old man himself, as it happened, was not altogether without means, being in receipt of a pension of 19s. a week— not to be scoffed at in those days—paid quarterly. When he drew it for the first time since Louisa's arrival she asked him to let her have the pleasure of giving it to Mrs Tregillis. By this time, no doubt, thoroughly bemused he handed it over—which is more than Louisa did. When he found that his money had never reached his wife, had in fact totally disappeared, Mr Tregillis was finally goaded into action, and the friend of the family was charged with theft. This development alerted the

doctor, who had hitherto regarded the solicitous Louisa as a Florence Nightingale, and he looked more closely into the old lady's condition. To his horror he discovered that she was being steadily poisoned with sugar of lead, and furthermore that Louisa had been obtaining the stuff, under pretext of skin trouble, from his own wife who managed a chemist's shop. Louisa was arrested and, the old woman dying soon after, charged with murder. Considering how small any monetary advantage would have been, and the fact that Louisa already had some sort of relationship with a man (a watercress-seller) nearer her own age, one can only puzzle over the strange workings of that human mind in Naylor's Cottages, Plumstead, some ninety years ago.

In St Aubyn's Road, Upper Norwood, near the southern corner of the Crystal Palace site, a particularly horrible murder took place on the last day of August in 1957. A girl of 4, Edwina Taylor, was reported missing from her home at 3 Tudor Road, and after a massive search was found dead in the basement of No 14 St Aubyn's Road, a few minutes walk away. The child was lying on a pile of coal; she had been killed by strangulation and damage to the brain. In the ground-floor flat lived a man of 31 named Derrick Edwardson, but when the police went to interview him on routine enquiries they found the place empty. In a pocket of his overalls, which were at his place of work, was a note saying that he had enticed the little girl to his flat and killed her with the intention of raping her after death. "But I realized," the note continued, "that I had killed someone that somebody must have loved and I felt ashamed of myself. . . . I will surrender tonite. I did not interfere with her." It was not until 9th September, however, that Edwardson was in custody, and then only because he gave himself up. After spending the afternoon at the local 'Odeon' watching the film *St Joan* he walked into Wealdstone Police Station and admitted his identity. Edwardson, who previously lived at 10 Grove Road, Willesden, had already been convicted of an indecent offence against a girl of 5 and of writing, as a threat, an exact description of the murder he later committed. The case, which involved one of the biggest police searches ever set up, caused some alarm at the realization of how freely a man with known dangerous sexual abnormalities could move around.

Our last crime of the district is possibly the best known—that of the Stauntons, which culminated in the death by neglect of Harriet Staunton, née Richardson, at No 34 Forbes Road, Penge. It is a fairly long and complicated story that has been fully recounted elsewhere (notably by Elizabeth Jenkins in *Harriet*) and is also included in the Notable British Trials Series, so we shall, as before, consider it only briefly here, noting as concisely as possible its geography and its complex family relationships. Harriet Richardson, born in 1841, was—in the euphemism of the day—somewhat 'simple'. Though not handsome she was neat, well-mannered and, apart from occasional sulky moods and outbursts of bad temper, generally amiable. She was, however, undeniably deficient mentally, could derive no benefit from ordinary education, could write only with great difficulty, could spell only the simplest words. At the age of 34 she left her mother's house to live with the Hincksmans at 53 Heygate Street, Walworth Road, near the Elephant and Castle. Mr Hincksman was a nephew of Harriet's mother Mrs Butterfield (she had since married again), and he had two stepdaughters, Elizabeth and Alice Rhodes. Elizabeth was married to a man younger than herself named Patrick Staunton. Patrick had a brother, Louis, aged 23, who was an auctioneer's clerk and perpetually short of money. In this respect Harriet, though short on brains, had one notable asset—she was the owner, in possession and reversion, of about £4,000, a sizable fortune in the 1870s.

Very swiftly, and much against Mrs Butterfield's wishes, Louis wooed and married Harriet, and they went to live at No 8 Loughborough Park Road (now Loughborough Park), Clapham. Mr and Mrs Patrick Staunton were next door, at No 9. Hearing rumours of the birth of a child, Mrs Butterfield went to Loughborough Park Road, to find both houses empty. The Louis Stauntons had in fact gone to Gipsy Hill, Norwood, where they stayed, with Alice Rhodes, until 1876. The Patrick Stauntons meanwhile were at the Woodlands (also called Frith Cottage) an isolated house near Cudham. An arrangement was made whereby Harriet's baby should live with Mrs Patrick and her two children, looked after by an orphan girl of 15 named Clara Brown. Clara was a cousin of Alice and Elizabeth.

In August Harriet herself went to stay at Woodlands (Louis paying Elizabeth £1 a week for her board), leaving her husband

and Alice Rhodes at Gipsy Hill. Thereafter no more was seen of Harriet by the outside world. Louis and Alice, now accepted as married, went to live at Little Gray's Farm, Cudham, about half a mile from Patrick's cottage. All this while Mrs Butterfield was chasing around from place to place trying to find out just what was going on. In April 1877 Harriet's baby was taken to Guy's Hospital by Patrick and Elizabeth, who said it was the son of a carpenter and was named Henry Stormton. It was a tiny, shrivelled being with only a faint spark of life, and in fact it died that same evening. The following Tuesday Louis, calling himself Harris, arranged for its funeral. Four days after the death of the baby, on 12th April, Louis and Elizabeth took apartments at No 34 Forbes Road, Penge, for an "invalid lady" from Cudham. Harriet, Patrick, Louis and Elizabeth, together with Alice Rhodes, arrived that evening. Harriet could scarcely walk and seemed totally unable to speak. She was put straight to bed, where the landlady, Mrs Chalklin, heard her groaning. The following morning, on the advice of Mr Chalklin, Dr Longrigg was sent for and found Harriet in a shockingly emaciated and revoltingly dirty condition. She died later the same day. On information from Louis, the doctor gave the cause of death as cerebral disease and apoplexy.

That evening, by sheer chance, a gentleman with the resounding surname of Casabianca was in the Forbes Road Post Office when a stranger entered to enquire where the Registrar of Births and Deaths could be found. On being told, he casually mentioned that it was in connection with the decease of a lady from Cudham. Mr Casabianca pricked up his ears, for he happened to be the husband of Harriet's half-sister and knew a lot about the anxiety among the family over mysterious events concerning a lady in Cudham. As a result of his enquiries and a visit to Dr Longrigg the death certificate was withdrawn and an inquest ordered to be held at the Park Tavern, 1 Station Road, Penge. A verdict of wilful murder was returned against Louis, Patrick, Elizabeth and Alice Rhodes, and a later one of manslaughter against the first three in respect of the child. The charge *re* Harriet really amounted to one of murder by neglect, the defence was essentially one of death by disease. All four were found guilty, but were later reprieved following petitions from a large number of medical experts. Alice Rhodes was released, the others given varying terms of imprisonment.

Patrick Staunton died while still in gaol, Elizabeth and Louis both survived to experience freedom again. The case had some legal importance in that it may well have influenced the passing of the Married Women's Property Act of 1882 and the Prisoners' Evidence Act of 1898.

The farm in Cudham and the cottage are no longer to be found, but the Park Tavern, where the inquest was held, may yet be visited in Station Road. Forbes Road changed its name on account of the unwelcome publicity, and is now known as Mosslea Road.

Such in outline is the story of one of the strangest, perhaps almost unintentional, yet in its quiet way the most callous of crimes, motivated by Louis Staunton's determination to have both Harriet's money and Alice's company.

12

A PAIR OF PISTOLS, A SACK AND A ROPE

The Outskirts, North of the River: Elstree, Watford, Potters Bar, Edgware, Ruislip, Brentford, Heston, Teddington, Ilford

In the final two chapters we shall be going further afield, to a number of places just outside the London postal district but still mainly within the bounds of the Metropolitan Police.

> They cut his throat from ear to ear,
> His brains they battered in,
> His name was Mr William Weare,
> He lived in Lyon's Inn.

The interest which the trial of Thurtell and Hunt for the murder of the above-named gentleman aroused, not only in the general public but in the writers and artists of the day, probably lay more in the picture it presented of the raffish sporting and gambling community of the period than in the chief characters concerned, all of whom—including the victim —were callous, worthless, stupid and shallow specimens even of their own types.

John Thurtell was born in 1794, son of a prosperous business man of Norwich. His family found him growing up high-spirited but increasingly unmanageable. In the end they sent him off on a naval career. He soon turned this in, and his long-suffering father set him up in business (he was still under 21) as a "bombasine manufacturer" in London. It was not long before he became an accepted member of the less reputable racing and boxing circles, where he met with a physically enormous and mentally minuscule man five years his senior, named William

Probert. Probert had married a physically repellent but financially attractive woman called Noyes and with the proceeds of the match had set up as a wine merchant, first in Coventry Street, Piccadilly and then at 112 High Holborn, where the venture failed. Shortly afterwards Thurtell's own business collapsed, as did his brother Tom's career as a farmer. This left everyone with more time for dissipation and many hours were spent at the 'Brown Bear', a sporting pub in Bow Street. Here Thurtell made the acquaintance of William Weare, an ex-waiter at the Globe Tavern, Fleet Street, who had saved a certain amount of money (most of which he carried around with him) and also acquired a certain skill at billiards. He was also a card-sharper of some repute. In 1822 Tom Thurtell became licensee of the Cock Tavern, Haymarket, with brother John as manager. The pair also concerned themselves with a number of minor business frauds, culminating in a dubiously originated fire for which the insurance company disputed liability. It was during this period that Thurtell also met, at one of the many inns he patronized, Joseph Hunt, an almost illiterate man of 26 with a criminal record behind him, whose only discoverable virtue was that he had a good singing voice.

The cast was now complete. So was the setting, for at about this time Probert had bought (with his wife's money) a small cottage at Gill's Hill, Radlett, near Elstree, where he installed Mrs Probert, her squint-eyed sister, Tom Thurtell's two children, and a couple of servants. He also installed an illicit still.

In October 1823 Tom and John Thurtell were lodging at the 'Coach and Horses', Conduit Street, and Weare arrived back in London from Doncaster with the proceeds of some good luck at the races. John Thurtell, Probert, Hunt and Weare could often be seen together at Rexworthy's Billiard Saloon at Spring Garden (now Spring Gardens), near Whitehall. It appears that on one occasion Thurtell won, or professed to have won, some money from Weare which was not paid. Whether this decided the events that followed is not clear, but on 23rd October Weare told his fellow players at Rexworthy's that he was going to the country with Thurtell the next day for a little sport, including some shooting. Early the next morning Thurtell and Hunt bought a pair of pistols, a sack and a rope, and hired a gig. Later Thurtell called for Mr Weare at his lodgings, which were on the second floor of No 2 Lyon's Inn. It is probably this address that gave rise to the totally groundless legend that Mr Weare was a respectable solicitor. Lyon's Inn had once been an Inn of Chancery and was situated in Wych Street at the corner of Newcastle Street, Strand, until replaced by the old Globe Theatre. All that squalid district, including Butcher's Row and Holywell Street (Booksellers' Row), was swept away around 1906 to make room for the new Aldwych and Kingsway. Weare was waiting with a gun of his own and a carpet-bag containing a change of clothes and a backgammon board. The pair set off, Probert and Hunt following in a second gig. There followed an extraordinary sort of stop-go race along the Edgware Road, Probert passing Thurtell, then stopping off for a drink while Thurtell passed him and so on, with nobody seeming to know who was in front of whom. Thurtell was eventually the first to arrive at Radlett. Probert dropped Hunt, for some reason, at Phillimore Lodge, about a mile beyond Edgware, and went on alone, meeting Thurtell near Gill's Hill Lane and learning what had happened during the past half hour or so. Just after turning into Gill's Hill Lane, Thurtell said, he had drawn his gun and shot Weare in the face. Weare had staggered out of the gig and taken a few steps along the road, whereupon Thurtell followed and cut his throat. Thurtell then sent Probert back to fetch Hunt. Weare's body was tied in the sack and hidden under some bushes and the trio went on to the cottage down the lane. After announcing their arrival to the ladies they returned to rifle the dead man's pockets. After dark (and supper) they went back once more, this time with a horse. They placed the body over the horse's back, took it along Gill Hill's Lane and threw it into a pond behind the cottage.

Early the following morning a workman saw blood in the lane, hunted around, and discovered a bloodstained pistol and knife, neither of which Thurtell had been able to find in the dark. A day or two later a neighbouring farmer told Probert about a shot he heard in the lane about the time of the killing. Probert, thoroughly alarmed, informed his companions (who had returned to London the next morning but were now back at the cottage) that the body must be removed to a safer place. They took it from the pond, put it in Probert's gig, and then in a brook that ran a little north of Elstree. Meanwhile suspicions of foul play in the neighbourhood had been growing rapidly and another farmer, from Battler's Green, Aldenham, told the

Watford magistrates that official enquiries should be set on foot. Two Bow Street Runners were despatched from London, and before very long all three villains were apprehended. Probert at once turned King's Evidence, and Hunt hurriedly followed suit by offering to show the whereabouts of the body. This was taken for examination to the Artichoke Inn, some three miles from Radlett on the road to London. There it was examined by Dr Ward of Watford.

From the moment the story broke the excitement had been intense and the behaviour of the press brought severe censure from the Bench. At the Surrey Theatre a melodrama was hastily concocted called *The Gamblers*, featuring Thurtell and Weare, and even—it was boasted—the actual horse and gig hired for the occasion. Prejudice or not, however, there could be little doubt as to the outcome. Thurtell was sentenced to death and hanged in front of Hertford gaol and a large crowd. Hunt also received a death sentence but was reprieved and transported to Australia. Probert seems to have eked out a miserable existence and was finally hanged at Newgate for stealing a horse. William Weare was buried in Elstree churchyard close to Martha Reay, mistress of the Earl of Sandwich, whose murder is related on page 54.

Hazlitt and George Borrow were among those who wrote of Thurtell and his associates, and William Mulready drew their portraits. Walter Scott scoffed at the crowds who collected twigs and shrubs from the cottage garden as souvenirs, but himself drove out of his way to see the site in 1828, when, he reported, part of the house was already destroyed and the pool had become a green swamp. Though built over and widened, Gill's Hill Lane still winds its way between Loom Lane and Watford Road, Radlett. Probert's cottage was towards the Watford Road end; the murder itself occurred a short way in from Loom Lane. The Artichoke Inn, to which the remains of Mr Weare were carried, still stands—though partially rebuilt—on the Elstree Road.

Moosh and Tiggy sound more like names for television puppets than murderers, but such indeed they were. In 1931 there was an area between the Watford and Barnet bypasses that was no more than a jungle of hastily erected huts and shacks, rubbish heaps, and general débris. Here camped a nomadic population of 'underground navvies' working mainly on sewer and drainage undertakings and travelling from place to place with the demand. In a slightly more permanent dwelling place than the majority (it actually had a tarpaulin roof) lived William Shelley, 57, and Arthur Newman, 61, known as (and only as) Moosh and Tiggy. Pseudonyms were the general rule and more conventional names rarely if ever used. Not far from their residence was a huge dump by the Scratchwood Sidings between Mill Hill and Elstree, used by the Midland Railway for burning rubbish.

On 1st June 1931, a man who inhabited a shack by the dump found the remains of a body protruding from the smouldering pile. The police, with Sir Bernard Spilsbury, were called in. It was discovered that a middle-aged man by the name of Pigsticker was missing from the camp, and it was not long before Moosh and Tiggy were arrested for his murder. Evidence was given by an acquaintance who had just made arrangements to share their hut, and who had actually witnessed the killing while pretending, prudently if not courageously, to be sound asleep. His name was the surprisingly commonplace and colourless one of John Armstrong. Moosh and Tiggy were surprised by the police while at home, and surrendered without trouble. It appeared that Pigsticker, who had only recently joined the community, was regarded as a born thief and troublemaker. Moosh and Tiggy decided to teach him a lesson by a beating, but their enthusiasm for reform got the better of them. They were perfectly frank about the whole thing, making no secret of having killed Pigsticker and firmly of the opinion that he deserved it. Both appeared totally indifferent to the sentence of death, Moosh muttering cryptically that it came twenty years too late.

Potter's Bar Golf Course, Middlesex, was the scene of two murders in the mid-1950s. The first, unsolved, was brought to light when the partial remains of Albert Welch, a railway fitter, were found in a pond in 1954. He had been missing for over a year, and nothing was ever made known as to what had happened or who was responsible.

The second crime occurred the following year, in April 1955. Mrs Elizabeth Currell, 46, took her dog for an evening run on the course, but did not return. When the dog came back alone her husband phoned the police. Her body was found near the 17th tee. She had been beaten to death with one of the iron tee markers, but there was no sign of sexual assault. The only clue was a palm-print on the murder weapon. With exemplary perseverance the police went from house to house in the neighbourhood collecting nearly nine thousand prints. At last the matching one turned up, that of Michael Queripel, who worked for the Potter's Bar Urban District Council. After only a momentary attempt at denial he admitted to having killed her. From his statement the murder appeared to have been an almost unrealized development from a purely casual encounter, after a feeble attempt at rape. It turned into a horrifying nightmare of blood, torn clothing and vicious blows. Queripel was under 18 years of age. Sir Richard Jackson uses this case to point the fact that any ordinary person "taking the dog for an evening walk, may be only a hedge's thickness away from murder". He heads his account (in *Occupied with Crime*) with the number of prints that had to be checked before the matching one was reached—4,604.

A complete lack of apparent motive adds an extra touch of horror to any murder—and this is deepened still further when it has been carried out with an appalling ferocity. Daniel Raven was a successful young advertising agent, a Jew aged 23, with a comfortable home at 184 Edgwarebury Lane, and a wife who had given birth to her first child only four days before his crime. Relations with her parents were apparently not particularly friendly—neither did they seem to be unduly strained. On the evening of 10th October 1949 he visited his wife at the Strathleigh Nursing Home, 79 Creighton Avenue, Muswell Hill. Her mother and father, Mr and Mrs Leopold Goodman, joined him there. They left a little before he did, and it seems that he followed and drove them back to their own home at 8 Ashcombe Gardens, before returning to Edgwarebury Lane only a few hundred yards away. About an hour later, around ten o'clock, a cousin of the Goodmans from Glendale Avenue, Edgware, went to see them. Becoming worried at getting no reply, he climbed in through a window. Both Mr and Mrs Goodman were lying dead, beaten with fiendish savagery about the head— with, it was revealed later, a television aerial base that had been in the hall—and the room was a bloodstained shambles. Raven, when summoned to the house by the police, put on a dramatic show of horror and remorse, saying that he should not have left the Goodmans. "Why did they tell me to go?" he cried. Something, however, struck Inspector J. Diller as not quite right about the young man. For one thing, he looked unusually smart and crisp after a day's work, and he had changed his suit after returning from Muswell Hill; his shirt, too, was fresh. The reason for all this dressing up was not long in becoming apparent. Bloodstained clothing was found in the boiler at Edgwarebury Lane; shoes, washed but similarly stained, in his garage. The blood group was that of the Goodmans. Raven then took the dangerous step of changing his story. He now said that he went out again after leaving the Goodmans house, saw their light on, and thought he would pay another visit. He saw the bodies and fled in a panic, and all his subsequent actions were the result of the fear that he might be suspected. The tale did not impress the jury and Raven was found guilty. The defence had suggested that the murder might have been an act of revenge by another hand as Mr Goodman had helped the authorities in the past on matters to do with currency, and no motive whatever could be suggested for Raven. When summing up the judge commented, "Men kill for many reasons. They do not kill and leave statements of motive by the body."

In October 1958 a house in Hayes, Middlesex, was visited by the police for a reason surely unique in the annals of crime—to demand that a man wash his hair. He was given a special shampoo because of their suspicion that he might have dyed his hair from blond to dark brown. Their action was taken in the course of an investigation of a murder that took place the previous August a few miles away in Denham, Bucks.

After her husband had left for work, thirty-one-year-old Mrs Joyce Green, a cheerful, happily married woman living at Dawn Warren, Old Mill Road, Denham, was in the garden hanging out her washing, helped by her seven-year-old son. Shortly after ten o'clock she had reason to return into the house. There she was suddenly confronted by a large, powerful man wearing "a dark suit". He at once attacked her and, despite her fierce struggles and the screams of her son who had followed her in, actually dragged her up the stairs into a bedroom, where he first raped and then strangled her. The terrified boy meanwhile ran into his own room and hid beneath the bedclothes. Later, when he ventured to look out, he saw the man running away. The latter told him not to worry—his mother was all right, and hurried from the house. The boy managed to run to a next-door neighbour, who was horrified to find Mrs Green, gagged and almost naked, lying on the bed.

Later, Detective-Superintendent Ian Forbes-Leith of Scotland Yard questioned the boy, but in his shocked state he was able to say only that the man was tall, dressed in a dark suit—and had fair hair. Exhaustive enquiries in the neighbourhood revealed that a man answering to this description had been seen arriving at Denham in a Green Line coach around ten o'clock, had actually asked a passer-by the way to Dawn Warren, and had then hurried towards it. About half-an-hour later he was apparently seen waiting in the queue for a coach making the return journey to Uxbridge. The police description of the man's clothes differed from that given by the boy in that it said he was wearing a blazer with a green badge. Despite such apparently hopeful details, however, nothing appeared to be forthcoming to help them to arrive at a solution. Urgent appeals were even made in America, (where Mrs Green had once lived), and France because two Frenchmen were known to have visited Denham on holiday during the period in question. It was discovered that Mrs Green had been married before and that the boy was her son by her first husband, but there was absolutely nothing to suggest any connection with the crime.

Eventually, after a fresh line of enquiry was set up under Detective Superintendent Glander, a photograph was found in the police files that appeared to fit the description of the wanted man, but its owner had an unshakeable alibi. Further investigation led to Hayes and the officially ordered shampoo. The man questioned (who was later arrested and convicted of housebreaking) was reported to have said to the police, "I can tell you what I was doing on the day of the Denham murder." The case remains unsolved.

Ruislip also is the scene of another recent murder—that of 29-year-old Mrs Gloria Booth, whose body was found on 13th June 1971 in the north-west corner of South Ruislip Park, a recreation ground bordered on two sides by West End Road and Masson Avenue, and on the other two by open space. Mrs Booth was known to have been alive at about 12.30 a.m. that morning; witnesses told the police they had seen someone who fitted her appearance waiting at a bus stop on the West End Road some time after the last one had gone. Her partly clothed body was found by a paper delivery boy on his early round and it was assessed that she had been killed around 2.30 a.m. The condition of the clothing suggested that she had been lying on the floor of a garage, and marks on the body indicated a frus-

trated sexual assault. Details of the crime, including an enactment of a reported meeting between Gloria Booth and an
unknown man at the bus stop, were broadcast on a police
television programme in February 1972, but as yet the mystery
is unsolved.

Some half dozen miles south-west of Ruislip, the grounds of
Syon House extend to the river. The house was originally a
nunnery founded by Henry V and—as might be expected—
suppressed by Henry VIII who grabbed it for the Crown. He
also imprisoned in it one of his unfortunate queens, Catherine
Howard, until just before he cut off her head in 1542. The
present building had a somewhat chequered history as the Tudors
went on their head-chopping way (it belonged to the Duke of
Somerset until he lost his), and for the past three hundred years
has been the summer home of the Percy family. Leading from
London Road into Syon Park, not far from the Union Canal,
is a lane running between high brick walls. It can never be
closed because Henry VIII's august if somewhat cumbersome
body was carried along it *en route* for burial at Windsor, and
it has long been popular as a Lovers' Walk.

At least one murder is thought to have occurred in it before
the discovery, on Tuesday 27th January 1948, of the body of
26-year-old Sylvia Styles. She was fully clothed, one glove still
on her left hand, the other lying against the wall. A half-crown
piece was by her foot. She had been strangled, and it was found
that the murderer had used his left hand only. There was no
sign of any attempt at sexual assault. During the war Sylvia
Styles, who lived at 28 Beech Avenue, a turning off London
Road almost opposite the lane, had been an A.R.P. Warden
in the district. At the time of her death she was working at a
bakelite factory in nearby Catherine Wheel Yard (a survival
of the old coaching days when Brentford was the first stage west)
and was regarded as a very quiet girl, with no known men
friends. She had, however, a vivid imagination—stimulated
perhaps by the many films she went to see—and used to tell
stories about someone called Danny who was never identified
and probably had no existence in real life. On Monday 26th
January she returned home after work and later left to go to a
cinema in Hammersmith. Most unusually, she left her handbag
behind, but was thought to be wearing an expensive wristwatch,

which was not seen again. Between 9 and 10 p.m. she was seen waiting in a trolley-bus queue in Hammersmith with a tall man in an overcoat and a trilby hat. At 10.40 she was seen again, getting off the bus at Brentford. The man, or one similarly dressed, accompanied her. Later in the night residents in the neighbourhood reported having heard sounds of a quarrel, but no-one seems to have been curious enough to look further.

A young man named David Bailey, when interviewed by the police, at first denied knowing her, then admitted that he had arranged to meet her on the Monday, or, if he found he couldn't make it that evening, on the Tuesday. In fact, he said, he didn't turn up on either day. Police toured the district in loudspeaker vans seeking possible witnesses, possibly the first time such a method was used, but the killer of quiet, lonely Sylvia Styles has never been discovered.

To Brentford also belongs the earliest (alleged) murder in our survey, that of Edmund Ironside, king of the English, who according to some accounts was in 1016 "treacherously slayne in Red Lion Yard, Brentford" probably with a sword or battle-axe from behind while downing a drink. The old Red Lion Inn stood on the corner of Brentford High Street and Ealing Road : it was rebuilt in 1906 and finally pulled down when the present one, on the opposite side of the road, was built. There was, around it, a yard. That is as close as we are ever likely to get, but, passing the present Red Lion, we may perhaps glance across the road and let our imagination be kindled by the legend of the killing by stealth of an English king fifty years before the Conqueror.

Moving nearer to the present day and further to the west we arrive at Whitton in 1923. In July of that year, in what was then called Whitton Woods, Mrs Ada Kerr, a young woman living apart from her husband, was found lying with her throat cut. Henry Griffin, aged 25, was charged with her murder. He told a strange story of having suddenly lost consciousness while walking with her among the trees and later finding himself lying on the ground with a gash in his throat. Mrs Kerr had disappeared. He then stoically bound up his wound and went off home. In support of what seems at first sight a very tall tale a doctor at the trial said there was a possibility that Mrs Kerr's own wound might have been self-inflicted. In other words, she might have tried to murder Griffin and then killed herself. Not merely one, but two juries failed to agree over the truth of this and each was discharged. The case was adjourned, but before the prosecution could decide what to do next Griffin solved their problem for them by dying of a heart attack in prison. Parts of the district are much changed, and the exact scene of this puzzling event is uncertain now.

On 11th December 1960 three boys playing cowboys and Indians on Yateley Common, Hampshire, discovered the body of a 12-year-old girl almost hidden in the grass. She had been strangled and sexually assaulted, though not actually raped, and was wearing a Girl Guide uniform. She was identified as Brenda Nash, who lived at Bleriot Road, Heston, and had been missing since 28th October. Six weeks previously, on 9th September, a young girl, aged 11, had been bicycling from a Girl Guide meeting to her home in the locality of Hanworth, when a man in a car stopped her and said he was a policeman and suspected her bicycle of having been stolen. He told her to leave it where it was and he would drive her to the police station. He then attacked and raped her, pushed her out of the car and drove off. She arrived home in a pitiful state, bruised and bleeding, but was able to describe the man with close accuracy. She had even noted the date and make of the car— a 1951–4 black Vauxhall.

During the following weeks the police were busy checking every owner of such a car in the district, and after the discovery that Brenda Nash was missing their efforts were redoubled. Towards the end of November they questioned a 44-year-old welder fitter named Arthur Albert Jones, a man with a wife and two children who lived at 23 Ely Road, Hounslow. He agreed that he had a Vauxhall car of the type referred to, but said that on both the crucial dates, 9th September and 28th October, he had been with his sister-in-law, Mrs Eldridge, at 303a Beckenham Road, Kent. These alibis were broken, however, when on 12th December a young woman named Lesley Carruthers reported to the police that Mrs Eldridge's daughter, Christine, who worked in the same hairdressing salon, confided her anxiety about a false story she said her mother had agreed to tell in order to shield her brother-in-law. Mrs Eldridge knew nothing, of course, about any possible connection between Jones and the young girls—he had told her that he had been out with a woman and did not want his wife to know. Christine now realized that her uncle resembled the description given by the youngster. Confronted with this, Jones changed his stories and said that on each occasion he had been out with prostitutes in the Holland Park–Notting Hill Gate area. Meanwhile other evidence had been building up against him on the rape charge: he was tried for this and given fourteen years imprisonment. The day after his conviction his photograph was published in the press and a Mr Frederick Holloway reported that it looked very like a man he had seen standing at the corner of Bleriot Road, Brenda Nash's home, and Brabazon Road. At an identity parade Jones was picked out not only by Mr Holloway but by another man who had seen him in the Vauxhall. On this and other evidence he was charged now with the murder of Brenda Nash, found guilty and sentenced for life. His trial took place at the time of the Homicide Act of 1957 and his killing of Brenda Nash, however ghastly, was 'non-capital'.

Due west of Hanworth lies Teddington, with its lock and towpath by the river. In 1953 both featured in sexual killings of maniacal ferocity, of which a 22-year-old labourer, Alfred Charles Whiteway, was convicted. The victims were Barbara Songhurst, aged 16, of 75 Princes Road, Teddington, and Christine Reed, aged 18, of 15 Roy Grove, Hampton. On the afternoon of Sunday 31st May the two girls went off for a bicycle ride. During the early evening they chatted and played around with three youths who were camping on the river, one of whom was a friend of Christine's. At about 11 p.m. they said it was getting late, packed up their belongings, and set off for home. Neither arrived. On the morning of 1st June Barbara Songhurst's body was found in shallow water about a mile north of the lock, opposite the grounds of St Catherine's Convent. She had been beaten, raped and stabbed. Marks on the river bank indicated that her body had been dragged into the water on the Richmond side of the lock gates. On the following day Christine Reed's bicycle was found in the river near the gates, but it was nearly a week before her body was recovered from the water, having floated two miles downstream. Nothing unusual had been heard by anyone near the towpath that Sunday night, but two people saw a couple of girls cycling past and heard one of them say they would get into trouble for being out so late. Barbara Songhurst's bicycle was never found, but the proprietor of a garage in Lower Ham Road, Kingston, reported seeing one that answered

to its description in his private roadway on the Monday morning. It disappeared equally mysteriously some time later that
same evening.

The gradual linking of the murders to Whiteway grew from
a complicated series of events best summarized as follows:

On 24th May, a week before the murder, a 14-year-old
schoolgirl was attacked and raped on Oxshott Heath, a few
miles from Teddington, by a man who overtook her on a bicycle.
She was able to give a fairly detailed description, noting in
particular his cleft chin, and that he had with him an axe or
chopper.

On 31st May occurred the murders of Christine and Barbara.

On 6th June a middle-aged woman, Mrs Birch, was attacked
and robbed in Windsor Great Park—the attacker also attempting
to assault her.

On 8th June a general appeal to the public was issued including a description of the man who attacked the schoolgirl
on Oxshott Heath—detectives having strong suspicions that
the cases were connected.

On 17th June a man who had previously worked with Whiteway saw him on Oxshott Heath—he noticed the strong resem-
blance to the schoolgirl's description, and notified the police.
Whiteway was taken to Kingston Police Station, but not as a
suspect in the murder case. During the drive he managed to
hide an axe in the back of the police car. (A constable subse-
quently took it to use at his home. When he realized its
significance he returned it, but considerable confusion and
embarrassment was caused and the unfortunate man collapsed
during cross-examination at the trial). Whiteway was allowed
to leave the station after questioning, but a little later it was
realized that his appearance matched that of the man who had
attacked Mrs Birch. He was arrested on 28th June and admitted
both offences.

On 29th June, during questioning by the detective in charge
of the murder enquiry, he said that he had known Barbara
Songhurst when she was 6—they had lived in the same road—
but had not seen her since.

On 30th July, according to the police, he confessed to killing
the two girls—a confession he later retracted.

On 20th August he was charged with the murders.

On 26th October his trial opened at the Old Bailey.

When first married Whiteway and his wife lived in furnished rooms, but had to separate when their baby was expected. Owing to housing difficulties he lived with his family at 24 Sydney Road, Teddington, she in King's Road, Kingston-on-Thames. He used to see her in Kingston, and on the night of the murder they had met at the usual place in Canbury Gardens, by the river. There were the usual uncertainties and conflicting statements when the question of timing was investigated, but much other evidence had accumulated against Whiteway. The garage where the bicycle appeared was not far from his wife's home, it was suggested that he might have ridden it from the scene of the crime and abandoned it there; some of the wounds on the girls' bodies could have been made by the axe hidden in the police car; he possessed a large collection of knives, and was in fact seen not long before the murder throwing some of them at trees by the river; the reason for killing Barbara Songhurst (as is customary, he was on trial for the one murder only), may have been that she would have been able to identify him after he had raped her. The jury took just over threequarters of an hour to find Whiteway guilty, and he was hanged at Wandsworth prison on 22nd December 1953. It seems clear that he had a history of other assaults behind him, and he had already served sentences for theft.

In the north-eastern part of our present district we have only a single murder to note, but it is possibly the most famous of all. On 3rd October 1922 Percy Thompson and his wife Edith visited a theatre in the West End. Afterwards, as they walked through De Vere Gardens, Ilford, on their way home to 41 Kensington Gardens a young man, Frederick Bywaters, ran up and stabbed Thompson to death—thus making Ilford the setting of one of the most discussed, dramatized, talked over and written up murders of the century.

Bywaters, a steward and clerk with the P. & O. Shipping Company, was 20 and had known Edith Thompson's family the Graydons, who lived at Manor Park, since he was a schoolboy. Edith Thompson was 28 and had been married for seven years to Percy, a shipping clerk. She had a good job as bookkeeper and manageress with a firm of wholesale milliners in London, and in fact earned, it seems, more than her husband. When Bywaters was in England she carried on an affair with him, when he was on a voyage she continued it in a flood of letters. Some of the contents of these letters played a large part in convicting her on a charge of incitement to murder, though Bywaters consistently swore she knew nothing of his intentions. Both were found guilty and hanged. The outcry against the execution of Mrs Thompson lasted long after her death, and numerous articles, plays and novels have argued the matter this way and that. It is in her character that the interest of the trial largely rests, a character revealed mainly in the letters to Bywaters. They have been held up as worthy of inclusion among the great love letters of all time. As available in the account of the trial, however, they come across as often amusing, interesting in a rather trivial way, at times genuinely tender and moving; but they are equally often the petulant outpourings of a bored, discontented, gushing and romance-sodden woman, swimming tediously in petty gossip and indulging in dangerous and callous make-believe. They reveal the sort of mentality in regard to the romantic novels of the period that today sends flowers to the weddings and funerals of characters in a radio or television serial. They can, in fact, be quoted to illustrate each conflicting point of view with equal effect. Percy Thompson remains a shadowy figure—nobody knows what *he* thought—he was there only to be despatched.

The theatre the Thompsons visited that night with their relatives Mr and Mrs Laxton was the 'Criterion', Piccadilly Circus. The play was a pre-Aldwych farce by Ben Travers in which they saw Cyril Maude, Binnie Hale, Jack Raine and (as An Old Woman) Hermione Gingold. It's title was *The Dippers*.

13

THROWN FROM BRIDGES
The Outskirts, South of the River: Richmond, Croydon, Chislehurst, Bromley

Without doubt the leading character in Richmond's criminal cast list is the atrocious Kate Webster, the 32-year-old Irish housekeeper who in 1879 dismembered her middle-aged employer, Mrs Thomas. Not much is known of Kate's early life, but she was born in Killane, County Wexford, Ireland, as Catherine Lawler, was briefly imprisoned for larceny at the age of 18, and on her release was shipped off to Liverpool to fend for herself. This she did by changing her name but not her activities, and as Kate Webster she received a four-year sentence for a similar offence. We next hear of her in 8 Brightwell Cottages, Rose Gardens, Hammersmith, now called—less prettily but more suitably—Cardross Street. There she made the acquaintance of some neighbours called Porter and through them obtained a job as a servant in the Notting Hill district. There, according to her own later statement, she was seduced by a man who kept an oil shop and "became in the family way". In 1874 she was in Kingston and gave birth to a boy on 19th April in a house in Acre Road. The following year she was arrested in Teddington on various charges of fraud and larceny and sentenced to eighteen months in Wandsworth Prison. In 1876 she took a step nearer her ultimate fate by going to live in Richmond, with her small son, at the house of a Mrs Crease, 8 Michel's Row, while she looked for work. Mrs Crease was charwoman to a Miss Loder whose neighbour, Mrs Julia Thomas, was in need of a housekeeper. On Mrs Crease's recommendation Kate Webster was interviewed and got the job. Mrs Crease generously offered to look after the little boy, and Kate moved in at the end of January 1879. The address was 2 Vine Cottages (renamed Mayfield just about the time Kate arrived there) in Park Road. The little house next door, No 1, was inhabited by a Mrs Ives and her daughter, who owned both houses and rented No 2 to Mrs Thomas. The latter lady little knew, when she opened the door to Kate and her few belongings, what she was letting herself in for: it was, in fact, the ultimate casting of her body, in small pieces, from various bridges over the Thames.

To be fair to Kate, Mrs Thomas does not seem to have been the easiest of mistresses. She was fussy and irritable, and never kept her servants for very long. The two women appear to have got along amicably enough at first, but inevitably the situation deteriorated. Kate's work grew slipshod, Mrs Thomas's nerves became frayed. By the end of February Kate had received her notice, though it seems that she asked and received permission to stay until Monday, 3rd March. On the Saturday before this Miss Ives saw Mrs Thomas doing a little work in the garden. On Sunday the mistress went to early service, the maid had a couple of hours off in the afternoon which she spent at the local pub. She returned in time to let Mrs Thomas attend church again in the evening. Some time between the two services a major row developed. Shortly after Mrs Thomas's final return that night Mrs and Miss Ives heard (but ignored) a heavy thud. It was the sound of their next-door neighbour being murdered by her housekeeper.

For the events of the next two days we have only the account (full but sometimes of dubious veracity) given by Kate just before she was executed. All that the occupants of adjoining houses noticed was an industrious servant busy with her Monday washing and dealing with the various tradesmen who called. What had apparently happened the previous evening was that Kate's rage had suddenly boiled over at some imagined slight and she had either hit Mrs Thomas with a chopper or flung her down the stairs and then strangled her. During the following forty hours, in between household chores, she dismembered the body, attempted to burn some fragments and boil others, and wrapped the remainder in a box and brown-paper parcels. On the Tuesday morning she cleaned all the windows of the house. In the afternoon she set off to Hammersmith to visit her friends the Porters, wearing a dress and jewellery belonging to

Mrs Thomas and carrying a heavy brown-paper parcel in a black shopping bag. While enjoying a pleasant chat and a cup of tea she placed the bag (which contained Mrs Thomas's head) under the table. She told the Porters she had recently married a Mr Thomas who had even more recently died and left her a house in Mayfield, Park Road, Richmond, which she was now anxious to sell. After tea Henry Porter and his 16-year-old son Robert set off with Kate to the station. She refused Henry's courteous offer to let his son relieve her of her heavy parcel. They stopped for a drink by Hammersmith Bridge and Kate said she had to cross over it to see a friend in Barnes. They waited while she paid what must have been a singularly brief visit, returning about thirty minutes later—without her shopping bag. On arrival at Richmond Henry Porter seems to have left his son to escort Kate the rest of the way; at any rate when they got to Park Road she asked Robert to help her carry a box to Richmond Bridge because she had to see a friend across that one also. Showing a polite lack of curiosity at Kate's busy social round of friends across bridges, Robert lugged the very heavy box to the centre. He was then sent back to the side they had come from. It was dark by now and he could not see much, but he heard a splash, and a moment later Kate reappeared saying she'd seen her friend and he could now go home. However, they found the last train had gone so she put him up for the night.

During the next few days she divided her time between Hammersmith and Richmond. Henry Porter introduced her to Mr John Church, landlord of the 'Rising Sun', Rose Gardens, who was interested in buying some of the late Mr Thomas's furniture. Meanwhile the box and its grisly contents had been found on the river bank, and the following day a foot turned up in a manure heap a short walk from Park Road. Knowing nothing of these developments, Mr Church accompanied Kate to Mayfield and agreed a price for the furniture—he also mixed business with pleasure by going boating with her, and stayed a night or two. On 18th March the heavens fell—it is only surprising that they had stayed up so long. As the furniture was being loaded into a couple of vans Miss Ives, somewhat belatedly awakening to the fact that something odd was going on, came out of her house and demanded to know where Mrs Thomas was. Kate became extremely agitated and said she had no idea. Miss Ives said she would "attend to it" and went back indoors. She then summoned her agent, who stopped the vans as they were about to leave, and got in touch with Mr Church. Kate fled precipitately back to her earliest haunts—Ireland—where she was found a week or two later still wearing her late mistress's effects. After wildly accusing several other people, including Mr Church, she was tried and found guilty. Just before her execution she made a full, though probably partially inaccurate, confession to the chaplain.

Kate Webster's actions after her crime—throwing pieces of her victim from Thames bridges as she paid lightning visits to 'friends', making arrangements to sell the house and belongings before the very eyes of the owner and the neighbours, must rank as supreme examples of the total lack of any grasp on reality shown, fortunately for the rest of us, by so many murderers.

The second notable name in the darker annals of Richmond's history is that of Dr Thomas Smethurst, accused of poisoning Isabella Banks, to whom he was bigamously married, on 3rd May 1859 at 10 Alma Villas, Richmond Hill.

During 1858 he was living with his lawful wife, an elderly lady some score of years his senior, at a boarding house, No 4 Rifle Terrace, Bayswater. This was then a small section of present-day Queensway, probably a single terrace of houses long since swallowed up. He first met Miss Bankes when she came as a boarder to the same house. At this time she was 43 and he was in his early fifties, but they seem to have fallen in love with a truly youthful ardour and celerity. Their unbridled passion, in fact, shocked the landlady into requesting Isabella to seek rooms elsewhere. She did so, at 37 Kildare Terrace, Bayswater, whither the infatuated doctor swiftly followed her —and from now on the lawful Mrs Smethurst is heard of no more. The date was 9th November. On 9th December Thomas and Isabella were 'married' at Battersea Parish Church and went to live as man and wife in unsuspecting Richmond, at 27 Old Palace Gardens, near the Green. On 28th March 1859, Isabella fell ill, with symptoms—such as vomiting—with which we have become unhappily familiar. On 3rd April she was worse. On 15th April they moved to 10 Alma Villas, Isabella being by now so ill that she had to be taken in a cab, and Smethurst wrote to her sister Louisa Bankes, at a now vanished address, 10 Langhart Villas, Maida Vale. On the 19th Louisa found her sister very ill indeed and two doctors called in by Smethurst diagnosed poisoning. On learning that he would inherit her estate they reported the matter to the local authorities. Smethurst was apprehended, released on account of Isabella's condition, but rearrested when, on 9th May, she died. The defence at his trial pointed out that no trace of poison was discovered and suggested that the cause of death was dysentery aggravated by vomiting—she was several weeks pregnant at the time. Smethurst was found guilty but the verdict caused some disquiet, particularly as no real reason could be found. He undoubtedly stood to gain financially from her death, but he already had ample means of his own. A prominent medical authority, Sir Benjamin Brodie, was directed by the Home Secretary to make a special investigation, as a result of which Smethurst was reprieved. Instead he was sentenced to one year's imprisonment for bigamy. On his release he went to live at 137 Tachbrook Street, Pimlico, and successfully applied for Isabella's estate.

It was at a boarding house in Pagoda Avenue, Richmond, that Patrick Mahon—33-year-old soda-fountain salesman, sportsman, charmer, and murderer of Emily Kaye on the Crumbles, Eastbourne—lived with his wife and daughter in 1924, the year of his crime. His mistress and victim, some years older than himself, lodged at the Green Cross Club, then in Guilford Street, Bloomsbury, and worked for a chartered accountant in Copthall Avenue where she met Mahon in the course of business. While they were spending a week-end together in a lonely bungalow near Eastbourne a violent quarrel broke out, in the course of which he killed her. He then dismembered the body, throwing parcels containing portions of it from the train between Waterloo and Richmond stations. His wife, who had suspicions about her husband's absences from home, found a Waterloo cloakroom ticket in one of his pockets and asked a friend, a retired member of the railway police, to look into it. A Gladstone bag was found to contain a cook's knife, bloodstained clothing and Emily Kaye's tennis-racket case. The bag was replaced and Mahon taken to Kennington Police Station when he called to collect it. The scene in the bungalow was appalling, but the crowning touch of horror was Mahon's description of how, as he was trying to burn Emily Kaye's head during a violent thunderstorm, the fierce heat of the flames caused the eyes suddenly to spring open. At the moment he was being cross-examined on this point at the trial thunder broke over the courtroom. Mahon was executed at Wandsworth.

Forty-five years ago Croydon was the scene of three linked deaths the secret of which has never come to light. In 1928 two interconnected families, the Sidneys and the Duffs, lived comfortably and happily in two of South Croydon's pleasantest and quietest streets, South Park Hill Road, running south of Coombe Road, and Birdhurst Rise, which branches away from Birdhurst Road. Mrs Violet Sidney, a widow of nearly 70, and her 40-year-old daughter Vera lived at 29, Birdhurst Rise; in nearby South Park Hill Road, at the southern end where it backs onto the railway, was the home of Vera Sidney's younger sister Grace, and her husband Edmund Duff, retired British Resident of Northern Nigeria, now working in a City business, and their two children, a girl of 14 and a boy of 3. Further along the same road dwelt Thomas Sidney, Mrs Sidney's son, and his family. All were on the friendliest of terms.

On an evening in April Edmund Duff returned home from a short fishing holiday, coming along a footpath from the station that ran alongside the bottom of his garden. A meal had been left ready for him and afterwards he joined his wife in the living-room. Later that night he had severe attacks of vomiting, dizziness and muscular cramp—the following evening he died. No poison was found, however, and a verdict of natural causes was returned at the inquest. About ten months later, on 11th February 1929, Vera Sidney at Birdhurst Rise was suddenly taken ill after lunch, and so was the cook, Mrs Noakes. The soup was suspected, but the fact that the family cat also became sick cast doubt on this as it was held unlikely that a cat would help itself to soup. Later it was thought that some veal, which also formed part of the meal, might have been to blame, but no steps seem to have been taken to discover if any particular food had been eaten by both the cat and its owners. On the following day the patients seemed to be a little better, but Vera Sidney later became very ill again and suffered very great pain. She grew rapidly worse, and died on 14th February. Mrs Sidney, prostrated with grief, was given a tonic by her doctor that contained a very small amount of strychnine. On 5th March, after taking her dose and complaining to the cook that it had a gritty taste, she herself was taken ill, with the usual symptoms of vomiting and muscular cramp, and died the same day. Verdicts of natural causes were again returned, but the outcry that followed resulted in an exhumation of the bodies of Mrs Sidney and her daughter, and later of Edmund Duff. In each case a lethal amount of arsenic was present. Weedkiller containing the poison was found in Duff's house and that of Thomas Sidney, but there appeared to be no reason to link either source with the deaths. Revised verdicts of murder against some person or persons unknown were returned for Vera Sidney and Edmund Duff. In the case of Mrs Sidney the possibility of either murder or suicide was recorded. No tangible motive, financial or emotional, ever came to light, though gossip set to its customary malicious work. The hint that Mrs Sidney, who apparently was not wholly in favour of her son-in-law, was the poisoner is dismissed as preposterous by Nigel Morland who not only was present in the district at the time but wrote up the case in detail afterwards in his book *Background to Murder*. All that can now be said with certainty is that the tragedies broke up what had hitherto been a friendly and popular family group.

Tamworth Road, Croydon, runs from Lower Church Street in the south to Waddon New Road in the north. At about 9 p.m. on Sunday 2nd November 1952, a dark, rainy evening, Mrs Edith Ware was putting her young daughter to bed in No 74, three or four houses along from the junction with Frith Road. Opposite her, as she drew the bedroom curtains, she could see the entrance to the warehouse of Messrs Barlow and Parker, wholesale confectioners. Two men were loitering in front of it, apparently anxious to avoid their faces being seen in the light of passing vehicles. A moment later one of them jumped over the gate, and then the other followed. Mrs Ware sent her husband to the nearest telephone box to call the police.

Thus was set in motion a series of events that reached their climax in a murder trial still the subject of controversy. When the police arrived at the roof of the factory to investigate they found two young men—Derek Bentley, aged 19, and Christopher Craig, 16. Both lived in Norbury, Craig at 9 Norbury Court Road and Bentley at 1 Fairview Road. Both had been in trouble before (Craig had been involved with another youth in an armed robbery), and Craig's elder brother, whom he worshipped, had been sentenced three days previously for armed robbery and being in possession of a gun with intent to endanger life. On this particular evening they had decided in company with three others to break into a butcher's shop further up the London road the safe keys of which, according to Mr John Parris, who defended Craig, had been stolen by Bentley the previous day. On arrival at the shop they found the owner still working there, so on Craig's suggestion they decided to try their luck at the Tamworth warehouse. Either two or three members of the group dropped out at that time.

Bentley was quickly taken in charge when the police arrived but Craig backed along the roof and started firing a gun. By the end of the confrontation, during which a reinforcement of armed police arrived, one officer—P.C. Miles—lay dead, another —Detective-Sergeant Fairfax—was slightly wounded, and Craig, having jumped from the roof of the building, was in hospital with injuries to his spine and breastbone. Both Craig and Bentley were charged with murder, though there was never any suggestion that the latter had a gun with him that night. Bentley was sentenced to death; Craig, on account of his age, to be detained during Her Majesty's pleasure. Bentley's appeal was dismissed, and despite public petitions the Home Secretary Sir David Maxwell Fyfe refused (rightly in the opinion of Edgar Lustgarten as expressed in his book *The Judges and the Judged*) to grant a reprieve.

What one believes to have actually taken place on that rooftop must depend on whether the words of the police or the lawbreakers carry most weight. According to the police Craig shouted abuse and defiance as he shot at them, while Bentley, as he was seized by Detective-Sergeant Fairfax, uttered the damning words, "Let him have it Chris." This could, of course, have meant "let him have the gun." Afterwards, according to the police, Craig maintained his attitude, both while lying on the ground and later in hospital. Craig's defence was that he did no such thing and had only been trying to frighten the police off—the fatal bullet was a ricochet. In his account of the case in *Most of My Murders*, John Parris says that as Craig was being taken down from the dock on one occasion during the trial he muttered to a warder, referring to Detective-Sergeant Fairfax, that he ought to have killed him too. Parris comments that it is as well his words were not overheard by the jury as they were "somewhat inconsistent with his defence". Parris also states that there was a third member of the gang on the roof that night and that Craig was holding off the police to enable him to escape. If that was so, it *could* have been he who said the words, "Let him have it". Bentley, Parris believes, did not tell even his family about this until the night before his execution. To have brought it out in the trial would of course have resulted in this third man being charged with murder.

There are a number of detailed accounts of the trial, including a very full transcript in the Notable British Trials series. A truncated version was also re-enacted on television in 1972. In the book on which the latter programme was based (*To Encourage the Others*), David Yallop puts forward the theory that the bullet which killed P.C. Miles did not come from Craig's gun at all. In pronouncing sentence Lord Chief Justice Goddard made it clear that he regarded Craig as the more guilty of the two. Bentley, though three years older, had a mental age of considerably less and had suffered from fits since he and his family had been bombed out of three houses during the war. According to the police, he said he knew Craig had a gun with him that night, but was not aware he was going to use it. Bentley himself, it was stated, was in possession of a knife and a knuckle-duster.

The case still rouses fierce arguments for and against the justice of Bentley's execution. Through all the fog of argument, emotion and cool reason, however, one fact stands out clear. P.C. Miles would have been alive today, and three families, his own, Craig's and Bentley's, would have been spared deep grief and suffering, but for the fact that the two youths, both with police records, set off on what they were perfectly aware was a criminal expedition to break in and rob—armed, between them, with a knife, knuckle-dusters and a loaded gun.

For our two final cases we move back again in time over one hundred and fifty years, and the dust of controversy has long been laid. Both, by chance, involve stately homes that still stand. The first concerns one John Clarke, convicted of murdering Elizabeth Mann, a dairymaid, on the estate of Charles Long, later Lord Farnborough. The mansion was Bromley Hill, Kent, in the Lewisham district, where the host, friend of Prime Minister Pitt, entertained such illustrious guests as George IV, William

IV and Queen Adelaide, and titled gentry. The house is to be seen today, developed but retaining something of its former appearance, as the Bromley Court Hotel, London Road. Clarke was hanged on Bromley Hill in the year of his crime, 1796.

Some three miles to the east was the equally notable Camden House, Chislehurst, the home in 1813 of a Mr and Mrs Bonnar. One morning during that year a female servant on going to wake her master and mistress found the former dead on the floor and the latter dying on the bed. Both had been violently attacked with a poker, which had been bent by the force of the blows. A physician, Dr Ashley Cooper, was sent for, but Mrs Bonnar was able to sigh only, "Oh dear!" before she too died. The footman sent to London to fetch the doctor was Philip Nicholson, the only male servant to sleep in the house. After delivering his message he rode on to see a man called Dale, a butler whom Mr Bonnar had recently dismissed for alleged misconduct. After telling Dale that "the deed was done" and that he, Dale, was suspected, Nicholson went on to inform the authorities at Bow Street, leaving behind him a puzzled—not to say alarmed—ex-butler. Dale was questioned but indignantly produced an unassailable alibi. By the time of the funeral the authorities were suspecting Nicholson himself, who had disappeared. He was found at an inn called 'The Three Nuns', Aldgate, and taken, after a brief, sharp struggle, to Giltspur Street Compter, drunk and incapable. Despite being under restraint he seems to have contrived to remain in a similarly intoxicated condition through several bouts of questioning by Mr Ashley Cooper and others. At the inquest a verdict of wilful murder was returned against him. Later he made a determined effort to cut his own throat but the ubiquitous Mr Ashley Cooper was sent for and with the help of local surgeons managed to patch him up. He protested his innocence a little longer, then on 7th June confessed that he was the murderer. The visits of several distinguished gentlemen to gaze at him, including Lord Castlereagh and Lord Camden, so irritated the prisoner that he burst open his wound in rage and had to be bound up anew. As a servant who had killed his master he was indicted for petty treason—see the case of the Swiss valet Courvoisier on page 75.

At his trial he enlarged his confession to give full details of the crime, saying he had no intention to rob, nor indeed any other motive, and blaming his act on a temporary fury from excessive drinking. He was executed on 23rd August 1813 on Pennenden Heath, near Maidstone.

Nicholson was an Irishman and a Catholic, and it was suggested afterwards that while serving at the dinner table he had heard his master expressing satisfaction at the failure of the Catholic Emancipation Bill, and had killed him in revenge— but this was not borne out by anything he later confessed.

Camden Place, named after a seventeenth-century antiquary, became famous later as the house of refuge for the Emperor Napoleon III and Empress Eugenie. It is now used as the club house of the Chislehurst Golf Club, well cared for and structurally the same despite some additions and inevitable minor interior alterations.

EPILOGUE
TYBURN

It seems fitting that we should conclude this brief tour of London
murderers at the spot where so many of them reached their
own conclusion.

The Tyburn is a left-bank tributary of the Thames now
wholly underground. The derivation of the name is uncertain:
it may signify Twyburn—i.e. two burns or streams—though it
also appears as Ayebourne. It had, in fact, a divided source, one
from a well by Fitzjohn Avenue, Hampstead, the other near
the old Belsize House. It ran southwards along Regents Park
and Marylebone Lane, crossing Oxford Street, its course south
indicated by Brook Street, to Piccadilly near the present Half
Moon Street, where at one time there was a bridge over it. It
then passed near the site of Buckingham Palace to enter the
flood plain of the Thames at a spot which is now uncertain,
possibly dividing into three branches one of which ran across
Tothill Fields.

Tyburn Gate, which more closely concerns us, stood a little
to the west of the junction of the present Oxford Street and
Edgware Road. It was erected in 1744 and demolished in 1829.
The date of the first executions at Tyburn is unknown but it is
believed to have been in use by 1196. Various claims for the
site have been put forward: 49 Connaught Square; a corner of
Upper Seymour Street; the junction of Oxford Street and Bayswater Road; the north side of Bryanston Street. All these, in fact,
may be correct, as the gallows was not always fixed in one
place. On occasion two uprights and a cross-beam are said to
have extended right across the Edgware Road. The site most in

favour at the moment for the permanent structure is in Connaught Place.

At the height of its use, when it was functioning so frequently that its removal between events was not considered worth the effort, it was triangular in plan, standing on three legs. This structure was demolished in 1759.

To 'go west', by Elizabethan times at least, meant to make the journey from Newgate to Tyburn; and not only murderers but felons, forgers, highwaymen and robbers travelled this way to their fate. Among the multitude were William Wallace (1305); Roger de Mortimer, the paramour of Queen Eleanor, widow of Edward II (1330); Perkin Warbeck (1499); Elizabeth Barton, the 'Holy Maid of Kent' who prophesied the early death of Henry VIII (1535—Henry himself carried on, beheading away to the last, for another dozen years); John Felton, who killed the Duke of Buckingham (1628); Lord Ferrers, for the murder of his steward John Johnson at his seat near Ashby de la Zouche (1760—Ferrers was an extravagant and dissipated man who ran through his estate. A receiver had to be appointed and he was allowed to choose whom he wanted. He picked his servant, thinking the man would be pliant and easy to influence. He was not. Ferrers drove his own carriage to Tyburn and was hanged with a rope of silk); Captain Macheath and Claude Duval, the highwaymen; Jonathan Wild, robber, receiver and informer; and others that we have met with in the course of this book. In 1772 the body of John Haynes, thief and horsebreaker, was taken after execution to be dissected by Sir William Blizard: the surgeon discovered signs of animation and restored Mr Haynes to life. Rival claims for the honour of being the last to be executed at Tyburn in 1783 are held by Mr John Austin and a man named Ryland, for forgery.

Today the traffic endlessly roars over the spaces once filled with open galleries where seats were let out at very high prices to the crowds 'come to see a man die'. In passing by we may perhaps think of those who paid the extreme penalty long ago. Let us spare a thought, also, for their victims.